Reclaiming the Gospel at Home:

Biblical Truths for Women

Charles A. Fowler, Editor

Published by
Innovo Publishing, LLC
www.innovopublishing.com
1-888-546-2111

Providing Full-Service Publishing Services for
Christian Authors, Artists & Organizations: Hardbacks, Paperbacks,
eBooks, Audiobooks, Music & Film

RECLAIMING THE GOSPEL AT HOME:
BIBLICAL TRUTHS FOR WOMEN

Library of Congress Control Number: 2016932076
ISBN 978-1-61314-223-3

Cover Design & Interior Layout: Innovo Publishing, LLC

Printed in the United States of America
U.S. Printing History

First Edition: February 2016

DEDICATION

To the faithful members of Germantown Baptist Church. The opportunity to serve you as pastor is an incredible joy! I pray that my ministry will always prioritize feeding you the Word of God, leading you to pursue His Mission for your lives, interceding faithfully for you and your family, and protecting you from the influences that would seek to harm or divide you.

To those who exercise their gift of teaching at Germantown Baptist Church—I pray that you always listen to the Voice of God speak into your life first, then, equip those whom you teach to hear His voice, understand His Word, and respond obediently.

To Sandra, my wife, for pursuing Christlikeness alongside me, and for providing a Christ-honoring example to our two daughters, Anna and Sarah. We pray that Anna will continue her pursuit of godliness in her marriage to Justin. We pray that Sarah will continue walking with Christ as a godly young lady into God's preferred future for her life.

May we all hear His voice, understand His will, and walk in it in the power of His Holy Spirit.

TABLE OF CONTENTS

ACKNOWLEDGMENTS

As is always the case, every book happens because many people see the value of its message and invest a portion of their lives and gifts into developing it. *Reclaiming the Gospel at Home: Biblical Truths for Women* is no exception. While I cannot name everyone and articulate their particular contribution, I do want to highlight some whose investment has been significant and has made this book possible.

First of all, I want to thank our writers. Carolyn Mrok, Marie Strain, Beth Reed, and Kay Reed are all incredibly gifted teachers and cherished friends. While I enjoy the distinct honor of serving as their pastor, God has used each of them in very specific ways to teach, encourage, and walk alongside me. My life, on both a personal and pastoral level, has been enriched because of each of them. All four of them have spent their lives studying the Word of God and pursuing His likeness. They all continue to grow, look for fresh opportunities to express their gifting, and are blessed with a platform of influence for the glory of God. I am inspired by each of them, and I thank God for their influence in my life and through this book.

On a day-to-day basis, no one has had a larger role in this book project than Brenda Doss. She has served as the communication hub for the entire project. It is her project management skills that helped keep our writers, our publisher, and me on task and informed. She has contributed significantly to the editorial process as well. I cannot say enough about her contribution. Her commitment to excellence and her gracious spirit has helped make this book project possible.

In addition, I want to express my heartfelt appreciation for Bart Dahmer, Terry Bailey, Darya Crockett, Rachael Carrington, Yvonne Parks, and the entire Innovo Publishing team. They have consistently demonstrated a Christ-honoring professionalism and commitment to excellence. Working with this team has been a joy. The flexibility and patience they have demonstrated when we have had to make adjustments in timelines has been remarkable. Thank you for not only being a publisher but being a true partner in the development and release of this book.

Finally, I want to acknowledge a tremendous blessing that has become increasingly obvious to me over the course of the writing, editing, and release of this book. It is the blessing of working with a team of writers, editors, and friends who demonstrate a love for the Word of God and a desire to see that Word transform the lives it touches. I thank God that as we have resolved details related to this book, I have dealt with individuals whose lives have been shaped by the Word of God, gifted by the Holy Spirit, and committed to seeing the life of Christ flow through them personally and professionally. This blessing is not one that I take for granted. I see the fingerprints of God adorning the lives of our entire team, and I trust that His presence is going to be evident throughout the pages of this book. I pray that the Lord uses this to encourage women to pursue Him with greater intentionality and express His precepts in their lives and families with greater power and consistency.

Reclaiming the Gospel at Home: Biblical Truths for Women has benefitted from the generous investment of time, wisdom, and biblical insight from so many. We pray and dedicate this book to the spiritual refreshment of women. Proverbs 11:25 states, "he who refreshes others will himself be refreshed." I pray that the Holy Spirit will not only refresh our readers but also the lives of those who listened to His voice and invested their lives through this project.

SUGGESTIONS FOR GROUP STUDY

Thank you for your interest in this project. We were blessed in its writing, and we trust that the Lord will bless you in its usage.

We wish to make you aware of several specific details concerning this Bible study. First and foremost, it was written to be a resource for use in group Bible-study venues. As you will quickly see, its format is somewhat different from many other Bible studies. However, we believe that it will be used of the Lord to lead many women to a more intimate knowledge of our God and the Lord Jesus Christ. This can be accomplished by each Bible study student reading the authors' comments on the many issues revealed by the book of Ruth and studying for themselves from God's Word the biblical principles that support our observations and conclusions.

We recommend the following Bible study format for the greatest spiritual profitability. The book was designed to be studied in a twelve-week time frame. Each week a person will lead a discussion on what has been studied the previous week. Each leader is to encourage their recruited class members to purchase a book with the intention to study one chapter a week by completing the included assignments. Even though the comments made by each author are valuable, the most spiritually profitable thing each student will do is to closely observe the included Scriptures and learn for themselves what God's Word reveals on every topic addressed.

We recognize that the size of Bible study groups vary from situation to situation. We believe the discussion format that would generate the greatest amount of interaction would be in groups of ten to twelve. Therefore, if your Bible study is larger, you may find it helpful to begin your time in a large group setting and follow that by dividing into smaller groups for more intimate discussion.

You may discover other helpful formats for your study. Ultimately, we desire that the women experiencing this study be encouraged to interact with the content in a setting that is open and intimate.

Even though there are summary questions presented at the end of each chapter, each leader is encouraged to stimulate discussion on any other topic addressed in that chapter that seems applicable to their particular group. There are many issues addressed in these chapters that are "everyday relevant" to today's women. An open and nonthreatening discussion of personal application of God's Word directed at these issues will be life changing for many, if not most.

The ministry of the Holy Spirit is of utmost importance in any study of the Scriptures. We strongly suggest that each student begin her daily study with a heart that desires to hear from God and a prayer that the Holy Spirit will minister to her in a very personal way and help her apply it to her life.

Our fervent prayer is that the Lord will do a deep and abiding work in the hearts of all whom He draws to this book—all for the glory of His great name.

INTRODUCTION

Reclaiming the Gospel at Home: Biblical Truths for Women is a book written by women for women. This is the second book in the *Reclaiming the Gospel at Home* series. The heart of this spiritual resource is a desire to gain some fresh insights into the biblical story of Ruth. Many read this book and see it primarily as a love story between Ruth and Boaz, her kinsman-redeemer. However, there is a richness in this text that explores the depths of family relationships in ways that few other biblical books provide, and we experience them all through the lens of Ruth's and Naomi's lives.

Some of these experiences include the loss of a husband and son, a move from one culture to another, the realities of physical, emotional, and spiritual struggle, and the sovereignty of a faithful God to care for His own. These plus many other circumstances that women and families face today are explored. Throughout the entire book the reality that life can be challenging and unpredictable is explored, but always in light of the goodness and grace of our heavenly Father.

The chapters in this book have been written by four women: Carolyn Mrok, Beth Reed, Kay Reed, and Marie Strain. There are a few common threads that link these women together in life and ministry beyond their contribution to this book. First of all, they are all godly women who continue to devote their lives to the study of God's Word. Second, they all have been given a gift of teaching by our gracious heavenly Father through His Holy Spirit. Finally, all four exercise these gifts through the ministry of Germantown Baptist Church.

As will quickly become obvious, this book was not written to just tell you about what God says in the book of Ruth, nor just to interpret the meaning of what He says. This book was intentionally written so that you would have an opportunity to examine biblical truths for yourself through questions asked in the text. At times, cross references are given to examine a greater understanding of the biblical truths being conveyed. Also there are places where the book will lead you to personal application of biblical truths, which, of course, is one of the most important aspects of all Bible study. However, the greatest desire of these four women is that, through this book, you would come to know the Creator God of the universe more intimately, and, thereby, be transformed more into the image of His Son, the Lord Jesus Christ.

As you walk through this Bible study, I pray that it stirs within your spirit a desire to walk with God and trust Him through every circumstance that occurs in your life and your family. Each new and unexpected situation provides a backdrop upon which you can declare the glory of God. Every person experiences hardship and pain. Those who have surrendered their lives to the Lord Jesus Christ have the opportunity to walk through those seasons of life differently than those without Christ, as a demonstration of God's power and faithfulness. Hopefully you will be encouraged and your faith strengthened as you walk through *Reclaiming the Gospel at Home: Biblical Truths for Women*. This book has been written to remind women of God's extravagant love and never-ending grace that He desires to flow through each of us every day.

Soli Deo Gloria
Charles

RUTH 1:1–5

During the time of the judges, there was a famine in the land. A man left Bethlehem in Judah with his wife and two sons to live in the land of Moab for a while. The man's name was Elimelech, and his wife's name was Naomi. The names of his two sons were Mahlon and Chilion. They were Ephrathites from Bethlehem in Judah. They entered the land of Moab and settled there. Naomi's husband Elimelech died, and she was left with her two sons. Her sons took Moabite women as their wives: one was named Orpah and the second was named Ruth. After they lived in Moab about 10 years, both Mahlon and Chilion also died, and Naomi was left without her two children and without her husband.

CHAPTER ONE

Kay Reed

Faithfulness Under Pressure

Introduction

"For whatever was written in the past was written for our instruction, so that we may have hope through endurance and through encouragement from the scriptures" (Romans 15:4).

God had someone pen the book of Ruth for you! What a thought! If you are in need of hope, endurance, and encouragement, this is the study for you. God has a message for you, and the Holy Spirit will apply it to your needs right now if you are listening. Look for Him to show up. Ask Him to keep your spirit alert, receptive, and responsive to His voice. Expect a blessing!

If you don't need a Word from God now, you will. Just live a little longer, love a few more people, experience a few more disappointments, face a few more crises, and you will need a Word from Him. Store up the truths that God wants to teach you from the Scriptures. Hide His Word in your heart, and you will be prepared for whatever the future brings.

An unknown author provides the background for the book of Ruth in the first verse: "During the time of the judges, there was a famine in the land." The time of the judges in the history of Israel is recounted in painful detail in the book that precedes Ruth in our Bible.

Even a cursory reading of Judges leaves one with the knowledge that God's chosen people had failed to appropriate His promised blessings.

God had intended that Israel, His holy nation, would live in the land of promise as a nation of priests. Instead, they misrepresented Yahweh to the Canaanites who lived among them as well as the nations that observed them from afar. They bowed their knees to heathen gods of other nations, and, as a result, their idolatry failed to present Yahweh as the One and only God.

During the time of the judges, immorality dragged the Israelites to the depths of degradation, until their conduct made them indistinguishable from the Canaanites in whose midst they lived. The commandments that God had delivered through Moses to their ancestors were ignored or disobeyed. God, in His mercy and grace, periodically raised up judges among them to deliver them, but each person had his own ideas about what was right and what was wrong, and the power and holiness of Yahweh were absent from their daily lives. National periods of repentance were followed by backsliding and God's judgment, which, in time, brought them back to repentance. And so the cycle of sin, judgment, and repentance continued throughout the time of the judges, which lasted about three hundred years. Although we cannot be certain, the events in the book of Ruth probably took place during the time of Gideon or Jephthah.

In the midst of national immorality and idolatry, God acted in great grace by including Ruth, a young Moabite woman, in the family line of the Messiah Who was to come. She pictures the later Grace, our Lord Jesus Christ, Who, through His death and resurrection, opened the door for believing Gentiles to come into righteous standing before Him.

The story of Ruth begins in the small village of Bethlehem in Judah. The Hebrew word translated Bethlehem means "house of bread." We are immediately reminded of the world-changing event that took place in that village over one thousand years later. That was when the "house of bread" was the setting for the birth of the Bread of Life, Jesus (John 6:35). But during the time of the judges, Bethlehem was suffering judgment.

Trials

During this season of national shame and depravity, God sent a famine as a means of discipline. His instructions, through Moses to the Jewish nation, had been explicit:

> If you carefully obey my commands I am giving you today, to love the LORD your God and worship Him with all your heart and all your soul, I will provide rains for your land in the proper time, the autumn and spring rains, and you will harvest your grain, new wine, and oil . . . Be careful that you are not enticed to turn aside, worship, and bow down to other gods. Then, the LORD'S anger will burn against you. He will close the sky, and there will be no rain; the land will not yield its produce, and you will perish quickly from the good land the LORD is giving you. (Deuteronomy 11:13–15)

Among those who suffered from the effects of the famine was a small family of four Israelites. The father was Elimelech, the mother Naomi, and the two sons were Mahlon and Chilion. We can imagine what this family was like by looking at the meaning of their names, for in the Bible, names were very significant, and they were often assigned because of personality or character traits. Elimelech means "my God is King" and Naomi means "pleasant." The names of their two sons, Mahlon and Chilion, mean "sickness" and "puny" or "pining." Imagine with me for a moment, that each had a personality like his or her name, and look at what the family dynamic may have been. Elimelech might have been confident and bold, his name proclaiming the greatness of Yahweh. Naomi would be delightful! She was compliant and caring, a joy to all who knew her. Perhaps Mahlon and Chilion had been sickly from birth. Seldom were both enjoying good health at the same time. Their physical condition was a constant source of concern for their parents, especially the mother who showered them with affection. There were only four of them in a community that counted children a great blessing from God and delighted in large families. Now put yourself in the place of the breadwinner for this family. Each day, Elimelech experienced a growing anxiety as he saw the family's store of food and other necessities diminish. As he looked about, he envisioned a bleak future, which led him to a difficult decision.

If he stayed in Bethlehem, he would continue to dwell among God's people and share their hardship. But he had heard that just a few miles away, in the land of Moab, everything was fine, and there was no famine. Perhaps he considered that the difficulties he and his fellow Israelites were experiencing were directly from God's hand. Maybe he was aware of his personal need for repentance before God but decided that he was no worse than his neighbors. He had heard stories about God's miracles on behalf of His people in the past, but that was in the past. He really wasn't sure that God could, or would, respond to his needs in the present. Difficult circumstances sometimes bring God's people to a stark choice—either react without consideration of God's will or look to God for help. Elimelech decided to leave the place of God's presence and provision and travel to Moab.

Faithfulness Should Be Learned in the Home

How different Naomi and Elimelech's lives would have been if the decision had been a faithful one instead of a faithless one! It is in the home that values are taught, by actions more than words. What an opportunity for Naomi and Elimelech to call on God in personal repentance and faith. It was the perfect chance to expect God to provide and to look to Him daily for provision. Apparently, that was what some of their neighbors had done because they were still there ten years later when Naomi eventually returned.

Moab was not a long journey, only about fifty miles eastward. However, it represented a decision of gigantic proportions! Elimelech and Naomi left family, friends, and community. They left traditions and everything that was familiar to become aliens in a strange land. The Moabites were descendants of Lot. Their god was Chemosh, whose worship demanded child sacrifice. This move was not a small thing, but an act of rebellion. Dwelling in Moab, Elimelech and his family were misfits, children of the true King among worshippers of a false god.

It is interesting to consider whether or not Naomi was fully complicit in the decision to move. It is possible that she really had no part in the decision but was simply told what her husband had decided to do. Women in that day had very little power within their families and none in society at large. Was she submitting herself to her husband's desires? Did she leave reluctantly? We are not given the answer to those questions, but knowledge of society in that day strongly suggests that the decision to move was Elimelech's. If that were the case, she was not the first woman to suffer greatly because of a decision over which she had no control, nor was she the last.

At first, their plan probably was to stay in Moab just long enough to ride out the famine, but verse 2 tells us that they settled there. This reminds us of the Moabites' ancestor, Lot, who first "set up his tent near Sodom" (Genesis 13:12), but later, we see Lot at the gate of the city sitting among its elders. (Genesis 19:1) Sin has a way of slowly drawing a person in, entrapping its victims in a cycle that spirals ever downward.

How matter-of-fact the text is, when it tells us that after settling in Moab, Naomi's husband, Elimelech, died and Naomi was left with her two sons. Only those who have suffered the loss of a spouse can fully appreciate the grief and disorientation that a spouse's death brings. In Naomi's case, the loss of her husband also meant the loss of her primary source of livelihood. It was unusual for a woman to have the resources to support herself, not to mention two sons.

Verse 4 states that Mahlon and Chilion took Moabite women, Orpah and Ruth, for wives. This was in direct disobedience to God's instructions concerning nations that served other gods. He had specifically forbidden marriage between His people, Israel, and idol worshippers.

> Do not intermarry with them. Do not give your daughters to their sons or take their daughters for your sons, because they will turn your sons away from Me to worship other Gods. Then the LORD'S anger will burn against you, and He will swiftly destroy you. (Deuteronomy 7:3–4)

Faithless Decisions Affect Multiple Generations

Mahlon's and Chilion's marriages dishonored God and illustrated their lack of dedication to Him. With the example of their parents' apostasy before them, Naomi and Elimelech's sons were drawn away by the Moabite women and the heathen culture in which they lived. This is exactly what God had warned them against, and God moved in judgment as He had promised.

Naomi had been in Moab for ten years when both of her sons also died, robbing her of the last of her family and leaving her with two widowed daughters-in-law. It is impossible to imagine her grief and sense of loss! Without her husband, there was no one to share the joys of the past, no protection for her in the present, and no provision for her in the future. Having walked away from the place of God's care, regrets and memories haunted her daily.

Without her husband and sons, Naomi no longer had an identity. They had been the center of her universe and her work. Waves of grief must have washed over her when she least expected it. A glance at someone who reminded her of her husband, the sight of a little boy at play, the setting of the sun that preceded the time for the evening meal, the quietness of her house, all reminded her of her solitude. In reflection, oh how she regretted the move away from God's people and God's land! There was no one now to help her make a decision about her future. She was ill equipped to make decisions, for that had been done for her all of her life. Yet she was alone now, a solitary, grief-stricken woman, no longer young, with no offspring to support her. She thought she was on her own, but she wasn't, for God had a plan that she could not see.

Grief Is the Ultimate Trial

The God Who made us knows us perfectly! Grief has the effect of drawing our attention toward God. Those suffering from grief seek the Lord because their hearts are so tender and desirous of answers and connection with Him. Naomi did not have the promises of the New Testament as we do. Nevertheless, there was a definite hope and assurance of resurrection in the Old Testament also. Job, in what is probably the oldest book of the Bible, stated with confidence: "But I know my living Redeemer, and He will stand on the dust at last. Even after my skin has been destroyed, yet I will see God in my flesh" (Job 19:25–26).

Truth

Teach by Words and Action

Naomi and Elimelech must have noticed that their sons learned how to walk by watching their parents walk. Mahlon and Chilion learned to talk by hearing their parents talk. They learned other life skills by copying their parents' actions. Did they expect that they would also adopt their parents' attitudes toward the most important thing in life, their God? Or did they not pay attention to their obligation to diligently teach their children? Did they become so distracted by the mundane affairs of life that they failed to follow God's directions?

> Imprint these words of mine on your hearts and minds . . .
> Teach them to your children talking about them when you
> sit in your house and when you walk along the road, when
> you lie down and when you get up. (Deuteronomy 11:18–19)

Failure to teach our children God's Word with both our words and our actions is a failure that will affect their lives and ours for years to come! Of course, no parent does this perfectly. It is wonderfully freeing to realize that God knew before He gave us children that we could not be a perfect parent or a perfect role model. What a comfort and encouragement!

Efforts to teach faithfulness or any other principle will fail if our actions contradict that teaching, for the Truth must also be shown by example. A clear example of human faithfulness was modeled by my uncle. My aunt suffered from Alzheimer's disease. Our family and friends watched my uncle care tenderly for her, day after day, through all the stages of the disease, for many years. Whereas she had been a gentle and loving woman, for a period of time she became angry, belligerent, hostile, and even violent. After she became bedfast and no longer

21

recognized him, he spoke gently to her, fed her, and patiently cared for her medical and personal needs. Finally, he hired professional help when her care became too much for him to handle. They had no children, and those family members who were closest to him urged him on several occasions to place her in a nursing facility because we saw that it was taking a toll on his health.

During that time, when family or friends remarked on his devotion to her, he often answered with, "I promised to love and keep her through better or worse, and that is what I am going to do." And that is what he did! During her illness, his own health declined rapidly, and he died a few years after she did. However, his faithful response to their wedding vows provided an amazing lesson on faithfulness for us all. Our family both heard and observed his testimony of faithful love.

I have also had the privilege of observing my mother care for my father when he had Amyotrophic Lateral Sclerosis (ALS), a neurodegenerative disease. For more than three years, she put her own needs aside and unselfishly cared for him as the disease progressively paralyzed him. Both of these examples of faithfulness by members of my immediate family are a part of my heritage.

◊ If everything your children or friends know about God had been learned only from your actions, what would their conception of God be?

◊ If everything your children or friends know about God had been learned only from your words, what would their conception of God be?

◊ Can you share an example of faithfulness that you have observed among your family or friends?

Decisions Affect Future Generations

When Mahlon and Chilion took Moabite women to be their wives, they took one more step away from the God of their fathers. Likewise, we can expect that our example of faithfulness or unfaithfulness to godly principles will have great effect on succeeding generations.

Help, LORD, for no faithful one remains; the loyal have disappeared from the human race. (Psalms 12:1)

It is very common today to hear David's complaint repeated. Who hasn't bemoaned the state of the society we live in? Unfaithful decisions and actions have changed the very nature of our world. Parents abandon their children physically, emotionally, or both. Husbands or wives leave their spouses, many times beginning a new relationship with someone else. Government officials abandon their high ideals for self-serving reasons. Elderly parents are cast aside when they call on their children for help and support. The examples of unfaithful decisions are all around us. One must ask if, in most of these situations, those choosing to be unfaithful have not already walked away from their devotion to God and His teachings. Unfaithful decisions are but a symptom of the greater problem—lack of faithfulness to God and His Word.

Faithless Decisions Often Cause Others to Suffer Consequences

Are you currently or have you in the past, been greatly affected by the consequences of decisions over which you had no control? Of course you have, for we live in a sinful world, and every day we must come to terms with circumstances that are thrust upon us. Are you the innocent victim of an unfaithful spouse? Has the illness of a loved one cast you into the role of caregiver? Has a rebellious child brought shame, financial strain, or constant stress into your life? Do you have physical problems that are the result of your genetic makeup?

Dear Sister, don't blame God, for that is the road to bitterness! Rest in His sovereignty and place your anger and disappointment in His hands. Few of us have suffered as much loss as Naomi did, but God had a great plan for her life that she could not foresee. Likewise, God has a plan for every one of His children that assures our sanctification if we will cooperate. God has promised to refine us even to the point that we will resemble Jesus. Take comfort in Romans 8:28–29, which says:

> We know that all things work together for good to those who love God: those who are called according to His purpose. For those He foreknew He also predestined to be conformed to the image of His Son, so that He would be the firstborn among many brothers.

As with Naomi, some difficulties are God's means of discipline. One of our first responses to illness and tragedy should be consideration of our spiritual condition. Sincerely seek your Father's face and ask Him whether there is a need for repentance in your life.

> My son, do not take the LORD'S discipline lightly or faint when you are reproved by Him, for the LORD disciplines the one He loves and punishes every son He receives. Endure suffering as discipline: God is dealing with you as sons. For what son is there that the Father does not discipline? (Hebrews 12:5b–7)

Grief and hard times have the effect of drawing our attention to God. Our hearts are tender and sometimes desperate for answers through connection with Him. It is often during such times that we seek God as never before.

You will call to Me and come and pray to Me, and I will listen to you. You will seek Me and find Me when you search for Me with all your heart. (Jeremiah 29:12–13)

◊ Can you remember a time when God's hand of discipline brought illness, difficulty, sorrow, failure, chastening of any type into your life? If so, prepare to share that with the group. If you do not wish to share your answer, at least acknowledge God's chastening in the space below.

◊ James says that God disciplines every son (and daughter) that He receives. If you have no awareness of God's discipline in your life, what might that indicate?

Consider the possibility that your heart needs to be more sensitive to the movement of God's hand in your life. Perhaps you have simply missed the significance of some life events. On the other hand, not all hard things in life are the result of someone's specific sin. In John 9:1–3, Jesus's disciples asked Him whether a certain man who had been born blind had sinned or whether his blindness was the result of his parents' sin. Jesus' answer was, "Neither this man nor his parents sinned . . . This came about so that God's work might be displayed in him."

Everything God created is affected by sin. Some difficulties, illnesses, and deaths are simply the result of man's fall. On the other hand, God sometimes uses hard things as a means of discipline. If we search for Him with all our hearts, we can know whether or not we are under God's judgment. If we are, quickly turning to Him in repentance is the only answer.

"God whispers to us in our pleasures, speaks in our conscience, but shouts in our pain: it is His megaphone to rouse a deaf world."[1] C. S. Lewis

Transformation

"If we are faithless, He remains faithful, for He cannot deny Himself" (2 Timothy 2:13).

Although Naomi and her family left the land that God provided for them, and in the process forfeited many of God's promises for an abundant life, they did not move away from the presence of the Lord. There in that foreign land, Naomi was not alone. God had not forsaken her; although, she moved away from His people and His will. He was about to show Himself in a mighty way. In fact, God always shows Himself at our time of greatest need.

God Is Faithful in Grief

"But mankind is born for trouble as surely as sparks fly upward" (Job 5:7).

If you are breathing, you can be sure that one day you will experience grief, if you haven't already. When that time comes, God will be faithful! Naomi experienced a level of grief that most of us can only imagine, but the result of the entrance of sin into this world resulted in the intrusion of death upon the human race. "For the wages of sin is death, but the gift of God is eternal life in Christ Jesus our Lord" (Romans 6:23). Most of us will bury our grandparents, parents, and perhaps other relatives and good friends as time goes by. Many of us will survive our husbands because, statistically, women live longer than men. One day, as surely as

---

1   C. S. Lewis, *The Problem of Pain* (New York: HarperCollins, 1940/1996), 91.

sparks from a fire fly upward, you will need the presence and comfort of God in the person of the Holy Spirit in your time of grief.

Let me give you my own testimony. My husband and I lost our oldest son to suicide as the result of mental illness. From the moment I knew about Mike's death, there was a deep abiding sense of the presence of God's Spirit. His death occurred at the end of his long seven-year downward spiral into schizophrenia. Shock, self-incrimination, shame, dismay, anguish, regret, and sorrow filled our nights and days but underneath were the strong arms of Jesus.

God spoke to me in comfort from His Word. Having committed the twenty-third Psalm to memory during my childhood, it was a great source of comfort. But in this time of grief, my understanding of that wonderful psalm expanded and became clearer. Verse 4 suddenly had new meaning: "Even though I walk through the valley of the shadow of death, I fear no evil; for thou art with me; thy rod and thy staff, they comfort me" (RSV). Previously, my conception of the valley of the shadow of death was a shadowy valley full of supposed danger through which the shepherd led his sheep. His presence directed them and his rod and staff, a symbol of his protection, were a comfort to them. I had always understood that valley as the time of my own death. There was assurance that Jesus, my Shepherd, would be with me all the way and that His protection would surround me on that last journey from earth to heaven.

But suddenly, my understanding expanded. I found myself descending into the valley of the shadow of death while grieving for our child. Grief clouded every day as I walked in the shadow of Mike's death. His untimely death clouded every day with grief and blocked out the sun for months. In that deep valley, every step, every day was a walk in near darkness. There was no skipping ahead or avoiding the pathway. It was dim, it was deep, and it was step by step.

But every day, God comforted me and gave me strength for that day. Many times, He used other people to bring comfort and encouragement. Every act of kindness, every card, every good wish was magnified. His presence was sweet and constant, for He is faithful!

God Is Faithful to Forgive

The most basic spiritual need that man has is the need for forgiveness. The Scriptures declare, "for all have sinned, and fall short of the glory of God" (Romans 3:23). Sin is not a male problem, nor a female problem; it is not a problem that confines itself to one race or one location on the planet. **All have sinned!** But God has provided a remedy for sin in His Son, Jesus Christ. "The Lord does not delay His promise, as some understand delay, but is patient with you, not wanting any to perish but all to come to repentance" (2 Peter 3:9). In addition, the author of Romans declares, "They are justified freely by His grace through the redemption that is in Christ Jesus" (Romans 3:24).

God Is Faithful to Renew and Restore

Have you made some faithless decisions like Naomi's family did? Return to God and He will return to you (Zechariah 1:3, paraphrased). Paul announced in 2 Corinthians 4:16, "Therefore we do not give up. Even though our outer person is being destroyed, our inner person is being renewed day by day."

For proof of Jesus' willingness to restore those who sin, we only need to look at one of His disciples, Simon Peter. After Jesus' arrest, during the time of His trial and condemnation by the Jewish religious leaders and Roman authorities, Peter denied Christ publicly three times. Yet, after His resurrection, Jesus spoke lovingly to Peter and elevated him to a position of leadership among his fellow disciples and other followers (John 21:15–19). Peter's boldness grew after Pentecost, and soon we see him being used by God to heal a man who had been lame since birth (Acts 3:1–10). Peter, the denier of Christ, became Peter the rock. Church history records the world-changing leadership that Peter exerted within the early church.

If you are now bearing the consequences of someone else's unfaithful decisions, God has also made provision for you. Ask Him to restore the years that the locusts have eaten (Joel 2:25). He is faithful; He will do it! That does not mean that He will remove the consequences.

However, God delights in using even the consequences of poor decisions in a believer's life.

God Is Faithful to Use Our Weakness

Naomi was powerless to change what had happened to her, and she thought her productive, happy years were behind her. She saw no hope for happiness or fulfillment in her future. But God is not limited by our lack of physical resources. When we are weakest, we are in the best position to see God move in our lives.

A good example of this happened many years ago in the life of a good friend. Glenda was my classmate at the same school for twelve years. We remained friends into adulthood and then our paths diverged. We both married, but she had no children. Although we both lived in the same area, we kept in touch only rarely over the years, and then tragedy struck. Glenda was diagnosed with a rare, incurable disorder that slowly stole her health away. Although she was weak and seldom left the house, she needed friends and wanted to grow spiritually. So with great effort, she attended the weekday Bible study that our church sponsored. She was very ill and weak, and her disability was so severe that she made a habit of resting and conserving her strength all week in order to attend our weekly meetings.

However, Glenda grew spiritually—by leaps and bounds! Her insights were deep; her compassion for problems and illnesses of the other ladies was boundless. She became a prayer warrior! Week by week she used her telephone, cards, and notes to encourage other group members. Her illness served to embolden her. She spoke unashamedly about God's blessings on her to friends, family, and strangers. By the time of her death, she had endeared herself to the entire Bible study group, and all of us had a great sense of loss. What an example she had set for the rest of us! Although her poor health was her weakness, it soon became her strength! Through her weakness, God taught the rest of us a lot and illustrated what He can do with a weakness that is submitted to His use.

God Is Faithful to Accomplish His Will

"He who calls you is faithful, who also will do it"
(1 Thessalonians 5:24).

God had a plan. There was nothing that Naomi, Elimelech, Mahlon, or Chilion could do to thwart His plan. They had a choice whether or not they would fit into God's plan, but even if they did not choose to cooperate, He would still perform His will.

God appeared to Abraham, their ancestor, and said, "I will make you into a great nation. I will bless you, I will make your name great, and you will be a blessing. I will bless those who bless you, I will curse those who treat you in contempt, and all the peoples on earth will be blessed through you" (Genesis 12:2–3). Throughout succeeding generations, God has patiently set events into motion to accomplish His promises.

God declared Himself to be faithful through Moses in Deuteronomy 7:9. "Know that Yahweh your God is God, the faithful God who keeps His gracious covenant loyalty for a thousand generations with those who love Him and keep His commands." Of course, the reference to a thousand generations means an immeasurable span of time. So there will never be a time when Yahweh will fail to keep His covenant with Abraham and his descendants, the Jewish nation.

Part of the covenant God made with Abraham was that all the peoples of the earth would be blessed through Him. Thus was born the hope of a Messiah, a Savior, among the Jewish people. Over two thousand years ago, God fulfilled that promise, and Jesus Christ, a descendant of Abraham, was born in Bethlehem. The enemy of mankind, the devil, spared no efforts to kill the child, but God was watching over His Promise to perform it. In due time, Jesus gave His life willingly to redeem mankind, and through repentance from sin and trust in Christ's redemptive work, everyone who is born again into the Jewish Messiah's Kingdom is blessed with eternal life.

God is faithful! He will accomplish His will! You and I have a choice. We can cooperate with Him and be blessed to work with Him and be used by Him to advance His will on earth. On the other hand, we may refuse to submit our will to His and miss His blessings. But either way, God will accomplish what He has set out to do. "For His dominion is an everlasting dominion, and His kingdom is from generation to generation. All the inhabitants of the earth are counted as nothing, and He does what He wants with the army of heaven and the inhabitants of the earth. There is no one who can hold back His hand or say to Him, 'What have you done?'" (Daniel 4:34b–35).

We began this study with a long look at a family that made an unfaithful decision. God had warned His people that their tendency would be to drift away from Him and His ways and conform to the ungodly ways of the heathen people who would surround them. A few generations after they entered the land of promise, Elimelech and his family left it and suffered God's judgment as a result. There is much more to this story, as we will see. However, at this point, we can draw a few conclusions that can be applied to our lives.

We have all made our share of mistakes and missteps, and we sometimes suffer God's discipline as a result. Other times, we bear disappointments, lifelong scars, and hardships through no fault of our own but because someone else disobeyed God. In addition, some of the most difficult times in our lives may be the result of illness or accidents, the natural result of living in a world where sin has warped God's perfect creation. The good news is that God has made provision to use all of these circumstances to bless the lives of those who follow Jesus.

> Praise the God and Father of our Lord Jesus Christ, the Father of mercies and the God of all comfort. He comforts us in all our affliction, so that we may be able to comfort those who are in any kind of affliction, through the comfort we ourselves receive from God. For as the sufferings of Christ overflow to us, so through Christ our comfort also overflows. (2 Corinthians 1:3–5)

The Christian community is the means by which we are often comforted in the painful times of life, no matter what the root cause of that pain. The comfort that God uses to work His best for His children comes most effectively through others who have desperately needed and received His comfort at some time in their lives.

The Christian community must be redemptive and supportive in nature in order for healing to take place. God would have us waste none of our sorrows. Instead, let us pass along comfort to others in the way God comforted us. Then, we become a messenger of help and healing within the community. In order for this to occur, however, we must be willing to share our testimonies of forgiveness and healing, and also our needs and shortcomings within our community of Christian friends. If we are unwilling to open ourselves to others, the flow of redemptive love the Holy Spirit sets in motion is blocked. God never intended for us to be isolated in a time of trial.

If you are in need right now, look to the Christian community for help. God has placed someone there who has experienced similar problems and sorrows. There is provision there for you. That is what Naomi decided to do, and it was a good decision. Read on. You will find fresh hope and healing.

◊ As you reflect on your life, can you pinpoint a time or times when God graciously saved you from the consequences of your own poor choices? If so, have you made it a point to thank Him for His divine deliverance? If not, do so now.

◊ Are you the type of person who hides your needs and trials from others? Are you closed to close relationships and open friendships? If so, consider why you are this way and how this tendency might have robbed you of God's best. How has your desire to remain isolated during times of pain impacted your life? How might it have been different had you experienced the difficulty in community with other believers? Do you have a sorrow or testimony that you would like to share, either for your encouragement or for the encouragement of others? If so, will you? If your answer is yes, ask God to provide opportunities.

RUTH 1:6–13

She and her daughters-in-law prepared to leave the land of Moab, because she had heard in Moab that the Lord had paid attention to His people's need by providing them food. She left the place where she had been living, accompanied by her two daughters-in-law, and traveled along the road leading back to the land of Judah. She said to them, "Each of you go back to your mother's home. May the Lord show faithful love to you as you have shown to the dead and to me. May the Lord enable each of you to find security in the house of your new husband." She kissed them, and they wept loudly. "No," they said to her. "We will go with you to your people." But Naomi replied, "Return home, my daughters. Why do you want to go with me? Am I able to have any more sons who could become your husbands? Return home, my daughters. Go on, for I am too old to have another husband. Even if I thought there was still hope for me to have a husband tonight and to bear sons, would you be willing to wait for them to grow up? Would you restrain yourselves from remarrying? No, my daughters, my life is much too bitter for you to share, because the Lord's hand has turned against me." Again they wept loudly, and Orpah kissed her mother-in-law, but Ruth clung to her. Naomi said, "Look, your sister-in-law has gone back to her people and to her god. Follow your sister-in-law."

CHAPTER TWO

Kay Reed

Spiritual Discernment—A Grace for All Seasons

Introduction

"She and her daughters-in-law prepared to leave the land of Moab, because she had heard in Moab that the LORD had paid attention to His people's need by providing them food" (Ruth1:6).

In her lifetime, Naomi had lived in her father's house, and in later years, in her husband's house. In both houses, she was probably protected and, perhaps, she was also cherished. We don't know what her marriage was like or how her husband and sons treated her. Perhaps she was treated poorly and given no more consideration than a servant. Maybe she was loved and highly esteemed by the men in her family, we don't know. We can be sure, however, that she had very little practice making decisions. First, her father, and then her husband, was the head of their household, the provider and the decision maker. Her job was to submit to them and look out for the daily needs of the household. Now, her husband and two sons were dead, she was in a foreign land, and she was the lone decision maker.

To whom could she turn for advice and counsel? Not her mother and father. If they were still living, they were not living in Moab. Not her friends, for it is highly unlikely that she had developed deep and lasting friendships among the women of Moab. She alone had to make the most urgent decision—how to survive as a widow with no means of support. The answer was clear—return to Bethlehem. In Bethlehem, there was provision for widows. In Bethlehem, there was the presence of extended family. In Bethlehem, there was food, and that was her most immediate need. So Naomi made the right decision, prompted by a wrong motive, and decided to return to Bethlehem.

You may remember that in the last chapter we made note of the cycle that occurred for about three hundred years during the time that judges ruled Israel. That cycle began with God blessing His people, after which they experienced a slide into sin. God would send discipline, they would repent, and afterward He would bless them again. Soon, the cycle repeated itself. It appears that repentance had again taken place among the Jewish people. So God sent food, as He had promised. Because Naomi was away from Bethlehem, living in a foreign land, she missed the blessings of corporate repentance. Had she and her family stayed in Judah, she would have been rejoicing with the rest of God's people over the forgiveness of sins that comes in time of repentance and revival. She would have delighted to see the renewal of joy and thanksgiving that accompanied God's blessing of provision. However, she missed all those good things while struggling with grief in Moab because of the loss of those she loved the most. Grief affects one's ability to make good decisions. What Naomi needed, but lacked, was spiritual discernment.

Trials

Lack of Spiritual Discernment During a Crisis

As we consider spiritual discernment, we should adopt a common definition. While this specific term is not found in the Bible, its generally accepted usage today describes the ability to view the world biblically and, as a result, receive spiritual direction.

While grief is designed to heighten our sensitivity to God's voice, sometimes our tendency in times of stress and sorrow can be to react in ways that do not reflect spiritual discernment. When experiencing grief, God would have us draw closer to Him and look to Him for direction. He desires that we would *act* in accordance with His direction and will. Instead, we often *react* to our circumstances and take actions that are the opposite of His will. That is what Naomi appears to have done. She made a decision to return to Bethlehem because of her physical circumstances, but there is no evidence that she sought the guidance of Yahweh or that she repented before Him for any part she might have had in leaving His people and His way. Therefore, she made a series of wrong choices.

At first, she had made a right decision for the wrong reason. Naomi must have developed a loving relationship with her daughters-in-law, for the Bible says they began to make preparations to leave Moab with Naomi. The three women actually disposed of their belongings, packed necessities, and began their journey back to Judah (Ruth 1:7).

At that point, however, she made a wrong decision and changed her mind. Perhaps despondency set in as she began to journey homeward. Maybe she wondered what she would find when she arrived. Would any in her extended family still be alive? Where would she live? Would she be a beggar for the rest of her life? Did she begin to anticipate her own humiliation because of the taunts of her former neighbors and other women of the village? Did she expect a chorus of "I told you so"?

There may have been an additional reason. Maybe Naomi began to be concerned for Orpah and Ruth's welfare. Perhaps she did not anticipate a warm welcome for them in Bethlehem. There was a history of animosity between Israel and Moab, particularly the women of Moab. In Numbers 25:1–15, during the time of Moses, we read that Moabite women enticed some of the Israelite men into fornication and false worship. That same problem with Moabite women repeated itself many times during the history of Israel as recorded in 1 Kings 11:1; Ezra 9:1–2; and Nehemiah 3:23. Maybe Naomi was afraid the presence of two young unattached Moabite women in the small village of Bethlehem might spell TROUBLE.

Whatever her reason, after they began their journey, Naomi abruptly changed her mind and instructed her daughters-in-law to go back to their childhood homes in Moab. It seems that her concern must have been their welfare, for her instructions are: "Each of you go back to your mother's home" (v. 8a). Her description hints that they needed what their mothers alone could supply—comfort and emotional support in their time of grief.

At this point, Naomi did invoke the name of Yahweh in a blessing. She called attention to the faithful love of her Jewish God and likened the love that Orpah and Ruth had showed to her late sons and to herself to Yahweh's love. She released them to marry again, wished them rest, peace, security, and blessing. She dismissed them with a kiss (v. 9), although they wept and pledged their love to her (v. 10).

In verses 11–13, Naomi explained her reasoning to Orpah and Ruth, citing the reasons they should return to Moab. Her argument was centered on their future marriages. She explained that there was no chance she would have another husband and more sons, and even if that were the case, they would be too old to be eligible brides to her sons. Orpah was persuaded by her argument and departed, but Ruth announced her love and loyalty to Naomi and to Naomi's God. The Scripture says, "Ruth clung to her" (v. 14).

In her time of trial, Naomi entirely missed the spiritual implications of her situation. When she urged them to return to their homes, she was sending them back to their heathen gods as well. Describing her life as "too bitter for them to share" (v. 13), she could not see the hand of God in her circumstances, possibly because she felt abandoned by Yahweh. But God is always at work in our lives, in good times and in the bad, in our good decisions and our bad ones.

An Old Testament Example of Spiritual Discernment

Having observed Naomi's failure to show spiritual discernment, let us consider an Old Testament example of a woman who acted wisely and with spiritual discernment in a different kind of crisis. The true story is recounted in 1 Samuel 25:1–42. Stop now and read these verses carefully, then consider this intelligent and beautiful woman of old.

Abigail was the wife of Nabal, whose name means "fool." The Bible defines a fool for us in Psalm 14:1: "The fool says in his heart, 'God does not exist.'" Her husband, the fool, insulted David after he had been anointed by Samuel to become king, but before he was actually crowned. During this stressful time, David and his band of men were living in the wilderness of Paran and being pursued by Saul.

Because David's men had protected Nabal's flocks and shepherds, he asked for a portion of Nabal's bounty as payment. But Nabal refused his request in an insulting manner, and David's response was to grab his sword and set out with four hundred men and plans to kill Nabal and all of his men. Abigail was warned about the situation. The messenger summarized the problem when he said about Nabal: "He is such a worthless fool, nobody can talk to him" (v. 17b.) So here, ladies, we have a real crisis! On the one hand, David and four hundred men are advancing toward Nabal and his encampment, while on the other hand, Abigail's husband is unlikely to change his mind and seek peace. Abigail took action!

"Abigail hurried, taking 200 loaves of bread, two skins of wine, five butchered sheep, a bushel of roasted grain, 100 clusters of raisins, and 200 cakes of pressed figs, and loaded them on donkeys" (v. 18). She intervened, met David, and persuaded him to accept the provisions that she had brought; she then apologized for her husband's behavior. Showing great spiritual discernment, she declared that it was the Lord Who had prevented David, to that point, from participating in bloodshed and avenging himself with Saul, who was trying to kill him. She prevailed on David to change his mind. Her final argument showed great spiritual discernment. "'When the LORD does for my lord all the good He promised, and appoints you ruler over Israel, there will not be remorse or a troubled conscience for my lord because of needless bloodshed or my lord's revenge'" (vv. 30–31a). David blessed Abigail for her discernment (v. 33).

When Abigail returned to her home, Nabal was hosting a great feast and was drunk, so again she showed discretion and told him nothing about the whole affair. The next morning, when she did tell him, "he had a seizure and became paralyzed. About 10 days later, the LORD struck

Nabal dead" (vv. 37b–38). When David learned of Nabal's death, he sent for her and married her. How is that for a happy ending?

Your time of trial may also end happily, if you employ spiritual discernment in your decision making. There is no guarantee that you may find yourself marrying a king, but by exhibiting spiritual discernment in decision making, you could avoid becoming the wife of a fool.

Truth

Developing Spiritual Discernment

Since spiritual discernment is essential to a God-honoring life, let us spend some time considering how such discernment is developed in a believer. In a nutshell, God gives spiritual discernment as a natural outgrowth of time spent in His Word and in prayer. God promised to David in Psalm 32:8: "I will instruct you and show you the way to go; with My eye on you, I will give counsel."

This promise is a reminder of a mother whose eye is on her children. She is always vigilant for their welfare, always aware of any approaching danger, and a step ahead of her children to guard them from their own foolish actions. Using her mother's instinct, she often knows what they will do, even before they do it. In the same way, God fulfills His promise to guide with His eye, for He promises to "instruct, to show (demonstrate)" the way to go. So, if we are truly seeking God's instructions and can't understand what He is saying, He promises to go one step farther and "show" the way. He further promises to keep His eye on us and give counsel. There will never be a time when a He will ignore a request for counsel and guidance.

By studying the Bible, His infallible Word, we learn what He is like. We learn His precepts; we learn to recognize His voice. Many times, when searching for guidance on a matter, God answers through Scriptures in a time of devotion or prayer. Sometimes, but not always, the answer will come through a Scripture that has been committed to memory. At times, the key to the answer is found in the advice of other Christians, or, at other times, a pastor or radio preacher will pronounce the answer through a sermon. The point is, however, that God will do what He promises! He will, we can be sure, give spiritual discernment if a believer is seeking it.

The means by which God guides our hearts and minds into spiritual discernment is the Holy Spirit. Paul says, in 1 Corinthians 2:12–16: "Now we have not received the spirit of the world, but the Spirit who comes from God, so that we may understand what has been freely given to us by God. We also speak these things, not in words taught in human wisdom, but in those taught by the Spirit, explaining spiritual things to spiritual people. But the unbeliever does not welcome what comes from God's Spirit, because it is foolishness to him; he is not able to understand it since it is evaluated spiritually. The spiritual person, however, can evaluate, everything, yet he himself cannot be evaluated by anyone. For who has known the LORD'S mind, that he may instruct Him? But we have the mind of Christ." Learning to recognize the voice of the Holy Spirit so we can receive all that God has for us is a necessary part of Christian maturity.

◊ According to 1 Corinthians 3:18–21, why is it important that we not take direction from the prevailing culture in seeking to make godly decisions?

◊ Why might unbelievers around us not understand why we make certain decisions?

41

◊ Is any decision too small a matter to bring before God for His counsel? Why or why not?

◊ What does Paul mean when he says, in 1 Corinthians 2:15, ". . . yet he himself cannot be evaluated by anyone"?

The development of spiritual discernment is necessary for many reasons and should be in progress before the crisis begins. It is highly unlikely that someone who has neglected the study of the Word, failed to develop the spiritual discipline of prayer, and, therefore, does not recognize the voice of God's Spirit, will have the discernment he needs when a crisis occurs. Believers must, above all else, know the Scriptures, God's Word. The Scriptures are the Truth against which all theories and teachings may be measured. "All scripture is inspired by God and is profitable for teaching, for rebuking, for correcting, for training in righteousness, so that the man of God may be complete, equipped for every good work" (2 Timothy 3:16–17).

It is urgent that the second part of the Great Commission be put into practice. Jesus left these instructions with His disciples in Matthew 28:19–20: "Go, therefore, and make disciples of all nations, baptizing them in the name of the Father and of the Son and of the Holy Spirit, teaching them to observe everything I have commanded you. And remember, I am with you always, to the end of the age." Making disciples is the first part of the Great Commission. The second half is teaching them everything Jesus commanded.

The New Testament Gift—Distinguishing Between Spirits

In Old Testament times, God guided His people through powerful leaders such as Moses and Joshua. Later, He called out judges to be their champions, and, still later, we see the era of kings and prophets who spoke God's Word to His people. In the New Testament, after the establishment of the Church, the Holy Spirit gave gifts of supernatural abilities to believers in order to meet all the needs of the Church. These supernatural abilities are known as spiritual gifts. The Greek word for gifts is *charisma*. It is defined in Strong's Exhaustive Concordance of the Bible as "a divine gratuity."[2]

First Corinthians 12:10 tells us that the Holy Spirit has also given, as one of the spiritual gifts, discerning of spirits (KJV), distinguishing of spirits (NASB), or distinguishing between spirits (HCSB). This gift is not necessarily the same as the skill of spiritual discernment that we have been discussing, although it certainly involves spiritual discernment. Kenneth S. Wuest, in his Expanded Translation of the Greek New Testament translates the description of the gift in this way: "and to another the correct evaluation of those individuals who give forth divine revelations . . ."[3]

Paul tells us that the spiritual gifts are "for the training of the saints in the work of ministry, to build up the body of Christ, until we all reach unity in the faith, and in the knowledge of God's son, growing into a mature man with a stature measured by Christ's fullness" (Ephesians 4:12–13).

This New Testament gift is to be exercised within the Body in order to protect members from deception by false prophets. The apostle John urged, "Dear friends, do not believe every spirit, but test the spirits

---

2   James Strong, S.T.D., LL.D. *Greek Dictionary of the New Testament. In the Comprehensive Concordance of the Bible: Together with Dictionaries of the Hebrew and Greek Words of the Original, with References to the English Words* (IA Falls, IA: World Bible Publishers, 1986), 77.

3   Kenneth Samuel Wuest, "First Corinthians." *In the New Testament: An Expanded Translation* (Grand Rapids: Eerdmans, 1961), 405.

to determine if they are from God, because many false prophets have gone out into the world" (1 John 4:1). By the time John wrote this letter to other believers, some fifty to sixty years after the establishment of the Church, the purity of Christianity was being threatened by many false teachings and by efforts to combine Christianity with prevailing philosophies. Throughout the history of the Church, false doctrines have assailed believers.

This is no less true today. How do we know whether we are hearing and seeing a false prophet or a true teacher of the Word? We must test the spirits. Such testing provides the basis upon which we can discern divergence from the truth that characterizes the teaching of false prophets. Luke, in Acts 17:11, commended the Christians in the church of Berea and called them noble minded because they received the Word with great eagerness and "examined the Scriptures daily to see whether these things were so" (NASB). Individual members of the local church must educate themselves in Scripture and examine the Scriptures carefully, but the Spirit has also given the spiritual gift of discerning between spirits to make certain that the Body of believers will not be led astray.

Recognition of the presence of this gift and those who have it is necessary so that when a crisis occurs, the Church will be equipped. "And I pray this: that your love will keep on growing in knowledge and every kind of discernment, so that you can approve the things that are superior and can be pure and blameless in the day of Christ" (Philippians 1:9–10). It is certain that deception will assail the Church during the last days, for there is a false prophet coming in the disguise of a spiritual leader who will seek to lead the world to worship the Antichrist.

Read these Scriptures and answer the questions that follow:

1 Timothy 4:1–2—Now the Spirit explicitly says that in later times, some will depart from the faith, paying attention to deceitful spirits and the teachings of demons, through the hypocrisy of liars whose consciences are seared.

Revelation 16:13–14—Then I saw three unclean spirits like frogs coming from the dragon's mouth, from the beast's mouth, and from the mouth of the false prophet. For they are spirits of demons performing signs, who travel to the kings of the whole world to assemble them for the battle of the great day of God, the Almighty.

Revelation 19:20—But the beast was taken prisoner, and along with him the false prophet who had performed the signs in his presence. He deceived those who accepted the mark of the beast and those who worshiped his image with these signs. Both of them were thrown alive into the lake that burns with sulfur.

Revelation 20:10—The devil who deceived them was thrown into the lake or fire and sulfur where the beast and the false prophet are, and they will be tormented day and night forever and ever.

1. Underline every appearance of the word *deceit, deceitful, deceived*. Draw a box around the word *signs* in these verses.
2. Notice the methods that will be used in the later days to draw people toward worship of the Antichrist. The meaning of the word *signs* is "miracles." This is the same Greek word, *semeion*, which describes Jesus' miracles. This tells us that the false prophet will perform miracles similar to those that Jesus performed when He was on the earth. Is it any wonder, therefore, that the gift of discerning between spirits will be absolutely necessary in the future?

The repeated use of the words *deceit* and *deceitful* describe the way the false prophet will persuade many to follow and eventually worship the Antichrist. Note that the tactics of the enemy, the devil, have not changed since the Garden of Eden. "For Adam was created first, then Eve. And Adam was not deceived, but the woman was deceived and transgressed" (1 Timothy 2:13–14).

Therefore, it is imperative that each believer develop spiritual discernment! The time is coming when deception will be quite prevalent within the established Church. The gift of discernment between spirits will be absolutely necessary then, and so will spiritual discernment. Without it, how will one know who to believe?

Transformation

The story is told in 1 Kings about a dream Solomon, David's son, had. David had died and Solomon was king when God appeared to him in a dream asking, "What should I give you?" (1 Kings 3:5). Solomon's answer was "'. . . give your servant an obedient heart to judge Your people and to discern between good and evil. For who is able to judge this great people of yours?' Now it pleased the LORD that Solomon had requested this" (1 Kings 3:9–10).

Just as it pleased the Lord that Solomon asked for a discerning heart instead of long life, riches, or the death of his enemies, we know any request we might make for discernment will also please God. In addition, God has promised that He knows how to give good gifts to His children who ask, and that He will never give a stone when we ask for bread (Matthew 7:9). Therefore, if you want discernment, know that God will graciously give it. But it won't fall as manna from heaven every morning. Instead, God will give the means by which you may develop it. Here are some suggestions:

1. Make prayer a priority. Ask for discernment in spiritual matters first, and you will find that you will also have wisdom in everyday decisions. Make a point of asking, seeking, and knocking until you are satisfied. If you need help to feel more satisfied with your prayer life, visit a reliable Christian bookstore and you will find much help there. Read about the great men and women of faith, and pay particular attention to their prayer lives. Your church may have a prayer ministry. If so, join it. In doing so, you will meet those in your fellowship who have a mature prayer life. Remember that even legends of the faith have seldom been satisfied with their own prayer lives, so don't be ashamed to admit your need.

2. Move past your past. Perhaps you have made some poor decisions. Maybe those decisions have cost you mightily.

Take those decisions and their consequences to the Lord in repentance. He will redeem them and use them for your good if your repentance is genuine. This process of repentance is pictured in the verses we are considering in this chapter about Naomi's decision to return to Bethlehem. The words *return* or *go back* are used over and over again in these verses. Naomi left her home in Moab, made a turnabout, and went back toward Bethlehem. In considering your past mistakes, go back in your mind to the time you made a decision that you now know was displeasing to God, and confess it. *Return* unto God and He will *return* unto you.

After you have repented of past sins, returned to God, and asked for spiritual discernment in the future, expect God to forgive, cleanse, and give the discernment for which you have asked.

Watch for the answers He will give. Ask God to help you recognize His answers when they come. Without a doubt, we often ask for something in prayer, and then fail to recognize God's answer when it comes. It is especially helpful to keep a journal of your requests and record the answer. If you have a good friend who is spiritually mature, ask her to tell you when she notices that you are making better decisions. It will be a wonderful day in heaven when we see the way God has answered our prayers because we miss so many of His answers in the busyness of our lives.

3. Seek to spend time with someone who is more spiritually mature than you. The most likely place this might happen is within your family or church family. Perhaps there is a more mature woman within your circle of friends or family who will be willing to mentor you in the faith. You don't have to plan a formal time for study or discussion, just go places together or do something that you both enjoy.

Our Bible study group, for many years, enjoyed the participation and developing friendship of a much younger woman in our midst. She was no longer living near her mother or grandmother and was looking for friendships with older women. What a blessing she was to us, and although she has now moved from the area, we came to love and delight in her children. Older women are able to help the young women, especially young mothers, to gain a perspective about their childbearing years and know from experience how fast the intense days of mothering pass. The Bible urges older women to ". . . encourage the young women to love their husbands and to love their children" (Titus 2:4).

4. Be willing to step out and stretch your faith. While seeking spiritual discernment, you may be surprised to find that other spiritual skills are developed as well. If you don't know what your spiritual gift is, be open to the Spirit's teaching as you become sensitive to His leading. The best way to discover your spiritual gifts is to take opportunities for service that interest you. It will then be much easier to evaluate the spiritual impact that the exercise of your gift will have. The Christian life is surprisingly exciting when one is operating in the empowering of the Spirit!

A New Testament Example of Spiritual Discernment

There is a fascinating account in John 12:1–7 of an incident that took place six days before Jesus' death. He was in Bethany at the home of Mary, Martha, and Lazarus, and they gave a dinner for Him. In the custom of the time, they were reclining at the table when "Mary took a pound of fragrant oil—pure and expensive nard—anointed Jesus' feet, and wiped His feet with her hair. So the house was filled with the fragrance of the oil. Then one of His disciples, Judas Iscariot, (who was about to betray Him), said, 'Why wasn't this fragrant oil sold for 300 denarii and given to the poor?' . . . Jesus answered, 'Leave her alone; she has kept it for the day of My burial.'"

We see here a most astonishing act of spiritual discernment. Mary, of all the people who were present at that dinner, recognized that the time of Jesus' death was near. Who was there? Probably all the disciples, maybe other invited guests, for the Scripture says ". . . they gave a dinner for him . . ." (v. 2). We know that Lazarus was there, for the Scripture says so. Martha was serving. Yet this one woman, out of all the men who had been taught by Jesus and traveled with Him for almost three years, was sensitive enough to God's leading that she anointed Him for His burial. Contrast her sensitivity with that of the disciples who, just a few days after that, were arguing among themselves about who should be the greatest in Jesus' earthly kingdom, which they thought was going to be established soon (Luke 22:24).

How do you suppose Mary developed this astonishing level of spiritual discernment? For the answer, let us look at another incident that had taken place a few months earlier. In Luke 10:38–42, we are told that Jesus, again, had come to Martha and Mary's house. Martha was concerned about her many duties as a hostess and grew annoyed because her sister, Mary, was not helping her, but instead was sitting at Jesus' feet listening to Him teach. She said to Jesus, "'Lord, don't you care that my sister has left me to serve alone? So tell her to give me a hand.' The Lord answered her, 'Martha, Martha, you are worried and upset about many things, but one thing is necessary. Mary has made the right choice, and it will not be taken away from her.'"

Jesus and Women

Ladies, don't miss what Jesus said to Martha. Contained in His mild rebuke of Martha was His commendation of Mary for the choice she had made—to sit at His feet and learn from Him instead of being "worried and upset about many things." In that day, women were not formally educated, especially not in spiritual matters. Fathers and mothers were instructed to teach their children, which included girls, but formal education was reserved for boys. Thus, Jesus' approval of Mary's desire to learn about spiritual things was highly unusual.

Jesus elevated the status of women in many ways during His earthly ministry. He openly healed and ministered to women, as in Luke 7:35–50, when He told the immoral woman that her sins were forgiven. In Luke 13:16, He called a disabled woman who had been bent over for more than eighteen years a "daughter of Abraham," thus elevating her to the level of a man. A group of women, including Mary Magdalene, Joanna, Suzanne, and others traveled with Him on occasion (Luke 8:1–3).

Also, the first witnesses to the resurrection were women, although a woman's testimony was considered unreliable and was not accepted in a court of law.

In the early church, women were very involved in the spread of the Gospel. There was Lydia, who was a seller of purple cloth (Acts 16:14–15), and Phoebe, "a servant of the church in Cenchreae" (Romans 16:1). Priscilla is mentioned five times in the New Testament. Priscilla and her husband, Aquila, are seen traveling with Paul in Acts 18:18, and in Romans 16:3, Paul calls them his coworkers in Christ and says they risked their lives for him.

Since the coming of the Holy Spirit, spiritual discernment and all the other treasures of the Kingdom have been as available to women as to men. Note that on the Day of Pentecost, when the Holy Spirit came upon the believers, Peter's sermon contained this quotation from Joel 2:28–29 "And it will be in the last days, says God, that I will pour out My Spirit upon all humanity; then your sons and your daughters will prophesy, your young men will see visions, and your old men will dream dreams. I will even pour out My Spirit on my male and female slaves in those days, and they will prophesy" (Acts 2:17–18). As a word of clarification, note the word *prophesy* means to proclaim the Gospel. Peter said that was the explanation for what was happening, and so he revealed that, beginning with Pentecost, we are in the "last days."

How wonderful that in these last days, both men and women have full access to the spiritual blessings of the Kingdom!

> Naomi said, "Look, your sister-in-law has gone back to her people and to her god. Follow your sister-in-law." (Ruth 1:15)

When we leave this segment of the story, Naomi was completely convinced that she was doing the right thing by insisting that Ruth follow Orpah and return to Moab. Naomi's spiritual discernment quotient was near zero. She had only the material possessions that she could transport on a fifty-mile journey. She and Ruth were homeless, uneducated women in a man's world, without money, power, or influence. None of this mattered to God! He had a plan to which none of them were privy.

They were living proof of the words of Paul, spoken many years later: "Brothers, consider your calling: Not many are wise from a human perspective, not many are powerful, not many of noble birth. Instead, God has chosen what is foolish in the world to shame the wise, and God has chosen what is weak in the world to shame the strong. God has chosen what is insignificant and despised in the world—what is viewed as nothing—to bring to nothing what is viewed as something, so that no one can boast in His presence. But it is from Him that you are in Christ Jesus, who became God-given wisdom for us—our righteousness, sanctification, and redemption, in order that, as it is written: The one who boasts must boast in the Lord" (1 Corinthians 1:26–31).

Although the Bible consists of sixty-six books, they all combine to tell one beautiful story. Beginning with Abram, who later became Abraham, the earlier books tell of how God chose a man, revealed Himself to him, called him out from his home and family, and began to make a great nation. The history of Abram's descendants, their children, and their children's children is an account of the outworking of our gracious God's plan to send a Savior into the world that had been corrupted by sin.

Beginning with the book of Ruth, God narrows the spotlight for the reader and points to one family that was a part of that nation. God is about to adopt a Moabite woman into the family that would, in three generations, produce King David. God's promises to Abraham, that he would be the father of a great nation and through him all the nations of the world would be blessed, are always in view as we read the story of God's faithfulness in performing His covenant.

We come in this wonderful story, unmatched in human history, to a time when two destitute women stand between Moab and Israel, contemplating their future. Who would guess that God would use what was foolish, what was weak, and what was insignificant in this world to bring great glory to Himself?

> "Sing to God! Sing praises to His name. Exalt Him who rides on the clouds—His name is Yahweh—and rejoice before Him. God in His holy dwelling is a father of the fatherless and a champion of widows." (Psalm 68:4–5)

◊ Spend some time giving praise to God for circumstances in your past that God has redeemed for His glory and your good. Write out your prayer of praise below:_

◊ What foolish, weak, or insignificant circumstance in your life needs to be redeemed?

◊ Has there been a time when another person had more spiritual discernment about a situation in your own life than you did? If it might help someone else, be prepared to share your answer with the group.

◊ How might the gift of distinguishing between spirits be misused in the Body of Christ?

RUTH 1:11–18

But Naomi replied, "Return home, my daughters. Why do you want to go with me? Am I able to have any more sons who could become your husbands? Return home, my daughters. Go on, for I am too old to have another husband. Even if I thought there was still hope for me to have a husband tonight and to bear sons, would you be willing to wait for them to grow up? Would you restrain yourselves from remarrying? No, my daughters, my life is much too bitter for you to share, because the Lord's hand has turned against me." Again they wept loudly, and Orpah kissed her mother-in-law, but Ruth clung to her. Naomi said, "Look, your sister-in-law has gone back to her people and to her god. Follow your sister-in-law." But Ruth replied: Do not persuade me to leave you or go back and not follow you. For wherever you go, I will go, and wherever you live, I will live; your people will be my people, and your God will be my God. Where you die, I will die, and there I will be buried. May Yahweh punish me, and do so severely, if anything but death separates you and me. When Naomi saw that Ruth was determined to go with her, she stopped trying to persuade her.

CHAPTER THREE

Kay Reed

Commitment—An Imitation of God

Introduction

"Better that you do not vow than that you vow and not fulfill it" (Ecclesiastes 5:5).

Yahweh is a God Who makes promises, and Who keeps every promise that He makes. He sets the standard. In this chapter, we will look at a vow that Ruth made to Naomi that has become quite famous. Refusing to be persuaded to leave Naomi and return to her childhood home, Ruth said, ". . . Do not persuade me to leave you or go back and not follow you, for wherever you go, I will go, and wherever you live, I will live; your people will be my people, and your God my God. Where you die, I will die, and there I will be buried. May Yahweh punish me and do so severely, if anything but death separates you and me" (Ruth 1:16–17).

Certainly, you have heard this vow repeated at weddings. You may have heard a song that contains these words, which is also a popular choice for wedding music. But did you know that these words were first spoken by Ruth to Naomi, her mother-in-law? The promise persuaded Naomi that Ruth was determined to follow her to Bethlehem in Judah, to live with her there, and to accept the poverty that Naomi would probably endure the rest of her life. Naomi could not doubt her daughter-in-law's sincerity when she committed herself to make Naomi's God her God and Naomi's people her people. Naomi gave up any idea of leaving Ruth behind when she heard her pledge, made freely and solemnly, in the name of Yahweh.

Orpah, Naomi's other daughter-in-law, had already made her choice and returned toward Moab. We don't know what happened to Orpah. When she left Naomi, she walked into obscurity. The story now centers on Ruth, and although we don't know what her appearance was, we do know that her name means "beauty" or "personality." Here she begins to live up to her name and becomes a shining example of a grace that adorns godly women, that of commitment. The kind of commitment that Ruth displayed in her vow portrays beauty of character. Her promise to Naomi closed all possible doors of escape, even reaching into the future past the day of her death, to the time of her burial.

Ruth's commitment to Naomi meant she would probably never marry again because Hebrew men were forbidden to marry anyone who was not also Hebrew. Therefore, she gave up all hope of having children of her own. The most important part of Ruth's vow, however, was a commitment to Naomi's God, Yahweh. Ruth's life would be completely different from that time forward. Her commitment to Naomi and Yahweh was complete. She withheld nothing. She walked away from all that she knew, abandoned the land of her birth, her friends and family, and the customs of her people to follow Naomi and Yahweh. Her commitment to her newfound God was so profound that to this day, female converts to Judaism often take the name of Ruth as their first name.[4] Note that in the oath she took, she called Yahweh by His covenant name, knowing that in so doing, she was turning her back on her false god, Chemosh.

Trials

An Example of Commitment

"Good news from a distant land is like cold water to a parched throat" (Proverbs 25:25).

---

4   Alfred J. Kolatch "The Synagogue." *In the Jewish Book of Why* (Middle Village, NY: J. David Publisher, 1981), 124–144.

Yes, Ruth had good news from a distant land when she learned about Yahweh! Apparently, she received it joyfully, but one has to wonder what she knew about Naomi's God. She had probably heard stories about some of the exploits of the judges who had been empowered by Yahweh to deliver His people at various times in the past. Northern Moab lay opposite Jericho, so it is probable that the miraculous way that Joshua led the Israelites to victory in Jericho was well known. No doubt travelers spread the news about such amazing happenings. But probably, most of what she knew came directly from Naomi or other members of her late husband's family. The Israelites' customs were different, their speech was different, and certainly their God was very different!

Chemosh was the god of the Moabites. His name means "destroyer, subduer, or fish god." He was an angry, vengeful god who demanded human sacrifice. Worshipping Chemosh might include offering one of your children as an sacrifice, as the king of Moab did in 2 Kings 3:27. Surely Naomi, or other members of her household, told Ruth about their God Who promised to bless His people when they obeyed Him and to be their strength and shield.

So Ruth made her choice. Abandoning Chemosh and the past, she pledged her future to Yahweh, Ruth, and the people Yahweh called His own. This was absolutely necessary because Yahweh demanded that His people worship Him and no other god. When He delivered the sons of Israel as a nation from Egypt and brought them to Mount Sinai, His very finger wrote in stone, "Do not have other gods besides Me. Do not make an idol for yourself, whether in the shape of anything in the heavens above or on the earth below or in the waters under the earth. You must not bow down to them or worship them; for I, the LORD your God, am a jealous God . . ." (Exodus 20:3–5a).

Our Call to Commitment

Some of us have made a pledge like Ruth's at the marriage altar. We may have used her very words. Such a pledge is a step into the unknown, for no one knows what will be required to fulfill that oath in the future. On the other hand, many are seeking to avoid such a commitment, being unwilling to bow to the demands that this vow or any other might make upon them. There is a trend today to avoid commitment, to the extent there is a name given to the fear that underlies the trend. It is known as commitment-phobia[5] or fear of commitment. So prevalent is the lack of commitment today that our entire society is affected by it. Churches, homes, businesses, and governments are all feeling the effects of failure to commit. Church programs suffer from lack of participation and financial support. Fathers and mothers walk away from their responsibilities as parents. Children, in turn, desert their parents when they become elderly and can no longer care for themselves. Adults of all ages fail to give a day's work in exchange for a day's pay. Our government is diminished and sometimes ineffective because of our leaders' failure to faithfully execute the duties of their office.

When Ruth left her heathen land and the worship of her false god, she pledged herself to Yahweh, and then immediately pledged herself to love and care for her mother-in-law. The second pledge was an outgrowth of the first. Commitment to God shows itself gloriously in commitment to others.

The Object of Our Commitment

Just as Ruth left all to follow Yahweh, Jesus calls the Christian to be willing to leave all and follow Him. His demands are far-reaching and unyielding.

> Don't assume that I came to bring peace on the earth. I did not come to bring peace, but a sword. For I came to turn a man against his father, a daughter against her mother, and a daughter-in-law against her mother-in-law; and a man's enemies will be the members of his household. The person who loves father or mother more than Me is not worthy of Me; the person who loves son or daughter more than Me is

---

5   Barton Goldsmith, PhD, "Understanding and Dealing with Commitment-Phobia." *Psychology Today*. April 25, 2013. Accessed June 01, 2014. https://www.psychologytoday.com/blog/emotional-fitness/201304/understanding-and-dealing-commitment-phobia..

not worthy of Me. And whoever doesn't take up his cross and follow Me is not worthy of Me." (Matthew 10:34–38)

This teaching of Jesus, no doubt, created consternation when it was first pronounced. It still does today. Since we live in a sinful world, our allegiance to Him will bring us into conflict with others who don't understand our commitment, and some of them might be members of our own families. This is Jesus' warning to count the cost because our decision will be costly, and it might even cost us our families. The cross is an instrument of death. It symbolizes death to our selfish desires, our resources, our time, or energies. We must be willing to subordinate our desires to His, make our resources His resources, and use our time and energy for His glory.

We are amazed when we consider the boldness of Ruth's promises and the unselfishness that prompted them. Such unselfishness is rare because of mankind's self-centeredness, also known as pride. Thankfully, from the time we commit ourselves to Yahweh and His Son, Jesus Christ, the Holy Spirit begins to work in our lives to rid us of pride, selfishness, self-centeredness, and other sins that constantly pull us back toward our old self-involved nature. "For those He foreknew He also predestined to be conformed to the image of His Son . . ." (Romans 8:29). An unselfish commitment to Jesus for God's glory is only possible because of the work the Holy Spirit accomplishes in our lives, and it is for God's glory alone.

The Testing of Our Commitment

It is sure that our commitment will be tested by God. There is a reason for that testing; God has a reason for everything He does. For insight in times of testing we are grateful for the wisdom the Holy Spirit gives through James 1:2–4: "Consider it a great joy, my brothers, whenever you experience various trials, knowing that the testing of your faith produces endurance. But endurance must do its complete work, so that you may be mature and complete, lacking nothing." Commitment requires endurance to prove that it is real, and in the process, maturity will be produced in the believer's life.

At one point in His ministry, Jesus' teachings grew difficult to accept. For example, in the sixth chapter of John, Jesus declared Himself the bread that came down from heaven (v. 41) and the bread of life (v. 48). He further said in the synagogue in Capernaum, ". . . I assure you: Unless you eat the flesh of the Son of Man and drink His blood, you do not have life in yourselves. Anyone who eats My flesh and drinks My blood has eternal life, and I will raise him up on the last day, because My flesh is real food and My blood is real drink" (John 6:53–55). At this point, many of His disciples turned back. "Therefore, Jesus said to the twelve, 'You don't want to go away too, do you?' Simon Peter answered 'Lord, who will we go to? You have the words of eternal life'" (John 6:67–68). At times, our commitment may be so thoroughly tested that we come to Peter's conclusion as our own. We stay because there is nowhere else to go! Our faith is in Him because by experience we know that He, and only He, has the words of eternal life. This is faith, and ". . . without faith, it is impossible to please God . . ." (Hebrews 11:6a).

Some commitments fail the testing. We all know people who have made a public decision to follow Christ but have walked away from that pledge. We cannot judge another's heart, nor do we have the privilege of knowing the future. Repentance may take place, allowing the prodigal to return. However, the apostle John in his first letter gives a standard by which it becomes evident whether or not one's commitment was sincere. "They went out from us, but they did not belong to us; for if they had belonged to us, they would have remained with us. However, they went out so that it might be made clear that none of them belongs to us" (1 John 2:19).

Choices have consequences; Ruth's certainly did! The story of her commitment is still revered by both Christians and those of the Jewish faith, but for different reasons. The book of Ruth is read annually by Orthodox Jews at the Feast of Pentecost, the time of the Festival of Harvest because her betrothal took place at the time of the barley harvest (Exodus 23:16). For Christians, her commitment symbolizes so much more. Among other things, it reminds us of God's faithfulness in keeping His commitments. Read on for more about this. It will encourage your heart!

Truth

No discussion of commitment can be complete without looking at the perfect Promise Keeper, God Himself. After God created man in His own image, man sinned and lost the right to rule over the world that God had given him in Genesis 1:28. Committing Himself to His fallen creation, God pronounced a plan of redemption. Furthermore, He has preserved the written record of His promise so that we may see and understand the kind of magnificent God He is! After pronouncing a curse on the serpent, the tempter through which sin entered the world, God looked forward through the ages to the time when His Son would become the redeemer of mankind. Speaking to the serpent, God said, "I will put hostility between you and the woman, and between your seed and her seed. He will strike your head, and you will strike his heel" (Genesis 3:15).

This is a very important prophecy and is called the *protoevangelium*, or "first good news." We must look more closely at the verse to understand why. Notice that the hostility that God pronounced is not only between Eve and the serpent, but between Eve's seed and the serpent's seed. This indicates that the hostility will go on from one generation to another. But notice also that in Scripture, the seed, meaning offspring, is never attributed to any woman but is always described as the contribution of a man. Yet, the birth of Jesus, the coming Redeemer, would not involve the seed of any mortal man. Rather, the virgin birth is described here as the seed of the woman. So we understand that this prophecy speaks of hostility for generations to come between the offspring of the serpent and the offspring of the woman.

The prophecy further pronounces, "He will strike your head, and you will strike his heel" (v. 15b). "He," the seed of the woman, will deliver a fatal blow to the offspring of the serpent. God describes two kinds of wounds here—a head wound that is fatal and a heel wound that is not.

Remember the words of this "first good news" because at this point we see God begin a work to redeem mankind. In addition, God has supernaturally preserved the written record of both His promise of redemption and the way He has fulfilled His commitment so that we may see and understand the kind of magnificent God He is!

Read carefully and let us trace the history of the movement of the hand of God through His chosen line.

◊ Adam and Eve had two sons, Cain and Abel. What happened to Abel in Genesis 4:8? Which of these two brothers was acting like the seed of the serpent? How do you know? (John 8:44).

◊ Why did Cain kill Abel? (Genesis 4:3–8; 1 John 3:12).

◊ What obituary does God leave with us regarding Cain? (Genesis 4:16).

◊ Remembering God's commitment to His creation and His promise that the seed of the woman would deliver a fatal blow to the seed of the serpent, how could this come about, since Cain had killed his brother, who was a true worshipper of God, and then had turned his back on Yahweh? (Genesis 4:25–26).

◊ Now let's come forward to the time of Christ in our thinking. "The seed of the serpent" is a collective noun, describing more than one person. Who would that be, according to John 8:44 and 1 John 4:3?

So the chosen line continued through Seth. Seth had a son named Enosh, and one of the descendants of Enosh was Noah (Genesis 5:7, 28–29). "Then God said to Noah, 'I have decided to put an end to every creature, for the earth is filled with wickedness because of them; therefore I am going to destroy them along with the earth. Make yourself an ark of gopher wood. Make rooms in the ark, and cover it with pitch inside and outside'" (Genesis 6:13–14).

In Noah, God again preserved a godly line. Noah warned about the coming judgment of God for 120 years while he built the ark, but only his family believed him. Noah had three sons: Shem, Ham, and Japheth. We can't know which of the three would be the line through which the seed of the woman would come, but God showed Noah. In Genesis 9:26a, Noah pronounced a blessing on Shem when he said, "Praise the LORD, the God of Shem . . ."

God carefully preserved the record of the descents of the three sons of Noah, and they are recounted in Genesis 10. We are particularly interested in verses 10–27 because they give the line of Shem down to a name we all recognize, Abram. In chapter 11, God called Abram to leave his land and his relatives and go to a land that God had chosen.

> "Now the LORD said to Abram: Go out from you land, your relatives, and your father's house to the land that I will show you. I will make you into a great nation, I will bless you, I will make your name great, and you will be a blessing. I will bless those who bless you, I will curse those who treat you with contempt, and all the peoples on earth will be blessed through you." (Genesis. 12:1–3)

List the things that God promised Abram:

1. "I will...

2. "I will...

3. "I will_____and you will be a blessing"

4. "I will...

5. "I will_____and all the peoples on earth will be blessed through you."

After Abram separated from Lot, his nephew who was the ancestor of the Moabites, God made a blood covenant with Abram. He promised that the land to which He would lead Abram to would belong to his descendants forever. God established the covenant sign of circumcision and changed Abram's name to Abraham (Genesis 17:5). God designated Sarai, whose name He changed to Sarah, as the mother of the chosen line and Abraham and Sarah's son, Isaac, and his descendants as part of the covenant (Genesis 17:19–21).

Isaac had two sons, Jacob and Esau. Which of the sons would be blessed to be the ancestor of the One Who would bruise the head of the serpent? God chose Jacob and confirmed the covenant with him in a dream (Genesis 28:13–14). Note especially verse 14b where God said, ". . . all the peoples of the earth will be blessed through you and your offspring." This is almost a word-for-word repetition of God's original statement to Abram. Jacob, whose name was changed to Israel, had twelve sons. They eventually found themselves in Egypt due to a famine in the land. One of Jacob's sons, Joseph, had been sold into Egypt by his brothers. Rising to be a ruler of the land, he was the instrument that God used to preserve Jacob and his descendants during the famine.

In Genesis 49, we find Jacob on his deathbed. He assembled all his sons and began to prophesy over them. In verse 10, he said, by God's Spirit, "The scepter will not depart from Judah, nor the staff from between his feet, until He whose right it is comes and the obedience of the peoples belongs to him." So Judah was the chosen line through whom "He whose right it is" would come.

Eventually, the descendants of the twelve tribes, the sons of Israel, became slaves in Egypt but were delivered by God, using Moses and his brother, Aaron. God met them at Mt. Sinai, but because of their sin of idolatry, they were condemned to wander in the wilderness for forty years or until the last of that generation died. Their descendants, led by Joshua and Caleb, who believed God's promises, were allowed to enter the land, which God had promised to Abraham centuries before. After they arrived in the land, they had no central government. Instead, God used judges to provide leadership.

That brief recap leads us to the time of Naomi, Ruth, and the story we are studying. How many years had passed since God promised a redeemer in the Garden of Eden? No one really knows, but certainly we can be amazed at God's commitment to His promise and His faithfulness to His commitment!

Over two thousand years ago, Peter marveled at God's timetable. He said". . . Scoffers will come in the last days to scoff, living according to their own desires, saying, 'Where is the promise of His coming?' Ever since the fathers fell asleep, all things continue as they have been since the beginning of creation" (2 Peter 3:3–4). "Dear friends, don't let this one thing escape you: With the Lord one day is like a thousand years, and a thousand years is like one day. The Lord does not delay His promise, as some understand delay, but is patient with you, not wanting any to perish, but all to come to repentance" (2 Peter 3:8–9).

Remember, it was this same man, Peter, who announced in Acts 2:17–21, that the coming of the Holy Spirit on the day of Pentecost showed that the last days had begun. So, paying close attention to 2 Peter 3:3–4, there should be scoffers around, scoffing at those who look for Christ's Second Coming.

◊ Do you know any scoffers or have you heard anyone scoff at the Promise of His coming again? If so, elaborate.

◊ What is the reason that Peter gives for God's delay?

◊ Stop now and pray for those you know or have heard who could be classified as scoffers. Pray for them, calling them by name if you know it. Pray that their hearts will be open to the Gospel, and then pray that you might have the privilege of witnessing to them. Write their names here so you can remember to pray for them often.

Transformation

"Now the scripture saw in advance that God would justify the Gentiles by faith and told the good news ahead of time to Abraham, saying, 'All the nations will be blessed through you. So those who have faith are blessed with Abraham, who had faith.'" (Galatians 3:8–9)

As we consider God's wonderful plan to redeem mankind, we can clearly see that the ancestors of the Redeemer were part of the Jewish race, descendants of Abraham. Through the Jewish people, sacred records were preserved that stretch back to creation. Now and then, Gentiles were included in the plan, as was the case with Ruth, the Moabitess. She is one of only four non-Israelite women who are mentioned in Jesus' genealogy in the first chapter of Matthew, and she foreshadows the mystery of the church that Paul confirms in Ephesians 3:6. "The

Gentiles are coheirs, members of the same body, and partners of the promise in Christ Jesus through the gospel." That is such good news! Through Christ, we Gentiles who have faith in Him may also inherit the blessings of salvation. Thankfully, along with salvation comes the indwelling of the Holy Spirit, Who is described by Jesus as the Helper. Therefore, the same power that we have seen keeping covenants and promises down through generations, the same wisdom that created the universe and maintains it, is available to each believer.

Christ Requires Commitment

> "Summoning the crowd along with His disciples, He said to them, 'If anyone wants to be My follower, he must deny himself, take up his cross, and follow Me. For whoever wants to save his life will lose it, but whoever loses his life because of Me and the gospel will save it. For what does it benefit a man to gain the whole world, yet lose his life?'" (Mark 8:34–36)

Christ demands first place, and requires that all other commitments be measured by the superior goal of following Him. His requirement for a follower is that one must first "deny himself." Right away, we see that this life of denying oneself will not be easy, for the believer's sinful nature is still alive. This is true, although the Holy Spirit lives in him, and through the Spirit, a believer has been born again. And so there ensues a lifelong struggle between the Spirit and the flesh. Paul described it beautifully when he said, "For I do not understand what I am doing, because I do not practice what I want to do, but I do what I hate" (Romans 7:15). Therefore, all subsequent commitments must be in harmony with the direction and example of Jesus. The flesh and the Spirit may struggle mightily at the prospect of each step in the maturing process, and the flesh may occasionally win, but the process of maturity will take place, with our loving Savior faithfully pruning the vine that abides in Him (John 15:1–2).

Jesus further said that it would be necessary for anyone who wished to follow Him to take up his cross, a demand that must have been more offensive to the hearers in that day than it is today, for they had a fuller understanding of what that would entail. To them, the cross was a frightful, fearsome instrument of torture and death. Yet, this is the demand Jesus put before the crowd that heard Him. In fact, the Scripture says that He summoned the crowd and His disciples to Him before He pronounced this ultimatum. If they wanted to follow Him, there must be no underestimating the commitment that would be required. Jesus never retracted that statement. It is still incumbent upon Christians today. Some followers will lose their lives literally, others figuratively. Therefore, if one has become a follower of Jesus, his greatest challenge, as well as test of wisdom and measure of spiritual discernment, will be deciding what commitments Jesus would have him make and how to keep the obligations that accompany those commitments. Just as Ruth's commitment to Naomi took her down a road she had never imagined, the same thing will likely happen to the devoted Christian today.

Christ Commits to You

"Come to Me, all of you who are weary and burdened, and I will give you rest. All of you, take up My yoke and learn from Me, because I am gentle and humble in heart, and you will find rest for yourselves. For My yoke is easy and My burden is light." (Matthew 11:28–30)

As an adolescent, I remember hearing my Sunday school teacher say this was his favorite Scripture. I was puzzled over that; I could not imagine what burden concerned him or why he would be weary. Now the passing of the years has endeared this promise to me as well. The events of life burden us with worries, cares, grief, concerns, and distresses. There is a misconception that as one grows older, the cares of life become fewer. It is not at all unusual to hear the elderly say their dream of a carefree, leisurely old age has not come to pass. However, the good news is that Jesus has promised to be our burden bearer if we learn of Him. That's the catch, and also the wonderful part! Learning of Him is a lifelong process. We will surely be weary of carrying our own burdens if we don't learn how to allow Him to bear them for us.

Not only does Christ portray Himself as a shepherd, but as a *good* Shepherd. Phillip Keller was, himself, a shepherd, and so he was beautifully equipped to write the book, *A Shepherd Looks at Psalm 23*. In it, he says, "It is the sheep owner's presence that guarantees there will be no lack of any sort: that there will be abundant green pastures; that there will be still, clean waters; that there will be new paths into fresh fields; that there will be safe summers on the high tablelands; that there will be freedom from fear; that there will be antidotes for flies and disease and parasites; that there will be quietness and contentment."[6] Christ promises, ". . . I will never leave you or forsake you" (Hebrews 13:5). He is committed without restraint to His sheep.

Jesus' commitment to us not only encompasses this life but extends to the next life as well. "I am the good shepherd. The good shepherd lays down his life for the sheep . . . My sheep hear My voice, I know them, and they follow Me. I give them eternal life, and they will never perish—ever! No one will snatch them out of My hand" (John 10:11, 27–28). Being assured of His care, as a good shepherd cares for his sheep, is the wonderful privilege of a Christian, not only in this life, but in the life to come.

Christ Desires Our Commitment to One Another

"I pray . . . for those who believe in Me through their message. May they all be one, as You, Father, are in Me and I am in You. May they also be one in Us, so the world may believe You sent Me." (John 17:20–21)

This is a short excerpt from Jesus' prayer in the Garden of Gethsemane on the night He was arrested. Earlier in the prayer, He prayed for His disciples. Then He continued in prayer for you and for me, "those who believe in Me through their message." Note that His prayer was for oneness for us, just as He and the Father are one! We can safely say this means we are to be committed to each other in the Body of Christ, the Church.

Our oneness should grow easily out of the fact we were all placed into the Body of Christ when we became believers. Spiritually, we have

---

6   W. Phillip Keller, "I Will Dwell in the House of the Lord Forever," *A Shepherd Looks at Psalm 23* (Grand Rapids: Zondervan Pub. House, 1970), 141.

the same Father and belong to the same family. Since Jesus considered our oneness to be of such high priority that it was the topic of His prayer at such a crucial time, doesn't it seem that we should give thought to how we are measuring up in this area in the sight of the Father?

After commitment to Christ, involvement with other Christians and our family through prayer and our physical presence should be next on the list of important commitments. It is impossible to be one with other believers if we withhold our love and involvement. Anyone who holds the church and its members at arm's length cannot possibly be pleasing God. Hear Jesus' words: "I give you a new command: Love one another. Just as I have loved you, you must also love one another. By this all people will know that you are My disciples, if you have love for one another" (John 13:34–35).

Searching the Scriptures for an illustration of outstanding commitment to God, I found examples of many well-known believers: Paul, Moses, David, the disciples, the prophets. However, my attention was finally drawn to a woman whose name we don't even know. Jesus knew her, though, and He cited her example.

> Sitting across from the temple treasury, He watched how the crowd dropped money into the treasury. Many rich people were putting in large sums. And a poor widow came and dropped in two tiny coins worth very little. Summoning His disciples, He said to them, "I assure you: This poor widow has put in more than all those giving to the temple treasury. For they all gave out of their surplus, but she out of her poverty has put in everything she possessed—all she had to live on." (Mark 12:41–44)

Pondering this scene, we can imagine Jesus as He observed the crowd. The Scripture says, "He watched how the crowd dropped money into the treasury" (v. 41). Note that "many rich people were putting in large sums" (v. 41b). One has to wonder how it was known that the rich were putting in large sums. Did they make a show of it? I doubt they enclosed it in an envelope because everyone knew that the widow gave "two tiny coins, worth very little." In comparison to the other gifts, she may have been ashamed to even drop her offering into the receptacle. At that point in the story, Christ summoned His disciples. He had a lesson for them.

Jesus cited, not the amount that she gave, which was the equivalent of about a half a penny, but the manner in which it was given. In giving everything she possessed, she kept nothing for herself. She made no provision for her future, even for her next meal. Isn't this the same temple where Jesus had driven out the money changers? Wasn't the priesthood corrupted by the political influence in the office of the High Priest? These things were true, yet she did not use any of them as an excuse for not giving her gift. In a supreme gesture of commitment of herself and of her future to God, she gave all that she had! Think of it; she cast herself and all of her future needs aside in one outstanding gesture of worship. Even though what she gave was a tiny amount, she is inscribed in the pages of Scripture as a model for giving. In the same way, Jesus measures our commitment to Him. We are not measured by what others give or do or how much they promise. We are not measured by how much we are able to give. Our commitment is measured by how much we have left over, that is, how much of ourselves we withhold.

> "But Jesus said to him, 'No one who puts his hand to the plow and looks back if fit for the kingdom of God.'" (Luke 9:62)

Ruth's commitment to Naomi is a beautiful thing. It won her a place in the hearts and in the sacred books of both Jews and Gentiles. However, it is no more beautiful than the commitment of a modern-day Ruth to her Lord, her family, and her church family. Christians are called to that same level of commitment when we surrender our lives to Christ. You and I serve the same Yahweh that Ruth served, a God Who delights in giving eternal rewards. Ours is a lifelong commitment to serve others to the glory of God that rises above all other promises. It brings one's life into harmony with God and undergirds all other righteous endeavors.

◊ How good are you at keeping your commitments? Is this an area in your life that needs to be brought before the Lord in repentance? If so, know that the Holy Spirit can supply the power for improvement. Thank the Lord for His grace.

71

◊ Over commitment may cause just as much problem within families as lack of commitment. If there are areas where you and your family are over committed, pray about it and then discuss it with the other members of your family.

◊ In what ways are you contributing to the welfare of Christ's Church as a whole?

KAY REED, AUTHOR OF CHAPTERS 1–3

Kay met the Lord in her early teens while in attendance at an old-fashioned revival meeting. Her primary spiritual gift is teaching, and she has been a Bible study leader and Sunday school teacher for almost fifty years. Her husband, Roy, and she are members of Germantown Baptist Church where he serves as a deacon. As the mother of four, grandmother of eight, and great-grandmother of one, she considers her family to be God's greatest blessing.

Kay Reed

Isaiah 55: 10-11

RUTH 1:19–22

The two of them traveled until they came to Bethlehem. When they entered Bethlehem, the whole town was excited about their arrival and the local women exclaimed, "Can this be Naomi?" "Don't call me Naomi. Call me Mara," she answered, "for the Almighty has made me very bitter. I went away full, but the Lord has brought me back empty. Why do you call me Naomi, since the Lord has pronounced judgment on me, and the Almighty has afflicted me?" So Naomi came back from the land of Moab with her daughter-in-law Ruth the Moabitess. They arrived in Bethlehem at the beginning of the barley harvest.

CHAPTER FOUR

Carolyn Mrok

What Is It That Defines Us?

Introduction

It should have been a day of rejoicing. Home at last! The two widowed women, Naomi and Ruth, had made the seven- to ten-day trek from Moab to Bethlehem, Naomi's family home. We are told their arrival caused a "stir" (Ruth 1:19). Instead of welcoming their former neighbor and this stranger with her, the women of the town were standing around whispering to one another, "Can this be Naomi?" (Ruth 1:19). What had caused such a remarkable change in the ten years since her friends had last seen her? It was not just that she was older; she seemed like a different person to them. A lot of details are left out of the narrative of this true story in the book named for Ruth, Naomi's daughter-in-law. We are not told how long ago or how far apart the three members of her family died. We do not know how long Ruth and Mahlon were married (the fact that there were no children might be a clue). We are not told what Ruth's state of mind was, only Naomi's. We know that Ruth was devoted to Naomi and Naomi's God (Ruth 1:16). Naomi's reply to their question revealed more than just a change in her appearance. She was not the same woman they had known. "Don't call me Naomi; call me Mara," was her response (Ruth 1:20).

It was the custom among Hebrew families to give their children names that had special meaning or described certain character or personality traits they envisioned for that child. Naomi's parents had ascribed the characteristic "pleasant" to their daughter. Her name means "pleasant." This is how her friends and neighbors had known her when she lived among them ten years earlier. What had happened to this woman to cause even her physical appearance to be so affected?

How had this believer in Jehovah gone from pleasant to bitter? (*Mara* means bitter.) Of course, she was a widow who was grieving the deaths of three family members, but what caused her to evolve from normal grief to an anger that then evolved into full-blown bitterness? Remember, her daughter-in-law was a grieving widow as well. The two women handled their situations very differently, and their identities were defined by the ways they chose to cope with their loses. While we don't want to be too hard on Naomi, nor do we seek to judge her as some might suggest, we'll see that as a child of God (as she was), we choose how we respond to the grace God offers for everything we face in life. Hopefully, we can learn from Naomi's negative example how not to let our circumstances define us and completely change our identity to bitterness.

Trials

Naomi explained her name change by adding, "I went out full, but the Lord has brought me back empty" (v. 21). She was not referring to the famine, which prompted her husband, Elimelech, to take his family away from Bethlehem to the pagan country of Moab. No, instead, she was telling the women gathered around her that when she last saw them, she was a woman full of family—her husband and two sons, Mahlon and Chilion. They were now dead; thus, she was empty! The three telling words that Naomi uttered—"call me Mara"—described more than her being bereft of family. She had ascribed to herself a new identity—bitter and empty. This was not just grief but utter hopelessness. She added the term "empty" not just to indicate a void in her life but to emphasize her emotional and spiritual state.

To be sure, Naomi (and let us not forget Ruth, as her mother-in-law seems to have done), had legitimate cause for grief. Naomi's grief seemed to have turned into anger, possibly at God.

Grief has various stages—denial, anger, bargaining, depression, acceptance—and one often moves in and out of these stages during the grief process. Naomi's words, as well as her physical appearance, seem to indicate that she had held on to these thoughts and feelings for so long that they had changed her, and even now, defined her. She was no longer pleasant; she was bitter. She had truly acquired a new spiritual and emotional identity. The anger and bitterness, which had come to define her, had even affected her countenance so that she was barely recognizable by her former neighbors.

Can bitterness really affect not only how we feel, but how we look as well? Do you know someone who has harbored bitterness for a long period of time? Doesn't it seem to harden, not only their souls, but their physical features as well? They are somewhat soured on life and present that attitude to those around them so that they are very unattractive, both physically and socially. Naomi appears to have become this sort of person. Apparently, this has not always been true of her. Her Bethlehem friends had known a different woman who perhaps lived up to her given name. Even her two daughters-in-law had at one time found something attractive in her, so much so that they both chose, at first, to follow her back home. Why had she let what had happened to her shape her identity in such a drastic way? What is the remedy for a bitter spirit? We know the cause of Naomi's. Apparently, she had let her losses eat at her for so long that she could not think beyond the scope of what life (think God) had done to her. What could she (or we) do to prevent her losses from controlling her life and defining who she was to become? Let's look to God's Word for answers so that we see clearly that we have a choice in what defines and shapes us. Naomi had that same choice and, unfortunately, at least for a time, she made the wrong choice.

Truth

It is natural for anyone who has suffered painful circumstances in his or her life to go through a grief process. It does not have to be the same circumstance as Naomi's—the loss of loved ones. It may be the grief caused by an unfaithful spouse, divorce, childhood or spousal abuse, or betrayal by a friend. It could be the loss of employment and the financial insecurity it brings. Maybe the rebellion or waywardness of a child has brought heartache and a type of grieving. Many are grieving the loss of their physical health due to a catastrophic medical diagnosis.

Whatever the source of the pain that causes us grief, God warns us that we are not to allow this root to grow into full-fledged bitterness. Look at Hebrews 12:15 and note what it says about the result of harboring a bitter spirit: "Make sure that no one falls short of the grace of God and that no root of bitterness springs up, causing trouble and by it, defiling many." Note what this verse indicates about the corrosive effect of bitterness—it defiles others, as well as the person who is harboring it. Where does bitterness come from? Some things that can lead to bitterness are anger (left to simmer too long) and unforgiveness of self, others, or even God. We have seen in Naomi's case the progression from natural grief to anger, despair, and depression brought on by unnatural, prolonged grief. Her anger at God, which had made her bitter, was so deeply rooted that it defined not just how she felt, but who she had become.

Naomi acknowledged that it was the "Lord Almighty" Who had been the source of her affliction. She said, ". . . the Almighty has dealt very bitterly with me" (v. 20), and ". . . the Lord has witnessed against me . . . and the Almighty has afflicted me" (v. 21). What does this seem to indicate? She certainly sees God's hand in her suffering.

It's very interesting, though, that she calls God by two very descriptive titles. The names she uses also indicate His character traits. She calls him "Lord Almighty" twice in Ruth 1:20–21, and she also uses the name "Lord." The Hebrew name (this is the language the Old Testament is written in) for the "Lord Almighty" that she uses is *El Shaddai*, which means the all-sufficient One, or literally the One Who sustains. Did she fail to see her Lord's sufficiency in her grief circumstance? She knew His name but failed to see what that name should mean to her in the particular situation. The other title or name she uses twice in verse 21, "LORD," indicates authority or control, in other words, His sovereignty. What part of that did she not see as applying to her? It seems that she knew His names but not the nature of the One Who bears those names. Although she took what had happened to her as having come from Jehovah, she failed to realize that He also had a plan for her that was good, that He was going to be her sustainer in her new walk as a widow, and that although she had suffered a terrible loss, her "LORD" was indeed in control.

Let's look at some other Old Testament examples of people who knew Jehovah by His covenant names and how they were sustained and found peace in that knowledge because they took them personally. God used the name *El Shaddai* (the sustainer, Genesis 17:1b) in speaking to Abraham about the covenant He had made with him. Abraham learned yet another aspect of God's nature when there appeared a ram in a thicket to be used for a sacrifice instead of his son, Isaac. He named the place "The LORD will provide" (Jehovah-Jireh). This name means God will provide. Knowing this name must have had a lasting effect on this patriarch, as God gave him other opportunities to believe Him for His hand of provision. That faithful man held on to God's promise of an heir for ten years by faith, believing that though he and Sarah were old, God was able to give them a child.

Unlike Naomi, Abraham clung to what he knew of God's character because he knew Him by His name—Lord Almighty. He applied what he knew about God to his circumstances. Naomi also claimed, "The LORD has brought me back." (Ruth 1:21). In this, she is declaring by the use of the name for Jehovah, which indicates that He is sovereign, that she knows He is in control of her situation. This did not seem, however, to bring her any comfort. While Naomi knew the significance of a name, she decided to change hers, instead of clinging to God's.

What is in a name, you might ask? The Bible has a lot to say about God's name. Let's look at these verses from Scripture and see how important it is to know Him by His names. Remember, it is His nature they describe. In Genesis 16:13, God is called "Jehovah-Roi," the God Who sees. In Genesis 22:14, He is "Jehovah-Jireh," the God Who provides. In Judges 6:24, we find the name "Jehovah-Shalom," God is peace. Naomi knew these, and yet that knowledge did not translate into trust. Instead, she chose to ignore the One she acknowledged and to be ruled by her emotions. Naomi not only failed to apply the significance of God's name to her situation, but she also failed to let her identity be defined by her relationship to Him. As a worshipper of Jehovah, she was His child and was under His watchcare. He had, after all, brought her back home to Israel just in time for the barley harvest. This was His providence.

The New Testament also reminds us of the power in the name of Jesus. We are told to pray "in Jesus' name" (John 14:13; 15:16). Why do think that is? Could it be that there is inherent power in that name? What are some of Jesus' other titles or names that also identify His character or attributes? We can call Him "Abba," which can be translated "Daddy" (Romans 8:15). We are called His "sheep," and He cares for us as the "Good Shepherd" (John 10:14). These, and many other names, indicate that He has our welfare at heart. Jesus is our Savior, which is what Joseph was told that His name would be when the angel visited him before the Christ Child was born (Matthew 1:21).

Not only are we told the different names of Jesus, but we are also given names that He applies to us as His dear children. We are called His friends (John 15:15). We are also described as His heirs (Galatians 4:7). The whole letter to the Ephesians is valuable to teach us who we are, because of who we are "in Christ." Ephesians 1:6 says ". . . He made us accepted in the Beloved" (NKJV). What does that do for you? How does that make you feel? It would be good for our sense of worth to read the whole book of Ephesians and mark every instance of the little phrase "in Him" (or "in Christ"). Doing this would help us to know who we are, because of who we are in Him.

In addition to who He is, and who we are because we are His, we are given so many other assurances that are meant to secure us in our identity. What about the promise in John 14:16–18 that assures us that He will not leave us without a Comforter (speaking of one of the roles of the Holy Spirit)? He further promises that He will never leave us or forsake us (Hebrews 13:5). In Jeremiah 29:11, we are given the principle of His sovereign plan for us "to give you a future and a hope." We have been granted peace *with* God (Romans 5:1), and the peace *of* God (Philippians 4:7). God's peace is one of His most precious gifts. This is what Naomi so desperately needed to receive from the hand of her God. Instead, she allowed her pain and sorrow to consume her and rob her of that ". . . peace of God, which surpasses all understanding . . ." (Philippians 4:7, ESV) that would have carried her in her grief in what some have called a "bubble of grace." This does not preclude the pain, but it makes it bearable and keeps it from becoming one's identifying characteristic.

Transformation

How are we to be defined? What influences how you see yourself, or, like Naomi, determines how others should see you? We, as women, assume many roles in our lives—wives, mothers, teachers, cooks, nurses, etc. What happens when our circumstances change and we are no longer those things? Our nests empty out, we lose our spouse, we no longer work—our life situations change. Have we been defined by these roles? Does the loss of them redefine our identity like Naomi? When trials come our way, do those adverse circumstances change our identity—the way we see ourselves? If our identity in Christ is based on Who He is and what He says about who we are, then although we grieve or temporarily despair or become depressed, we do not allow bitterness to take root in our hearts and overshadow our personalities and overtake our very lives.

What is it about knowing the Lord's names that gives us security and peace? Think about what we said earlier that was true of the given names of children born in Old Testament times. Just as those parents were envisioning the character they hoped the child would assume, so God's names express aspects of His character. Knowing God by His names means that we know Who He says He is and what He says He will do. Daniel was a man who knew his God and was able to stand strong as a youth in a strange land with forbidden practices. In the words Jehovah spoke through this faithful man who became God's prophet, He reminds us: "But the people who know their God will be strong and take action" (Daniel 11:32). So you see, it is vital that we know our God intimately by His names as well as through His words to us—the Bible.

How intimately acquainted are you with God as He expresses Himself through Scripture? It's His love letter to us. Have you opened it to see how lavishly you are loved? It is His unconditional, sacrificial love that will hold us when the storms come (and they will come to all). He has told us that He loves us with an everlasting love (Jeremiah 31:3). We are also assured that there is nothing that can separate us from that love (Romans 8:35–39). Do you know that you are loved in that way? That kind of love spells security for us. We all desire to be loved in that way, and as His child, we are. Are you His child? Do you feel the comfort of a loving Father Who knows you intimately and loves you infinitely? Naomi could have thrown herself on the breast of her El Shaddai and found comfort in His loving arms. Why wouldn't she?

Our fallen nature (due to sin) sometimes seeks its own fleshly remedy for the things we suffer. We buy the lie that Eve bought from the serpent (the devil—2 Corinthians 11:3) that God does not have our best interest at heart, or this thing would not have happened to us. We are then tempted to think that we must resort to our own devices in order to cope with the situation at hand. If we fall into this trap because we don't know our God or His Word well enough to know better, then we may become angry, like Naomi, because the God Who is supposed to love us has caused us to suffer in this way. There are many people who attended church, once upon a time, and professed to know God, but due to some circumstance, they no longer assemble with believers on Sunday because something happened to hurt their feelings, or make them angry, and they've never let it go. They have stewed and brewed over that slight, or whatever happened, to the extent that they have allowed exactly what Hebrews 12 refers to as "a root of bitterness" to take hold in their hearts, and it has eaten away at them, sometimes for years. They tell the story of what happened with all the emotion that they felt at the time it happened. You would think it had happened yesterday; it is so vivid and raw for them. This is the way with bitterness. It eats and eats at you until you are consumed. Those who live with, or near, a bitter person are adversely affected by it as well. Isn't that also what that passage tells us?

Do you know someone like that, perhaps a spouse, a parent, or a friend, who exudes the poison that comes from unforgiveness, which can lead to bitterness if not dealt with? As we stated earlier, it may be the refusal to forgive another person, or it may be self-directed unforgiveness. In Naomi's case, it seems to be directed at God. She blames "Adonai," Whom she knows to be in control, and yet, He hasn't prevented the deaths in her family.

What could she do? She was all alone now, left to fend for herself. Or was she? Did she not have a loving daughter-in-law, Ruth, who seemed better to her than her own two sons might have been? In her vulnerable state of protracted grief, where she seemed to prefer self-pity to comfort, she gave an opening to the enemy through the sins of anger and unforgiveness. We do the same thing when we despise or refuse the grace of God for something that happens in our lives. We, like Naomi, are sure that God could have prevented it, but He hasn't for His own reasons.

There is a saying that goes, "Sometimes the Lord calms the storm; sometimes He lets the storm rage, and calms His child." It is true, indeed, that bad things happen to good people, even to God's own people. Matthew 5:45 reminds us that, "He causes His sun to rise on the evil and the good, and sends rain on the righteous and the unrighteous."

What then can keep us from the same traps of anger, unforgiveness, and bitterness that Naomi succumbed to? First of all, we must know our God, the One we say we trust. God does, indeed, test our faith (think Job). It is in the trials of life that our faith is forged. Faith is not real until, or unless, it is tested. How do we or anyone else know whether we have saving faith unless it is demonstrated in the laboratory of life? James 1:2–3 tells us that trials yield proven character. In that same chapter in verse 12 it says, "Blessed is a man who perseveres under trial; for once he has been approved, he will receive the crown of life . . ." (NASB). Knowing God and His ways, by knowing His names (His character), will help us to take the things that happen to us as coming from the hand of the One Who knows us intimately and loves us supremely. We know that in accordance with that love, He has promised that it must result in good for me (Romans 8:28). The thing itself is not good, but our God, Who is a Redeemer, will bring beauty from ashes (Isaiah 61:3). He is the only One Who can, and He delights to do so. Not to spoil the end of the story, if you are not familiar with the book of Ruth, but He does it for Naomi before all is said and done.

Not only do we need to know our God by His name, and through His Word, but we must know our position in Him. He holds us securely in His hand (John 10:28) and will never let us go. We don't have to hold on to Him; instead, He holds on to us. That's security! Not only is our eternal destiny secure, but He also delights to give us an abundant life here and now (John 10:10). If we are confident that He is Who He said that He is, and also in who He says we are in Him, then we will see our Savior's hand in everything that comes our way—good or bad. We will be able to take from that nail-scarred hand whatever He sees fit to send our way because we know that He is entrusting His child with something out of infinite love, which will "work together" for our ultimate good. This is genuine trust.

There is the old illustration that you may have heard explaining what true faith or trust looks like. There was a tightrope walker who dared to cross the Grand Canyon on a wire. He asked his audience if they believed he could do it, to applaud. They politely clapped. He succeeded in his attempt, and they erupted in wild applause! Next, he proposed to do it again while pushing a wheelbarrow in front of him. His audience was once again asked to express their belief in him. After his second successful attempt, they cheered much more enthusiastically. Finally, he asked for a volunteer to sit in the wheelbarrow as he repeated the walk across the wire. He was met with a deafening silence. Where was their former faith or trust in his ability? Do you get the message? When we are just a spectator in life, we boast great faith in God. When we are pulled out of the stands, so to speak, and are put in a position where we either trust or fail the test, what is our response? That's our choice. That was Naomi's choice too. She failed the first time. Chances are she was given another opportunity before her life was over to have a retest. God desires for us to pass the test on the first try, but He is a patient Teacher Who gives make-ups so that we can become approved.

Ladies, are you reading this and realizing that you have failed, like Naomi, some test that God has allowed or caused in your life? It's not too late. Because you have picked up this book to read casually, or you are involved in a study of the book of Ruth, it is no accident. God desires to show you how you can let go of the grip of bitterness that you may have held on to for years. The antidote for the bile of bitterness, which sours our outlook and affects how others see us, is to know our God intimately and be confident in His character and His ways. Naomi knew His names and even saw His hand in her adversity, but she did not know her God's heart. Do you? Take the opportunity that He is giving you because He is speaking to your heart to make it a priority of your immediate future to get to know His heart toward you. There is a beautiful Christian song that reminds us: "When you can't trace His hand trust His heart."[7] Ladies, let that be the theme song of our lives.

◊   How do you see yourself? If your name was not _____, what emotional tag would you ascribe for yourself?

◊   Do you think that Naomi has gotten a bad rap? How so?

◊   How do you think Naomi's emotional and spiritual state affected her physical appearance? Have you seen this happen? Has it happened to you?

---

7   Eddie Carswell and Babbie Y. Mason, "Trust His Heart," Word, Inc., 1989.

◊ If your family and friends were asked to name a trait that defines you, what do you think they would say?

◊ How well do you know your God? Are you secure in His love? Can He trust you with a trial? Would you pass or fail? Why?

◊ Look up 1 Corinthians 10:13. Also look up the word *temptation* in a Strong's dictionary. Discuss what all this teaches about trials or temptations and how we can "escape" them (hint: is it "out of" or "through").

◊ What does 1 Thessalonians 4:13 tell us about how true believers are to grieve? What can keep it from becoming all-consuming like Naomi's?

◊ When Ephesians 4:26 tells us that it is possible to be angry yet not sin, what does that mean? Also in that same chapter, in verse 31, it says that as His disciples, we are to "put away" our anger and bitterness. Look at the context (what comes before and after) of this verse to see how this might be possible.

◊ Look for as many of God's names as you can find in the Old Testament and see what you can learn about His character and His ways (hint: they begin Jehovah-____). This will be one of the most rewarding studies you can ever do. What did you discover?

◊ Do a study on the attributes of God. If you are willing to spend the time, here they are (look up these Scripture references and explain in your own words what they are saying):

a. Omnipotent—Genesis 18:14; Job 42:2; Jeremiah 32:27

b. Omniscient—Job 37:16; Psalm 139:1–6

c. Omnipresent—Proverbs 15:3; Jeremiah 23:23–24

d. Eternal—Deuteronomy 32:40; Isaiah 57:15

e. Immutable—Psalm 102:25–27; Malachi 3:6; Hebrews 13:8

f. Incomprehensible—Job 11:7; Romans 11:33; Isaiah 55:8

g. Self-existent—Exodus 3:14; John 5:26

h. Self-sufficient—Psalm 50:7–12; Acts 17:24–25

i. Infinite—1 Kings 8:27; Psalm 145:3

j. Transcendent—Isaiah 43:10, 55:8–9

k. Sovereign (This is a long one, but it will bless your socks off!)—Genesis 45:5, 7–8, 50:20; Deuteronomy 32:39; 1 Samuel 2:6–8; 2 Samuel 16:5–11; Job 1:6–21; Isaiah 5:1–7, 14:24, 27, 45:6–7, 46:9–10 (evil equals adversity); Daniel 2:20–23, 4:34–35; Matthew 18:7; John 19:10–11; Romans 8:28–29; 1 Corinthians 10:13; James 1:2–4; 1 Thessalonians 5:18 (How do these last three relate to His sovereignty?)

l. Holy—Leviticus 19:2; Job 34:10; Isaiah 47:4, 57:15

m. Righteous—Deuteronomy 32:4; Psalm 119:142

n. Just—Numbers 14:18, 23:19; Psalm 89:14

o. Merciful—Psalm 62:12, 89:14, 116:5; Romans 9:14–16

p. Longsuffering—Numbers 14:18; 2 Peter 3:9

q. Wise—Isaiah 40:28; Daniel 2:20

r. Loving—Jeremiah 31:3; Romans 5:8; 1 John 4:8

RUTH 2:1–3

Now Naomi had a relative on her husband's side named Boaz. He was a prominent man of noble character from Elimelech's family. Ruth the Moabitess asked Naomi, "Will you let me go into the fields and gather fallen grain behind someone who allows me to?" Naomi answered her, "Go ahead, my daughter." So Ruth left and entered the field to gather grain behind the harvesters. She happened to be in the portion of land belonging to Boaz, who was from Elimelech's family.

CHAPTER FIVE

Carolyn Mrok

Putting Feet to Your Faith

Introduction

Here she is in a strange setting. What is she supposed to do now? Her mother-in-law, Naomi, still seems to be paralyzed by her grief. Ruth is also a widow with no apparent means of support. What can she do as a stranger in town with no relatives to rely on except Naomi, who for now is not even able to sustain herself?

In Ruth, chapter 2, we shift our focus from Naomi and her self-absorbed grief and bitterness, to Ruth. By way of contrast, she seems to have put aside her own grief over the death of her husband, Mahlon, to care for his mother.

Even though this young woman from a pagan background is relatively new in her faith in Jehovah, she exhibits a maturity far beyond what we might expect. Ruth must rely on what she has apparently heard or overheard about Jehovah to give her wisdom for her situation. Perhaps she has been told of the Hebrew custom of "gleaning" based on the law of Moses found in Leviticus. "When you reap the harvest of your land, moreover, you shall not reap to the very corners of your field nor gather the gleaning of your harvest; you are to leave them for the needy and the alien. I am LORD your God" (Leviticus 23:22, NASB). Ruth is not only a quick learner but a humble, yet decisive young convert. Though respectful of Naomi as her elder and mentor, she must believe that this is the plan by which her Lord Almighty (El Shaddai—the all-sufficient One—Ruth 1:20–21) will meet their needs.

Neither Ruth nor Naomi seem to be aware that their Lord (Adonai—Ruth 1:21) has led them back to Bethlehem in order to bless them. At the end of chapter 1, though it seems rather insignificant, it is noted that the two women just *happened* to arrive back from Moab "at the beginning of the barley harvest" (1:22). This is, of course, no accident, nor is it just a timely coincidence. Not only has God's providence brought Naomi back to her ancestral home, but that same providence will also direct Ruth's path to the field of one who will be God's instrument of blessing to them and to their posterity (2:3). The one who penned this account of Ruth (perhaps Samuel) introduces in the first verse of chapter 2 a man named Boaz, who we will not consider in the narrative of these three verses.

Instead, as previously stated, we will focus on Ruth, the widow of Naomi's son, Mahlon. She has chosen not only to follow Naomi back to Israel but to follow her God as well (1:16). We will observe how the young Moabite's faith is seen clearly by the steps she takes in order to provide for the physical needs of this family that has been reduced from five people to two. Ruth does not intend to be a burden on Naomi, but she seems to be intentional about her desire to unselfishly attend to her mother-in-law's needs. She shows her faith by the actions she takes in accomplishing this. Ruth's character shows in her diligence and submissiveness, but she proves, first and foremost, that even one newly converted from pagan gods is changed by that conversion so that she reflects the character of the One she worships. In these short verses in Ruth 2:1–3, we will, by using her as our example, look at her coming to faith and how that influenced not just who she was, but also, what she did. We will take faith from its inception to its working out in daily living. The change that occurred in Ruth's life with all its ramifications is the same for us who live in a very different culture than this young woman. Differences notwithstanding, our God is the same Jehovah that she came to know and serve, by serving Naomi. Faith informed everything we see in Ruth's life. The same must be said of every true believer in any culture or in any century.

Trials

In chapter 2, verse 2, Ruth seeks permission from Naomi to go and glean (gather barley) in someone's field. It seems a little strange that Naomi wouldn't have been the one to suggest this practice since she was surely more familiar with it than Ruth. Did it not occur to this older woman, one presumably more mature in her faith, not to mention her knowledge of the law, that gleaning could be the practice by which Jehovah might sustain her and Ruth? In her bitterness, Naomi's spiritual senses seem to have been dulled. On the other hand, Ruth exhibits a faith that has opened her heart to the possibilities of God's provision. Though she has had only recent opportunity to see God's hand at work, she seems to be more willing to trust His heart.

Perhaps when she learned of the custom of gathering the leftovers from another's field (gleaning), Ruth was stirred by God's Spirit to act. Even though the law specifically includes the poor and aliens in its instructions, Ruth is apparently apprehensive about how she, a foreigner, might be received by a native landowner and his workers. She suggests that it will take "favor" for her to be treated kindly by the reapers who might resent her as a newcomer in town.

After receiving Naomi's approval, Ruth sets out to put into practice what she has learned about how Jehovah's law makes provision for meeting the needs of the poor among His chosen people. Though this was a whole new concept to this transplanted young woman, she exhibits a faith in God's plan that is remarkable to all those who come in contact with her. Her faith overcame any fear she must have felt.

Think about it. Ruth had never seen a copy of this law that she had only heard about; yet she was willing to step out of her comfort zone and apply the wisdom that God had applied to her heart. She was both practical and purposeful, which is the epitome of godly wisdom.

Naomi gave her no instruction on what to do, or how to go about gathering grain to feed them. She was not told by her mother-in-law where she might find this "favor," though Naomi should obviously have known who their near-kinsmen were. Ruth was on her own, except for the One Who had already shown her His favor and Who would surely grant her favor in the eyes of others.

In our culture today, many fail to exhibit Ruth's work ethic or her determination to do whatever it takes to provide for the needs of their family members. Even in the church, sadly, there are some who abdicate their God-given role of provider. Then, on the other end of the spectrum, there are those who, in the name of providing, work excessively to the exclusion of meeting other needs of their families. These unmet emotional and spiritual needs are essential to a healthy family life.

Truth

Where did Ruth's newfound faith come from? She had, in all probability, heard her husband's family speak of their God and His law. Maybe she had watched her mother-in-law, in particular, live out the role of a godly wife and mother prior to the deaths of Naomi's husband and sons.

Let's get a personal look at this thing we call "faith." How did any of us come to faith? We know from the New Testament that the Spirit of God was wooing this former worshipper of idols as He did with us. This young Gentile from Moab probably didn't even realize what exactly prompted her to leave everything and everyone that was familiar to her in order to heed the tug at her heart to trust Naomi's God and forsake her own. John 6:44, 65 says, "No one can come to Me unless the Father who sent Me draws him . . . no one can come to Me unless it has been granted him from the Father" (NASB). Notice who takes the initiative in getting our attention.

Our faith, like Ruth's, comes from God as its source as He "draws" us to Himself. What next? Ruth somehow, and we are not told how, heard from God. We read in Romans 10:17 that "faith comes from hearing" (NASB). Hearing what, you might ask? We hear or read the Word of God—the Bible. Okay, so we are drawn by the Spirit, and we hear His Word, and then what? Ephesians 2:8–9 explains how we are saved as it states plainly, "For by grace you have been saved through faith; and that not of yourselves, it is the gift of God; not as a result of works, so that no one may boast" (NASB). What did we do that resulted in our salvation? Did you say, "Nothing"? Read those two verses again. Do you understand from what you read that it is a gift that can't be bought or earned? It explains that it was by *grace* that any of us were saved. That word means unmerited favor. Sound familiar? We'll examine that word again in just a minute. It is a gift that must be accepted or received intentionally by an act of our wills as we surrender our will to His.

Ruth may not have known that she had been forgiven, in mercy, of all her sins, but we know this because He tells us in 1 John 1:9, "If we confess our sins, He is faithful and just to forgive us our sins and to cleanse us of all unrighteousness" (NASB). So grace is giving us what we don't deserve, and then mercy is withholding from us that which we do deserve, namely, death and hell. Hallelujah!

Now back to Ruth. How do we know she trusted and surrendered her life to Jehovah? Look at her own words in Ruth 1:16. She confessed! Not only that, but she put feet to her confession by following Naomi and her God to a land she knew nothing about and to a people to whom she would be a stranger. In Romans 10:9–10, we read: ". . .that if you confess with your mouth Jesus as Lord, and believe in your heart that God raised Him from the dead, you will be saved; for with the heart a person believes, resulting in righteousness, and with the mouth he confesses, resulting in salvation." What does it say about confessing? Doesn't it indicate that confession seals the belief that is in our hearts? Because we have trusted the Lord, we confess it!

What did Ruth do that convinced Naomi or anyone else that she had become a believer? She put feet to her faith. What does that mean? She moved!

In 2 Corinthians 5:17, we are reminded *that* ". . . if anyone is in Christ he is a new creature; the old things passed away; behold, new things have come" (NASB). We can see evidence of this in Ruth's life. She was changing more than just her address. Her thoughts, her plans, her speech, and her way of doing things were all undergoing a radical shift. Further proof of the transformation in Ruth's life is evidenced by the initiative she takes in following God's law—the law of gleaning. She was already a believer in Jehovah, but she was becoming a "doer of the Word."

This phrase is used repeatedly in the New Testament book of James: "faith without works is dead" (James 2:20, NKJV). He is *not* saying that our deeds have anything to do with our *becoming* saved, but rather, they are the very *evidence* that we truly *are saved*. Read the entire passage in James 2:17–26 and ponder it for a few moments. Also, read James 1:22–25 and note the difference between those who just *hear* and those who both *hear and act* (doers).

We also learn that *true faith* is more than just *believing* (in the mind), or just giving lip service to one's faith. Guess who believes in God and His Word, and yet is not saved? James 2:19 clears up the matter of simply believing by telling us, "You believe that God is one; you do well. The demons also believe and they shudder." Are you surprised? So you see, there is a kind of faith that will *not* save. It's the kind that Satan and his demons have.

It's important for us to understand that while, in the English language, the word *believe* means something we give mental assent to or something or someone that we feel strongly positive about, this is not the case in the Greek language (the language the New Testament is written in). The words *pisteuo* ("believe," a verb) and *pistis* ("faith," a noun) have a three-fold meaning. The first is mental assent. Hebrews 11:6 says, "And without faith it is impossible to please Him, for he who comes to God must believe that He is and that He is a rewarder of those who seek Him" (NASB).

Pay attention to what the first part of that verse says about what it takes to please God. What is it? The next two parts of the meaning of the words *believe* or *faith* are a change of heart, which, in turn, prompts a change in behavior. The New Testament calls it our "walk," literally meaning lifestyle or habit. Ephesians 5:8 and 15 tell us, "For you were formerly darkness, but now you are Light in the Lord; walk as children of Light" and "Therefore be careful how you walk, not as unwise men but as wise" (NASB).

We see in Ruth, a fairly new believer who surrendered to what she thought was the will of Jehovah for her and did not just profess it but proved the genuineness of her faith by becoming a doer of the Word. She had a change of mind, a change of heart, and then her "walk" proved that she had been transformed.

This is the process described in Romans 12:1–2. Listen to the words the apostle Paul penned under the inspiration of the Holy Spirit:

"Therefore I urge you, brethren, by the mercies of God, to present you bodies a living and holy sacrifice, acceptable to God, which is your spiritual service of worship" (NASB). The word *present* indicates surrender. Now let's look at the rest of the passage in Romans verse 2: "And do not be conformed to this world, but be transformed by the renewing of your mind, so that you may prove what the will of God is, that which is good and acceptable and perfect" (NASB). What does the last part of that verse say about God's will? Do you really believe that? Ruth acted as if she did. She followed what she believed to be God's will for her. Remember, we also said that she evidenced a transformation by acting on what she believed, didn't we?

Let's also consider this idea of "favor" that Ruth 2:2 mentions. ". . . in whose sight I might find favor" (NASB). What's that about? The word *favor* may also be translated "grace." Earlier we learned that grace means "favor" or, in salvation, unmerited favor. So we see that grace is not *just* a New Testament term. One example of its use in the Old Testament is found in Genesis 6:8. It says about Noah that he "found favor in the sight of the LORD."

How does your Bible translate *grace* or *favor*? It does not matter; it's the same word. Here are two other Old Testament examples: Genesis 18:3–4, Esther 2:17. Abraham uses the word *favor* in speaking to "three men" who were paying him a visit. Queen Esther was seeking the favor of her husband, the king. Look these up and see how favor is found with both God and man. Ruth had already found grace (favor) with Jehovah as a believer; now she was seeking the favor of some landowner who would allow her to glean in his field.

In the New Testament, we have seen that it is God's grace that saves us. Then what? Is that the end of our need of His grace or favor? Certainly not! Read 2 Peter 3:18 to see the command that is given there for us to also "grow" in grace. So, grace begins our faith journey; then we grow (or mature) in it as we walk with the Lord by faith. Then there's yet another aspect of grace that the New Testament refers to. Look at Paul who needed God's grace in order to face something in his life that he did not specify. Many believe that was some physical infirmity. He asked God to remove it, but instead, God told him, "My grace is sufficient for you." Read the whole context of these powerful words in 2 Corinthians 12:1–10.

So we see that we need God's grace or favor from beginning to end throughout our lives. Our faith journey, like Ruth's, begins with His unmerited favor (grace) that saves us. Then His grace enables us to grow in maturity in our faith. Also, His grace is sufficient for us to face life's trials or anything God allows to touch our lives as His beloved children. Last of all, the Lord grants us favor in the sight of others in accordance with His purpose or will for us.

Let's look at a couple of New Testament passages that tell us who God delights to grant His grace to and why. James 4:6 says, ". . . God is opposed to the proud, but gives grace to the humble" (NASB). Then, in verse 10, he adds the admonition, "Humble yourselves in the presence of the Lord, and He will exalt you." First Peter 5:5 has some very similar words to James (remember, God was the inspiration for both).

So who is it that God resists granting grace to? The proud! On the other hand, who garners His favor? The humble! What kind of attitude did Ruth display? She displayed submission to Naomi and her God, and humility so remarkable and attractive that it had the whole town of Bethlehem taking notice of her.

Bethlehem was also going to take note of Ruth's diligence in taking whatever steps were necessary, no matter how humbling, to provide care and food for her small family unit consisting of two widowed women. Each other is all they had. Why do you think Ruth believed it was her responsibility to step up and seek provision? Wasn't she the dependent one? Shouldn't she have waited and expected her mother-in-law to do what she was capable of doing to provide for her son's widowed wife? Ruth did not have the admonitions that we have in the New Testament, but she seems to have lived out their words nonetheless.

In 1 Timothy 5:8 we read, "But if anyone does not provide for his own, and especially those of his household, he has denied the faith and is worse than an unbeliever" (NASB). Did you know God makes it perfectly clear that He expects us to provide for our families? Another plain teaching on the value God places on working and providing is found in 2 Thessalonians 3:10. It rather bluntly reads, ". . . if anyone is not willing to work, then he is not to eat, either" (NASB). Were you familiar with that? A retired Polish grandfather once expressed that message to his grandson in his very limited English as a way of explaining his refusal to consume enough food to sustain him. He shrugged and offered, "Me no work, me no eat!" Did he even know that was scriptural, though not meant to be applied in the way that he was using it?

Not only are we admonished to work but to work diligently as though God Himself were our boss. Now isn't that one definition of the word *Lord?* He is our boss, and our work is to honor Him by its excellence and the attitude we have in accomplishing it: ". . . as for the Lord. . ." Look at Colossians 3:23. "Whatever you do, do your work heartily, as for the Lord, rather than for men" (NASB).

Transformation

This has been a lot to take in and all from just three short verses in the very small book of Ruth. How can we apply what we've read about in the biblical account that bears the name of a young Gentile woman who has come out of a pagan background to embrace faith in Jehovah God, the God of her in-laws? Are you, like Ruth, a fairly new believer or a more seasoned one, like Naomi? Do you recognize God's voice when He is calling you to move into action, which requires faith? What is your response? Are you, like Naomi, crippled by some circumstance in your life right now that is drowning out His voice and overshadowing His hand? Are you so consumed with the affairs of your everyday life that the still, small voice of the Spirit within is overwhelmed by all the noise of the activity around you?

Let's start the application process by settling the primary question that Ruth answered in Ruth 1:16 when she confessed that she intended to follow Naomi and Naomi's God. Have you confessed Jesus as the Lord of your life? That's more, remember, than saying, "I believe in God." Have you, or has anyone else, seen a difference in you since you were saved? This should definitely happen, you know. Even if you came to trust Christ at a young age, you became a new creation, according to the passage we looked at in 2 Corinthians 5:17. Something changed! You might have become a more obedient child (which would have definitely been noticed), or maybe you were more conscious of and sorry for the wrong you did, or any number of things that would have evidenced the new nature you were given. A husband would see a wife who was being more submissive. Children might notice a calmer mother. Some other signs of being born again are a love for God's Word and the ability to understand what you read as one of the recipients of God's love letter to His bride. There is also an ability to love others that might have been difficult before. Do these characteristics describe you?

Do you know with absolute assurance that the faith you say you have is the saving kind? That is, it is a faith that works! Have you surrendered your will to His as Ruth did? Can you say, like she seemed to be expressing by her actions, "Whatever, whoever, wherever, whenever, Lord?" This is what it means to "confess Him as Lord."

Okay, if you're sure you belong to Him as His beloved child, then what is He asking of you that you've not been willing, up to this point, to do? Have you ignored that impression that there's something you are missing or supposed to be doing with your life that you just can't seem to define? Do you, like Ruth, need God's favor in some matter having to do with another person, maybe your mate or your mother-in-law? Hello! Have you prayed and asked God to grant you that favor? Remember, He's the source of it all. He delights to grant good gifts to His children even more so than we do as earthly parents. Speaking of our children, do you pray for God to grant favor to them? God said of His Son in Luke 2:52, "And Jesus increased in wisdom and stature, and in favor with God and with people." Wouldn't that be a powerful request for us to make for our children or grandchildren?

What is your attitude toward work? What needs to change in your attitude? Are you diligent like Ruth? Would your family or friends call you a hard worker who exhibits a Christlike attitude toward the work you've been given to do, whether at home or in the workplace? Read Proverbs 31 to see another example of a diligent woman who cares for the needs of her family. What about your family? Is there a balance brought between too little or too much in terms of stuff and activities? Are other needs unmet?

Let's take a look at Ruth's example, as well as what other Scriptures teach us about how faith influences all aspects of our lives from our relationships to our work. We want to see what it really means to "put feet to our faith."

Are you growing in your faith so that you live and move and have your very being in Christ (Acts 17:28)? Did you get saved and have just been sitting ever since, so to speak? This might actually indicate that you need to "Test yourselves to see if you are in the faith." (2 Corinthians 13:5).

Some might have experienced what pediatricians say of some newborns, that there was a "failure to thrive." You've only tasted milk, and you should be eating solid food by now. If this sounds like it fits your situation, read these Scriptures to see what the Bible has to say about you (1 Peter 2:2; 1 Corinthians 3:1–3; Hebrews 5:12–14, 6:1–2).

Then there is the matter of the sufficiency of God's grace for the tough times we, like Ruth and Naomi, all face. It may not be the loss of a loved one but may be any other situation where we need God's grace to get through. A woman may go through a season of depression, perhaps like Naomi, that renders her unable to function as she would like. This may have some physical source, or it could be a tool of our enemy, Satan. God could also use it. Whatever its source, it can be used as a humbling tool for the purpose of discipline for disobedience or pruning for greater usefulness in God's service. Remember, we said that God resists the proud. Paul had his "thorn in the flesh," which kept him from pride due to all he had seen and experienced. Perhaps you, too, are experiencing something similar in the way of infirmity. Have you ever thought that God might be using your circumstance, or even your pain, to speak to you or to get your attention? Have you asked Him to remove whatever it is, and He hasn't done so? Maybe, like Paul, He is saying to you, "My grace is sufficient for you" (2 Corinthians 12:9). Naomi's grief seems to have caused her to become bitter (see previous chapter) and somewhat immobile as far as seeking God's will for the next phase of her life. God, however, in His grace, gave her a loving daughter-in-law to help sustain her even in her bitterness toward God. Ruth, on the other hand, responded differently in her grief. She let her newfound faith be the motivation in responding to what God had surely allowed in both their lives. She, like Paul, took the grace God offered and in humility walked by faith into whatever circumstance she found herself in.

Do you see God's hand in everything that happens in your life? Because, if you are His child, that is true. He either causes or allows everything that touches the lives of His dear children. What He allows is for our ultimate good and for His glory. Do you believe this to be true? Do you know that He has a plan for your life and that His will for you is perfect?

We would do well to look at the life of Joseph in Genesis chapters 37–50 to see how even the sin of his brothers resulted in good in the hands of Jehovah. Look at Joseph's own words to that effect in Genesis 50:20. He told his brothers when they were reunited, "You planned evil against me; God planned it for good . . ." This is echoed in the New Testament through Paul's writing in Romans 8:28: "We know that all things work together for the good of those who love God: those who are called according to His purpose." How would it change your response to the things that happen to you if you really believed that and acted accordingly? Ruth shows us how.

Isn't it amazing what we can draw out of three short verses? God's Word is like that. It's supernatural! He is able to take the simplest truth and make such a profound application from it. The Bible is the only book that has that kind of power. Only He can take the account of one young woman's life and cause us to see how we measure up or fall short in terms of putting feet to our faith like Ruth. She didn't get to choose the circumstances that she found herself in any more than we do, but she took those circumstances as from the very hand of her God, in whom she had recently trusted. She seemed to have been attuned to His leading, and she moved into action, proving the faith that she had. She had, like Naomi, a reason to be bitter because of the hand life had dealt her. She chose, by an act of her will, not to give in to her flesh, which was surely tempting her to self-pity. She accepted God's grace, not only to make her a new creature, but she also proved the reality of Jehovah's grace toward her by becoming a doer of the Word, which she had only heard about, not read.

What have you learned from Ruth so far that you are going to apply to your life? It's not just a Bible story, you know, to be read and enjoyed for the happy ending. God had it recorded and preserved all these centuries just for us. We are to learn about our God and His ways with His children, and we are to take heed that we don't fail to act on the principles that are taught in the particular account we are reading (Romans 15:4; 1 Corinthians 10:11). Don't be a forgetful reader, but put into practice what you've learned from Ruth's example. She put feet to her faith, and then she bloomed where God planted her.

◊ Why do you think the last thing mentioned in chapter 1 is the timing of Ruth and Naomi's arrival in Bethlehem? Is it important?

◊ What do you think is the point of mentioning Boaz in chapter 2 verse 1?

◊ What do you think was Naomi's plan for obtaining food? Had she even thought about it? Did she believe it was her responsibility? Was that an act of faith or what?

◊ What did you learn about God's view of work? Are you a Proverbs 31 kind of woman?

◊ Is your faith just in your head, or have you surrendered, like Ruth, so that you move when He calls?

◊ According to all the New Testament Scriptures you've read, explain how a faith journey begins and how a person can know for sure that his faith is real. Use the Scriptures to support your answer.

◊ What about the passages in James we read? Discuss the role our deeds have in our salvation. Do James' words conflict with Paul's? Why or why not? Discuss with your group what part providence plays in the life of a child of God. Try to think of instances in Scripture where we find this principle at work (hint: Joseph). Think of some other examples.

◊ What part does humility have in finding favor with God? Discuss Paul's "thorn in the flesh" (2 Corinthians 12:1–10). Why can't God use a proud person? Have you ever seen what you believe to be a humbling taking place in someone's life (maybe even yours)?

◊ The words *favor* and *grace* are used interchangeably in this account. What is "unmerited favor" How does it provide a blanket that covers the life of a believer? Find Scripture to support your answers, **always**!

◊ What life lesson is your take-away from these three short verses in Ruth 2:1–3? How do you intend to apply what you have learned so that your faith story (testimony) might benefit others?

RUTH 2:4–6

Later, when Boaz arrived from Bethlehem, he said to the harvesters, "The Lord be with you." "The Lord bless you," they replied. Boaz asked his servant who was in charge of the harvesters, "Whose young woman is this?" The servant answered, "She is the young Moabite woman who returned with Naomi from the land of Moab.

CHAPTER SIX

Carolyn Mrok

Finding Favor and Reaping Grace

Introduction

It is harvest time in Bethlehem. Ruth just happens to find herself gleaning in the field of a near-kinsman to her deceased husband. Though we can see the providence of God in this situation, this new believer in Jehovah has yet to realize that not only has He led her to this very field, but it is here that He intends to reveal Himself to her in the person of Boaz. We will, likewise, come to recognize in this wealthy landowner the grace of God extended to Ruth.

She sought favor in the eyes of one who would allow her to glean for food for her and Naomi, but God had a much bigger plan for her than she could ever realize. This is true for every child of God. We, like Ruth, have no idea what He has in store for us.

We are initially introduced to Boaz in the first verse of chapter 2. As we pick up the narrative of this account in chapter 2 verse 4, we find him visiting his fields where his workers are reaping barley. His attention is drawn to a strange young woman among the gleaners, and he inquires about her. "Whose young woman is this?" he asked (v. 5b). After learning her identity, he realizes, as he later confesses to Ruth, that he has, indeed, heard about her. The care she has shown to Naomi, her mother-in-law, has been gossiped about so her reputation has preceded her.

With this as the backdrop, let's see how God weaves His plan through these two people. Don't forget, this is not just an account about the lives of real people who lived and died as we all do, but God has seen fit to include this in His book because it shows us, centuries later, that our God works in the lives of His children in every era and in every culture. We are to see His hand and His heart through His dealings with these individuals and know that He is the same today.

Trials

Though Ruth has feared that she might be resented as a stranger when she goes out to glean, we see that she, indeed, has been allowed to gather along with others after the reapers in Boaz's field. She seems to have found the favor she was seeking as she set out to make some provision for herself and Naomi.

How could such fortunate circumstances befall this young Gentile woman who is now living as a foreigner among her late husband's Jewish relatives? Why would this formerly pagan young woman from Moab become the recipient of Jehovah's blessings and eventually be included in the very genealogy of Jesus Christ (Matthew 1:5)?

Let's consider in this passage (Ruth 2:4–16) how, just as God dealt with Ruth through Boaz, He has also given to us a Redeemer, Jesus Christ, to be our near-kinsman. In fact, Boaz becomes to Ruth what is known as her kinsman-redeemer. In Boaz, we see an Old Testament "type" of Christ. Pay close attention, as you read the rest of this short book, to how Boaz's care for Ruth typifies Jesus' care for us. As we watch Boaz seek Ruth out and pursue a relationship with her, we are reminded that our God does the same for us. Boaz treats Ruth with such kindness and speaks words of encouragement to her; likewise, God shows loving-kindness (a covenant term) to His own, and His Spirit is the One Who comes alongside us with encouragement. Just as Boaz instructs Ruth as to what she must do, so also, God has provided us with a resident teacher within and the instruction of His Word (1 John 2:27). God is our Protector and our Provider; this is the same role Boaz assumes with Ruth. Let's see, as this story unfolds, how the typology reminds us that our Kinsman-Redeemer has done for us all that Boaz did for Ruth and so much more. May this reminder bless our socks off!

Truth

The law of the kinsman-redeemer can be found in the Levitical law in Leviticus 25 and Deuteronomy 25. This was for the protection and provision of the widowed and the poor among the children of Israel. We are going to examine in detail the ways that Boaz presents to us some of the very same characteristics as Christ. Let's look at some New Testament passages that teach us what Jesus, our Redeemer, has bought for us, His kinsmen, with His death and resurrection.

As you look at this passage in Ruth 2:4–16, do more than just read the words. Do what is referred to as reading with a purpose. That is, as you read, look for certain things to note mentally; or, better yet, write down what you observe. The more of your senses you employ in the learning process, the greater the chance of your retaining what you learn. So, read aloud, if possible, to involve the ears and mouth, and write to include the mind and hands. Now, you're reading to remember! Let's get started!

In this passage, look for and record in this book or your Bible:

1. Who went in search of whom?
2. Who instructed and encouraged who?
3. Who arranged protection for whom?
4. Who met whose needs?

What did you learn from these preliminary observations? Ponder this as we look a little deeper at the principles to be learned from this beautiful, true love story that God has included in His Word so that we may learn of Him and His ways.

In answering the previous four questions, you surely found that Boaz was the answer to them all. It was this wealthy landowner who found Ruth and pursued her in his field. It was Boaz who instructed Ruth as to where she should go and what she must do. Likewise, he encouraged her with his words and even blessed her. He also promised this young woman that he would, indeed, provide for her needs, as well as those of Naomi, her mother-in-law. Unknown to Ruth, he had also instructed and warned his workers that they were not to harm or insult her. In other words, he had seen to her protection. Boaz seems to have thought of everything!

Does this sound familiar to you? Are you beginning to see Boaz in a different light? Who, but our Lord, pursues us until we find Him? Who, but our Redeemer, buys us out of the slave market of sin? Who else, but God, the Holy Spirit, instructs and encourages us? Who, but our Savior, promises to meet all our needs, and even beyond that, give us eternal and abundant life. Our Kinsman-Redeemer has done all that Boaz did for Ruth and so much more. He has made every provision for His children even though we, like Ruth, were strangers and aliens before He saved us. Ephesians 2:12–13 reminds us of this, but it also uses words of contrast. Read these verses and note the words that express the "before" and the "after" of your situation when you encountered Christ.

Remember, we said previously that verse 1 of chapter 2 mentions that Boaz is a man of great wealth. This is further evidenced by the fact that he is a landowner. Likewise, both the Old and New Testaments record for us the fact that our Kinsman is also wealthy. In fact, He owns it all! Look up Psalm 50:10–12. What does God say that He owns? You might want to highlight this verse in case you are ever feeling like your needs are beyond Him. Then, compare this with Philippians 4:19 to learn what Jesus says through the apostle Paul about our needs and His supply. You *definitely* want to underline this one for future reference. That little phrase *according to* might be translated "in proportion to," or "out of." Our God is not poor, nor is He stingy! If our Kinsman is wealthy, what does that make us? Let's see what the Bible says.

The word *testament* (as in New Testament) may also be translated "covenant." So when we are reading this portion of God's Word, we are reading, for all practical purposes, Jesus' last will and testament to His heirs. That's who we are. Isn't that exciting? Read it for yourself in Romans 8:16–17 and Galatians 4:7. We are His sons and daughters, and, therefore, His next of kin. He wants us to know our position in His family and what our inheritance is in accordance with that. A will is not read, nor is it valid, as long as the person who made it is still living. Jesus died for us so that we might be able to inherit everything that is

His. Hebrews 9:16–17 explains this as it refers to the covenant that was validated for us through His death. So, Jesus did for us spiritually what Boaz did for Ruth physically and materially in becoming her kinsman-redeemer. This is one reason he is regarded as a type of Christ.

Let's go through this comparison one step at a time. Be sure to stop and read each reference so that you can apply the message of Ruth and Boaz and see how to personalize what our Kinsman-Redeemer has done for us. If this Truth is grasped, it will forever change your spiritual net worth.

Instead of anonymously arranging to make provision for Ruth, the stranger in his field, Boaz sought her out personally. She did not approach him first. The same is true in our meeting Christ. He seeks us out and pursues *us*, not the other way around. Jesus states His mission in coming to earth as recorded for us by Luke. He said, "For the Son of Man has come to seek and to save the lost" (Luke 19:10). You probably remember the story in the Bible of the one lost lamb that Jesus, the Good Shepherd, left the ninety-nine of His fold to pursue. This is the same Shepherd Who came seeking us as the lost sheep, even when we were unaware and unworthy of that pursuit.

Unlike Ruth, who had become known to Boaz by her reputation as a caring daughter-in-law to Naomi, God sought us out when there was not one commendable thing about us. In fact, the Bible tells us in Romans 5:6–10 that we were His enemies when He died for us. Who would do that for us? Only Jesus, our Redeemer.

Next, we see that as Boaz seeks Ruth out to speak with her, his words are kind and encouraging. In this way, he also typifies our Comforter, the Holy Spirit. Read and make a list of all that John 15:26 and 16:13 have to say about the role that He plays in the life of a true believer. While you're at it, look up Romans 8:14–17 to see one of the ways that we know we are saved.

In Ruth 2:8–9 and 14, we read Boaz's words of instruction to Ruth as he tells her "stay here with my maids," "drink from what the servants draw," and "come here that you may eat" (NASB). In these words of instruction, Boaz is revealing to Ruth what she has available to her now that she has found favor with a near-kinsman of her deceased husband. Our instruction comes from the words of Scripture where we are given commands and precepts to show us who we are, what is ours, and how we are to live. God's Spirit has been given to us as our internal instructor and guide. Read John 14:17 and 14:26 to note what it says about this Teacher. Also, what do you learn about Him from 1 John 2:27? Make for yourself a handwritten concordance beside these passages in your Bible so that by finding one of them, it will show you where to find comparable verses on the same subject. Don't just depend on a concordance you might have printed in the Bible you are using. If you write it with your own hand, you will more likely remember it and be able to locate it when you're looking for it. Try it! You do write in your Bible, don't you? Please say yes! It is your textbook on life. Mark it all up and live what you mark. Get a new Bible when you can't read the one you've marked up. Don't transpose those old markings and notes in the new one either. Please! Jim Eliot, the martyred missionary, and husband to author and Bible teacher Elizabeth Eliot, once said of his Bible that he got a new one every year so that he would not just depend on old insights and notes, but he had to continue to look to God for new ones to live by. Wow! Now, there's some real wisdom to take to heart.

It is crucial for us, as believers, to know our Kinsman-Redeemer through His Word. We are told In 2 Timothy 2:15 to "Be diligent to present yourself approved to God, a worker who doesn't need to be ashamed, correctly teaching the word of truth." We need to have a good handle on Scripture so that we "handle" it correctly. One doesn't have to be able to quote chapter and verse or recite long portions verbatim. We just need to be able to "give an account for the hope that is in you" (NASB) to others and to defend and share our faith (1 Peter 3:15). It's necessary to know and understand the principles and precepts taught, even in the Old Testament, and not just the stories we learned as a child in Sunday school. This is what will also enable us to walk (live) in a way that is consistent with Scripture and that will be pleasing to the One Who has given us all we need ". . . pertaining to life and godliness . . ." (2 Peter 1:3, NASB).

Read what the psalmist had to say about the importance of God's Word in his life. Remember, he didn't have the New Testament either. He had the law and maybe one prophet's writings. In the longest chapter in the Bible, Psalm 119, the writer records over and over again how wonderful it is for him to know his God by knowing His Word. Stop now and be blessed by these words, which should also be convicting to us who take our easy access to the very words of the One Who instructs and encourages us so lightly. Once again, read with a purpose. Mark every word or phrase that he uses to refer to the Word of God (hint: ordinances, etc.). There are quite a few of them!

Now, back to the analogy of Boaz and Christ. In this same passage, we see that Boaz offers Ruth his protection. In three separate instances, he warns and instructs his workers with words such as: ". . . not to touch you" (v. 9), ". . . don't humiliate her" (v. 15), and "Don't rebuke her" (v. 16). In this way, Boaz is careful to insure that Ruth feels secure, safe, and protected by this near-kinsman. Our Redeemer also assures us of our security in Him in John 10:27–30, with words such as ". . . they will never perish—ever! No one will snatch them out of My hand." How protected does that make you feel? He reiterates this in the very next verse by saying emphatically ". . . no one is able to snatch them out of the Father's hand." This is one of many passages that teaches us about eternal security of the believer. In other words: once saved, always saved. You will surely want to mark these verses in your Bible so that if you, or anyone you know, ever doubt this important doctrine of Scripture, you will know where to find these pertinent passages. There's nothing like having marked them for yourself to help you to be able to find them again when you need them. Keep marking. It gets to be a good habit. Along the same lines, read Jesus' prayer to His Father in John chapter 17. Mark the phrase, "those You have given Me," and all similar words to see what Jesus says about those who are in a relationship with Him as His heirs and a part of the forever family of God. If that doesn't make you feel secure, what will?

In addition to securing Ruth's physical safety, Boaz addressed her emotional needs as well. His workers were not to speak to her in a negative or hurtful way. Let's see what Scripture says about how our spiritual Kinsman does the same for us. First of all, in Hebrews 13:5–6, God is quoted from the Old Testament in Deuteronomy as saying, "I will never leave you or forsake you." It also goes on to say that we do not have to fear what anyone might do to us. That is so clear and reassuring, isn't it? Mark that verse as well for future reference.

Though we are certain of our God's protection, we, as believers, must realize that we have an enemy, the devil (or Satan), who is seeking to "devour" us (or as we might say in modern vernacular, "eat our lunch"). This is what we are told in 1 Peter 5:8. Read that and see for yourself. We actually have three enemies: Satan, the world (that system that opposes God), and our old sinful nature (our flesh). Our battle is mostly internal (in the mind)—that's the battlefield. That's why we are told in 2 Corinthians 10:5 to ". . . take every thought captive. . ." This means that we must not let our minds feed on unhealthy things. Just like what bad food does to our stomachs, so with our minds bad stuff will come back to haunt us. When we least expect it, there it is at the doorway of our minds seeking to come back up! You've certainly heard the saying: "Garbage in, garbage out!" It's so true. We are instructed on how to keep our minds and hearts peaceful in both the Old and New Testaments. Read Isaiah 26:3 and Philippians 4:6–8 and note the secret to a clean heart and a mind that is at peace as well. The words *heart* and *mind* are often used interchangeably in Scripture. What is the key to having peace of mind and winning the battle fought between our ears? It has been described before as a process of filtering our thoughts at the doorway of our minds before we invite them in to be entertained! That's a great way to picture the way we should "take our thoughts captive." This way of handling our thought life has also been described as looking out the peephole in the door of our minds, like you would before swinging open the door of our homes to see who's there. This, too, is a graphic picture of how we might remember that every thought, like every visitor, might not be suitable to be entertained. Use Philippians 4:8 as the checklist for the process. Ask yourself when a thought first presents itself, "Is it true?" (sometimes it will pass this test, but don't stop there; keep going). Next on the list to ask is, "Is it honorable, right, pure, lovely, etc.?" It must pass the whole test, or else it is not to be invited in. This has been proven to work for many; it will work for you if you begin to practice the habit of "frisking" and "peeping" with your thoughts. Try it for yourself and see. By the way, don't forget to make yourself that personal, handwritten concordance with these important verses too. You're going to need them.

Though we have a personal enemy in Satan, he is subject to our Protector, the Lord Jesus Christ. He must have permission to tempt or try us. Read 1 John 4:4, NASB, for a confidence booster about who has the upper hand in so far as our peace and safety is concerned. Does it need to be repeated? Mark it and draw a red pitchfork over that second "he" (the one not capitalized), for you know who!

In addition to being Ruth's protector, her instructor, and encourager, and also being the one who pursued her, Boaz also takes on the role of her provider. He gave her a meal that was more than she could eat so she had leftovers to take home to Naomi. Later, he gave her an abundance of his crop to more than sustain them. This is, once again, so true of our Provider, Jesus. A verse that we looked at earlier, Philippians 4:19, reminds us that He is able to supply *all* our needs. You might want to underline the word <u>all</u>. There is another passage that's not quite as familiar found in 2 Corinthians 9:8. Read that and you know the drill by now: write Philippians 4:19 beside it in the margin of your Bible. Aren't you impressed with how colorful your guidebook for life is becoming? It will come to be such a blessing to you! Keep going. As earthly parents, we delight to shower our children with not only their needs but even their little heart's desires. God, as our heavenly Father, delights to do the same, only according to His infinite wisdom. He only withholds that which He knows would not be for our good. Scripture says that He is an abundant provider. Read Ephesians 3:20 and see what that tells you about how He goes above and beyond in everything He does for us. This is the picture we get from Boaz as he exceeds her needs and provides so much more than she could have even dreamt of. His kindness and generosity are such pictures of our Provider.

Another verse that you will certainly want to mark, and maybe even memorize, is Psalm 37:4. There, David notes that if we are delighted in the Lord, it would be His delight to grant us the desires of our hearts. That's a loose paraphrase, but go read it for yourself. It really says that! That almost sounds like a blank check, doesn't it? "How can that be true?" you might wonder. Well, If we are truly delighting in Him, and the things that He delights in (His will), then what *we* desire and what *He* desires *for us* should be one and the same. That's an incredible conditional promise! Fulfill the condition: be delighted in Him and watch how He delights to "delight" you with some of the most incredible things (desires) that you had hoped for, and become overwhelmed when He grants them.

Transformation

That brings us to a real-life example of how God has done just what has been described in the previous section. We believe that Psalm 37:4 is the only explanation. God has provided this writer's long-time heart's desire that is about to be realized one week from this writing. Our whole family is taking the trip of a lifetime together to the Holy Land with a group from church with our pastor as our leader. "Wow!" doesn't even begin to express how overwhelmed you feel when you see His hand of provision, not for just a need, but for a year's-long prayer and desire. The practical side of us knew it would not be possible, but our God is the God of the impossible! He made it a reality through a mother-in-law's legacy to us. We had no idea, but we know that He knew! How grateful we are for a Kinsman-Redeemer Who has pursued us, protected us, encouraged and instructed us, and Who has certainly provided us with even our hearts' desires.

Now let's get personal. Did you even know that you had a Kinsman-Redeemer? When you read the book of Ruth, did you ever see Boaz as a type of Christ? Were you *familiar* with the typology of Christ in Boaz? If it's new to you, you're not alone. It was news to all of us at some point until God opened our eyes through some teaching. Hopefully, that has happened for some of you. Before we call it a wrap, let's see what each of us needs to apply from this study so that we realize our true inheritance.

First and foremost, before you can inherit anything, you have to know that you are related to a near-kinsman who has provided for you in His last will and testament. Do you have a relationship with God through His Son, Jesus Christ? Do you have the assurance of your salvation? Is your eternal destiny secure in Him? Those are all ways of asking the same thing—do you know for sure that you have been born again (John 3:3)? Are you saved? If you have any doubts about that, there may be valid reason for those doubts. If you can convince yourself one minute that you're okay, but before you know it the doubts return, then you need to deal with the doubts once and for all. You'll never have peace until you do. Talk about it with a wise Christian friend whom you trust. You can certainly call any one of the women who have written this study, and they would be thrilled to help you gain assurance of your salvation. We can walk you through the Scripture to show you what the Bible says about what a truly saved person is like. Don't put it off. Do it now! There is nothing more peaceful than having the matter of your eternal destiny settled.

If you already know that you are secure in Christ, did you know that it was not you who pursued Him, but that He came after you? It's kind of like He had been chasing you, and you suddenly stopped in your tracks to see who was on your heels—and there He was! He was there all the time; you just never turned around until then. Not only does He pursue us, but He is also the One Who does the holding on, or the keeping. Remember those verses about not "snatching out of My hand"? Scripture teaches that it is God Who saves us, and God Who keeps us. Not one is ever lost again. You did read John 17, didn't you? Read it again. Once a true believer, always a true believer. Those you hear talking about "losing their faith," as if it has been misplaced and might be retrieved, are not talking about the kind of faith that saves in the first place. They are not speaking biblically. You cannot lose what Someone else is holding on to. Think about it. Those verses we read clearly teach that it is God Who holds on to us, not the other way around. There is a tongue twister that puts it rather plainly: "Faith that fizzles before the finish had a fatal flaw from the first!" Say that three times real fast. It's true, though. It may *not* be Scripture, but it *is* scriptural. Those who give up on God or lose their faith so that they no longer believe in Him are described for us clearly in 1 John 2:19. Read that passage to see that those who leave Him were never truly His to begin with.

Galatians 5:22–23 lists the fruit (singular) of the Spirit. That's what is found in the life of every person who has God's Spirit living in them—all who are saved. Ruth was different and remarkable because she had surrendered her will for her life to Jehovah. What about you? Are you different?

As we learned in lesson five, Ruth "put feet to her faith." Have you been applying what you know to be God's will for your life? Now that you know you are an heir and have an inheritance, what are you going to do with all that you've been given? It will take commitment and consistency, not perfection. He provides all we need to be all He expects. Don't squander the riches that have been entrusted to you. Invest your inheritance from our Kinsman-Redeemer in kingdom-worthy pursuits. Spend time in the Word—not hours and hours as if you're going to be tested, but at least make that "handle" your goal. It will end up holding you when you need it to.

Are you resting in the peace and protection that's ours as His beloved children? Are you anxious about anything? Reread Philippians 4:6 and remember the part about thanksgiving. Don't leave that out of your requests in prayer. It's the sure-cure prescription for anxiety.

Is the enemy of your soul eating your lunch because you didn't even realize that you're in a battle? Put on your armor and stand firm against him. Ephesians 6:10–17 tells you how.

Are your needs being met? Who do you look to, or rely on, for this—man or your Provider? Do you pray for and about everything as you've been commanded to? Try it! There was a nameplate on a man's desk once that read: "Work as if everything depends on you, and pray as if everything depends on God." That is good counsel. Everything does ultimately depend on God, but He expects us to put feet to our prayers as well. Pray, wait to hear, and then move! If you're not sure that you've heard from Him, keep praying, but do that which seems wise and consistent with His Word and, perhaps, godly counsel. We're not specifically told that Ruth prayed, but she acted wisely according to what she knew to be a provision of His law, and He blessed her beyond measure. He will do the same for us.

Hopefully, now we can all see how Boaz, who became Ruth's kinsman-redeemer, is an Old Testament type of Christ. Ruth's rescuer was a real man who did each of the things that we've read and talked about for a real woman named Ruth. God chose their real-life story to teach all who read it a lesson about our Rescuer, Jesus Christ. We should feel moved to respond as she did after Boaz had shown her such favor and had extended to her more grace than she ever could expect to deserve. It is recorded for us in Ruth 2:10: "Then she fell on her face, bowing to the ground and said to him, 'Why have I found favor in your sight that you should take notice of me, since I am a foreigner?'" (NASB). We might say as we fall on our knees in our worship of our gracious Redeemer "Why have You chosen to redeem me, a wretched sinner, and take me to be your own, making me an heir of all that You own?"

Boaz's prayer of blessing for this vulnerable young woman is recorded in verse 12: "May the Lord reward your work and your wages be full from the Lord, the God of Israel, under whose wings you have come to seek refuge" (NASB). This reflects God's heart for us as well. Our reward and our wages will come from our Lord one day also because we too have taken refuge under the wings of our Kinsman-Redeemer.

Lord, You have told us that You will cover us if we seek our refuge in You because Your faithfulness is a shield for us (Psalm 91:4). Thank You for the blood of Jesus that covers us as feathers to protect us from our enemies. We bless You for all Your provision for us in Christ. For all Your instruction and encouragement, we are truly grateful. Most of all, we are humbled and in awe of You for pursuing us when we were running in the other direction. We bow low in our hearts to say, like Ruth, "Who am I?" Praise You for making me an heir of the King's estate. I am rich in Your grace and mercy. Hallelujah! Amen.

◊ What part of Boaz's treatment of Ruth is especially meaningful to you? Do you know why that is so?

◊ How have you experienced providence in your life circumstances that can be explained no other way except that God arranged it?

◊ How did you like the idea of reading with a purpose? Did you like looking for specifics? Do you think that it helped you make more accurate observations?

◊ Do you feel the loving-kindness of your Redeemer in your life? What are some ways that He has protected, provided for, encouraged, and instructed you recently? You might want to write Him a short thank-you note.

◊ Look up the word *seek* in a concordance (preferably Strong's) to find as many passages as you can about people seeking the Lord. Then look up Romans 3:11b, which tells us something contrary to those verses you found. How do we reconcile those things that seem to contradict? Have a lively discussion, but remember that God's Word can never contradict itself.

◊ We know that the Holy Spirit did not come to indwell believers until Pentecost. How do you think Ruth got her instruction and encouragement from God? Have fun with that one too! Remember to cite chapter and verse to support your answer!

◊ We are told that one of the basic needs of women is security. We can handle *anything* (we've had babies); we just need the security of knowing what's what. Discuss what the Bible says about our eternal security.

◊ Consult your concordance for passages concerning the heart and the mind. What's the connection? Discuss what the verses you've found have to say about our hearts.

◊ Write down everything that comes to mind about our inheritance as joint heirs with Christ. What all has He bequeathed to us in His last will and testament?

◊ What has the "story" of Ruth taught you so far that you may not have known before? Be specific.

CAROLYN MROK, AUTHOR OF CHAPTERS 4–6

Carolyn was twenty-eight when she surrendered to the Lord, and He became her Savior. Her family has been members of Germantown Baptist Church for thirty-six years. Her main spiritual gift is teaching the Bible, which she has been doing for over fifty years. She graduated from the University of Georgia with a BA in French and received an MA in English as a Second Language from Memphis State University. Carolyn married her sixth-grade sweetheart, Eddie, and on August 2, 2014, they celebrated fifty wonderful years of marriage. "He is still my boyfriend!" They have two grown sons, two precious daughters-in-law, and five wonderful grandchildren.

RUTH 2:17–23

So Ruth gathered grain in the field until evening. She beat out what she had gathered, and it was about 26 quarts of barley. She picked up the grain and went into the town, where her mother-in-law saw what she had gleaned. Then she brought out what she had left over from her meal and gave it to her. Then her mother-in-law said to her, "Where did you gather barley today, and where did you work? May the Lord bless the man who noticed you." Ruth told her mother-in-law about the men she had worked with and said, "The name of the man I worked with today is Boaz." Then Naomi said to her daughter-in-law, "May he be blessed by the Lord, who has not forsaken his kindness to the living or the dead." Naomi continued, "The man is a close relative. He is one of our family redeemers." Ruth the Moabitess said, "He also told me, 'Stay with my young men until they have finished all of my harvest.'" So Naomi said to her daughter-in-law Ruth, "My daughter, it is good for you to work with his female servants, so that nothing will happen to you in another field." Ruth stayed close to Boaz's female servants and gathered grain until the barley and the wheat harvests were finished. And she lived with her mother-in-law.

CHAPTER SEVEN

Beth Reed

Overcoming Bitterness: From Blaming to Blessing

Introduction

"May the Lord bless the man who noticed you . . ." (Ruth 2:19).

Transformation. Spiritual growth. Life change. The terms are familiar enough. They roll readily off the lips of those who have been taught basic Christianity. But what do they really mean? What do they look like in real life? Exactly how does that process work? The second chapter of Ruth provides an authentic, historical example of God's power to change a human life through changing a human heart. As the narrative of Ruth unfolds, the principle of redemption emerges as the overarching theme. Layer upon beautiful layer, the foundational Truth of redemption is built. But in its simplest form, a wounded and wandering soul is called back to her original destiny. A woman of God who had lost her way is restored to the position and disposition God intended for her all along. A woman who was bound by the pain of her past was set free to rejoice in the hope of her future. A woman whose lips were peppered with blaming becomes a woman whose words are sprinkled with blessings. Hers is a story of progression. Hers is the tangible portrait of a deep, spiritual truth: *the heart of God intends for His people to be progressively transformed into the image of His marvelous Son, Jesus Christ.* Her story (and indeed, her life) moves through increasing levels of spiritual maturity . . . from glory to glory . . . from faith to faith. The story is Naomi's. But it is not exclusively her story. It is the story of countless women who have broken free from the pain of their past and embraced the hope of their future. It is the story of all who have walked away from bitterness and have begun to walk in blessing. Is it your story? It could be. This very day could be your turning point, your line in the sand. This could be the day that you reclaim your joy and leave bitter baggage behind. Are you willing to walk a while in Naomi's footsteps? Are you willing to follow her example? Are you ready for a divine trade? The offer presents itself to you today. Agony and sourness can be replaced by contentment and sweetness. How would your life be different if you accepted the trade?

Trials

Have you ever known someone who became jaded, hardened, and bitter? Well, Naomi was THAT woman. She suffered loss and grief, and over time she spiraled downward to a state of complete bitterness. To fully appreciate the depth of her decline, it is helpful to return to her previous position and disposition. Naomi's name means "pleasant." Her husband's name (Elimelech) means "my God is King." She lived a pleasantly quiet life in Bethlehem with her husband and two sons, Mahlon and Chilion. Bethlehem means "house of bread." It is safe to assume that Naomi lived in a God-honoring home in a fertile town known for its abundance of bread. In the eye of the casual observer, she certainly led a blessed life . . . until the famine. When famine struck the "house of bread," this tight-knit Jewish family migrated to the land of Moab. Previous chapters in this book have recounted her losses, but to summarize, she lost everything most precious to her. She lost her husband. She lost both of her sons. She lost her security. And, most devastatingly, she lost her faith. "Naomi had lost her faith—not in God, indeed, but in the goodwill of God for her"[8] In that dark place of abandoned faith, pleasant Naomi soured. And from a sour spirit, she spewed blame and

---

8   Samuel Cox and Thomas Fuller, *The Book of Ruth* (Klock and Klock Publishers, 1982), 98.

bitterness toward Almighty God. "'Don't call me Naomi. Call me Mara,' she answered, 'for the Almighty has made me very bitter. I went away full, but the Lord has brought me back empty. Why do you call me Naomi, since the Lord has pronounced judgment on me, and the Almighty has afflicted me?'" (Ruth 1:20–21). Bitterness. Aristotle defined bitterness as the resentful spirit that refuses reconciliation. Bitterness is what happens when unforgiveness is allowed to ferment. "Bitterness occurs when we feel someone has taken something from us that we are powerless to get back."[9] Can you relate?

Think about your world today. Think about your friends, coworkers, and neighbors. Opportunities for bitterness abound everywhere. Broken families provide fertile and festering breeding grounds for broken and bitter people. Losing a spouse leads to the type of broken-heartedness that can balloon into bitterness. Distressingly, there are now multiple dimensions of losing a spouse. Each day spouses are lost to death, divorce, and addictions of all kinds. Losing a child carves a gaping wound in the heart of a mother, and it leaves an aching emptiness that is vulnerable to a root of bitterness. Families all throughout your community suffer loss every day—loss of jobs, loss of financial security, loss of reputation and honorable name. What flavor of loss have you suffered?

Bitterness is not the inevitable outcome of loss and offense, but it is the predisposition of the human heart. Why? Because the human heart is averse to pain, and it is slow to forgive. The human heart, in its fallen state, wants to shift responsibility and shift blame. According to the Word of God, the human heart is "more deceitful than all else and is desperately sick" (Jeremiah 17:9, NASB). No wonder it wants to lick its own wounds and keep record of wrongs. No wonder it wants to lay responsibility at the feet of anyone other than itself. And so the root of bitterness takes hold. Perhaps you have been wronged or betrayed. Perhaps someone broke their word to you. Perhaps someone brought harm to you or someone you love. And now, the damage replays in your mind day after day, month after month, year after year. Perhaps all that negative emotion is directed toward an individual or a group. Perhaps

9   Dr. Gregory Popcak, www.patheos.com/blogs/faithonthe couch/2013/11/overcoming-bitterness-5-steps-for-healing-the-hurt-that-wont-go-away/

(though you dare not speak it) that negative emotion is directed toward God. Have any of these descriptions struck a raw chord in your spirit? Are feelings of bitterness and discouragement being brought to the surface? If so, lift your chin, dear sister. Great news hastens toward you! "The present may seem unbearable to you, and your future may look even worse; but remember one thing. When Jesus Christ steps into the picture, everything changes."[10]

Truth

"Bless the Lord, O my soul, And all that is within me, bless His holy name. Bless the Lord, O my soul, and forget none of His benefits. Who pardons all your iniquities, who heals all your diseases; who redeems your life from the pit, who crowns you with loving kindness and compassion" (Psalm 103:1–4, NASB). Praise and glory to the One Who doesn't leave you in the pit! Praise God that He did not leave Naomi in the pit. Praise God that He offers to rescue you from the pit. Naomi had fallen into a deep pit of despair and bitterness. But God specializes in redeeming people from the pit! Naomi's story not only offers encouragement, but it also offers a practical pattern. Her story offers tangible steps toward freedom and joy—the redeeming of a heart that was never designed to be bound and bitter. Four foundational principles emerge from Naomi's transformation. Each applies today as it did in her day. Characters may change, circumstances may change, but the Redeemer never changes. Nor do His precepts. "Jesus Christ is the same yesterday and today and forever" (Hebrews 13:8, NASB).

Ripples of bitterness reverberate through multiple layers of life. Naomi returned to her homeland filled with bitterness. Her bitter disposition took its toll physically, emotionally, and spiritually. She was so altered by the clutches of bitterness that she was barely recognizable to her friends and family. Citizens of Bethlehem heard of her return, and it caused quite a stir. As curious women actually laid eyes on her, they replied with shock, "Is this Naomi?" (Ruth 1:19, NASB). Bitterness takes its toll without exception. No one is immune to its consequences. Take a few minutes to study the consequences of bitterness for yourself.

---

10   Warren Wiersbe, *Put Your Life Together* (Victor Books, 1985), 60.

◊ Read Hebrews 12:5 and record the effects of bitterness.

◊ Read Ephesians 4:30–32. According to the admonition and instruction, why are you instructed to put away bitterness?

As you see in God's Word, bitterness is harmful and its effects are far-reaching. An increasing number of medical studies report their findings related to bitterness and unforgiveness. Studies suggest links between bitterness and depression, high blood pressure, elevated cholesterol levels, and sleeplessness. Simply stated, it just seems downright unhealthy to harbor a bitter spirit. While there are physical consequences, there are also emotional consequences. Current and future relationships are placed in jeopardy by the toxicity of bitterness. In relationships, bitterness causes trouble and can defile many (Hebrews 12:15). It spreads like cancer and is a destroyer of fellowship. But the most toxic consequence of all occurs on a spiritual level. Bitterness hinders your relationship with the Lord, and it grieves His spirit. Bitterness is sin, and sin grieves the Spirit of God (Ephesians 4:30, NASB). How can a woman expect the fullness of God, the power of God, and the presence of God if she has grieved His Holy Spirit? She cannot. How can a woman expect the fullness of joy and the fruit of the Spirit if she has grieved the Holy Spirit? She cannot. Therefore, Paul says get rid of bitterness! Put it away. There is no rightful place for it in the life of a believer. It is a malicious snare and a toxic trap. "Let us lay aside every encumbrance and the sin which so easily entangles us, and let us run with endurance the race that is set before us" (Hebrews 12:1, NASB). Precious sister, the pain of your past cannot compare with the glory of your future (2 Corinthians 4:17). Cut loose the bonds of bitterness! Run the race before you . . . not the one behind you. Yes. Your heart cries out. Yes! But then follows the next logical question: how?

Repentance is the catalyst for renewal. Such a simple statement, such a deep truth. To be sure, Naomi had been hurt. She suffered great loss. Her wounding was deep. But hurt and wounding were not her greatest problem. Her greatest problem was a response birthed from a heart of discontent and ingratitude. Her greatest offense was that she simply forgot Who God was and is. She failed to remember His character. Remember her earlier days. She had been fearfully and wonderfully made by her God (Psalm 139:14, NASB). Her name befitted her disposition—pleasant. She lived in a home where God was recognized and honored as King. She had partaken of His bountiful blessings. But when her circumstances changed, so did her attitude. So did her perspective of God. And she stepped dangerously out of the will of God. Perhaps you are wondering, "What is God's will in the face of heartbreaking, earth-shaking pain?" I'm glad you asked.

◊   Read 1 Thessalonians 5:18 and record your insights.

◊   Read James 1:2–4 and record your insights.

◊   Read Acts 5:41 and record your insights.

◊   Read Romans 8:17–18 and record your insights.

◊   As you consider the verses above, how has God clarified His will for you in your current circumstance?

Does it seem harsh to conclude that Naomi stepped out of God's will? After all, she traveled a rough road. She experienced a radical reversal of fortune. Who could blame her for feelings of discontentment and ingratitude? No one. And herein lies the poignant truth. The point of examining Naomi's attitude is not for the purpose of condemnation; it is to expose her desperate need for change. By harboring and feeding negative emotions, Naomi had all but separated herself from the abiding presence of God. She had all but shut out heaven. Her misery and agony cried out for redemption, for restoration of joy. But first, there must be a change, an inner change. She needed a change of heart. Repentance, at its core, is a change of mind or a change of heart. The Greek word for repentance is *metanoia*. It is defined as a change of mind. In fact, it is such a change of mind that it would reverse the effects of its own previous state of mind.[11] Did you catch that? Repentance is such a complete turning that it reverses the effects of the previous state of mind. Newness! Restoration and renewal are the fruit of repentance.

---

11   W. E. Vine, Merrill F. Unger, William White, Jr., *Vines Expository Dictionary* (Thomas Nelson Publishers, 1996), 1320.

◊   Read Psalm 51 and record what you learn about repentance.

According to King David, repentance is directed toward the One Whom we have chiefly offended. "Against You, You only, I have sinned and done what is evil in Your sight so that You are justified when You speak and blameless when You judge" (Psalm 51:4, NASB). David recognized a powerful truth. Actions will hurt those around us and behaviors will harm individuals, but the ultimate offense every time is against Sovereign God, the King of kings. Repentance begins with Him. And it begins with acknowledging and agreeing that He is right—all the time, every time. "The decrees you issue are righteous and altogether trustworthy" (Psalm 119:138). King David agreed with God, confessed his sin, and asked for a clean heart. "God create a clean heart for me and renew a steadfast spirit within me . . . restore the joy of Your salvation to me" (Psalm 51:10, 12). How beautiful is the fruit of repentance! What would it mean to you to have your heart cleansed, your spirit renewed, and your joy restored? It all begins with repentance. And so it began with Naomi. And so the question arises, with all that bitter baggage, what prompted her to repentance? She was prompted to repentance not by pain or agony but by the goodness of God expressed through a redeemer.

Redeeming love and the goodness of God lead to repentance. Naomi's hard and bitter heart began to melt as she recognized grace (undeserved favor) spilling over to her and to Ruth. Out of absolute necessity, Ruth had gone out to gather grain behind the harvesters. Unknowingly, she landed in the fields of Boaz, a relative of Naomi's. After working all day, Ruth carried home fifty pounds of barley (close to 5½ gallons.) The sight must have overwhelmed Naomi. It was an abundant haul for two widows who had nothing. In addition, Ruth offered Naomi the portion of the meal she had purposely saved for her mother-in-law. Can you imagine Naomi's delight as she examined the bounty? As she surveyed this glorious grain, her mind must have calculated the surprising amount. She recognized that the load was oversized compared to the time of labor. She began to comprehend that this provision was only partly due to hard work. An intentional act of kindness contributed to the overflowing sack of grain. Naomi knew full well that the generosity of the master determined the value of the gleanings. "Where did you gather barley today and where did you work? May the Lord bless the man who noticed you" (Ruth 2:19). A new word formed on Naomi's lips. BLESS. *May the Lord bless the man who noticed you*. Naomi responded to the display of goodness on two distinct levels. Out of her wounded heart, she recognized the *generosity* of the land owner, and she connected it with the Lord. She accepted the measure of grain as a gift, both from a generous land owner and a generous God. Then Ruth revealed the name of the benevolent land owner. Boaz. The mention of the name must have transported Naomi back to a long-lost era. The name was indeed familiar. Even more than familiar, the man was family! Her heart recognized *kindness* as a long-forgotten grace. "May he be blessed of the Lord, who has not forsaken his kindness to the living or the dead" (Ruth 2:20). And there it was again. Naomi repeated her new word. BLESS. She blessed the kindness of this gracious land owner, and her mind recalled his previous acts of kindness prior to the death of her husband and sons. "If we show kindness to those who seem to have forgotten our previous favors, perhaps it may help to revive remembrance even of those which seem buried."[12]

At the same time as Naomi's calloused heart was softening, her spiritual eyes were opening. Like one who wakes from a long nap and wipes sleep from the corner of her eyes, things were coming into focus for Naomi. "The man is a close relative. He is one of our family redeemers" (Ruth 2:20). She began to see God's plan unfolding. The eyes of her heart recognized the *familial connection* of the generous and kind land owner. She began to embrace the implications of a redeemer. She must have surmised that Boaz's kindness toward Ruth was more than obligatory. For the first time (in a long time) a flicker of hope kindled in her spirit. For the first time since the death of her husband and her sons, she could cling to the knowledge that God's plans were not to harm her

---

12   Blue Letter Bible, "Commentary on Ruth 2," http://www. blueletterbible.org/Comm/mhc/Rth/Rth_002.cfm?a=234019

but to give her a future and a hope (Jeremiah 29:11). HOPE. And so her transformation continued. The entire process was initiated by, and sustained through, the goodness of God as expressed through Boaz. Yes, God was the Author of this beautiful work occurring in Naomi, but she was open to recognize and receive the work of His hands—the requisite for redemption.

Finally, Ruth shared the last morsel of conversation between herself and the kindhearted land owner. "He also told me, 'Stay with my young men until they have finished all of my harvest'" (Ruth 2:21, NASB). As if Boaz's *generosity, kindness,* and *connection* were not enough, God added Boaz's *encouragement.* With his statement, Boaz offered continued provision, protection, and preservation to Ruth . . . and by extension, Naomi. Her heart could hardly deny his intentions. Boaz, as master and land owner, was the lord of his harvest. The lord of this harvest had shown affection, tender care, and favor to a seemingly helpless and hopeless widow. Oh, the marvelous grace of God as expressed through merciful Boaz! As Boaz expressed kindness, the door of mercy was thrown open to Naomi. He is an Old Testament picture of the ultimate Redeemer, Jesus Christ. Jesus, Who stands as the eternal Lord of the Harvest, still sets His affection on the helpless and the hopeless. He shows kindness to those who deserve it the least. He opens wide the door of mercy. Indeed, it is the goodness of God that leads to repentance (Romans 2:4).

Naomi serves as a powerful Old Testament example of a woman transformed by the goodness and kindness of God. But she is certainly not alone in Scripture. Several women in the New Testament share a similar story.

◊   Read John 8:2–11 and record the facts of the narrative.

◊   As you examine the interaction between Jesus and the woman, how does Jesus display kindness?

◊   What does He instruct her to do?

◊   How do you believe she responded? And why?

◊   What lesson do you take away from their encounter?

◊   Read John 4:3–26 and record the facts of the narrative.

◊   How did Jesus deal kindly with the woman at the well?

◊   How did she respond to His kindness? (Read John 4:39–42 for additional clarification.)

◊   What lesson do you learn from their interaction?

◊   With the previous narratives in mind, read Romans 2:4. In light of Jesus' interaction with the Samaritan woman and the adulterous woman, how do you interpret and apply Romans 2:4?

Rescue and redemption exemplify a repeated pattern of provision from an ever-merciful God.

Would you agree that we live in an era of increasing hopelessness? Addictions, suicides, and incidents of self-harm point to a generation permeated with hopelessness. The weight of heaviness and oppression can seem crushing at times. But you, dear sister, have reason for comfort and confidence. You have reason for faith and fortitude. Why? Because Almighty God specializes in seemingly hopeless situations. His name, El Shaddai, declares that He is the All-Sufficient One. He is able to overcome any obstacle. He is able defeat any foe. He is able to redeem any life from any pit. And He is able to rescue any woman from any crisis. Will you trust Him with your crisis? Will you trust Him with your challenge?

◊　Take time to read Genesis 21:8–19 and record the key facts in the narrative.

◊　Describe Hagar's hopeless situation.

◊　Describe God's provision for rescue.

◊　What lesson do you learn about God?

◊ Now turn to the very next chapter and read Genesis 22:1–14. Record the key facts.

◊ Describe Abraham's seemingly hopeless situation.

◊ Describe God's provision of rescue.

◊ What do you learn about God from these verses?

Transformation

"... where the Spirit of the Lord is, there is freedom" (2 Corinthians 3:17). Freedom. It is a beautiful word. It is a lofty word. But how do you bring it down to earth? What does it look like with flesh on? It is best viewed in the context of a story, in the picture of a human life, and through a window to an individual soul. Perhaps no better explanation is required than the testimony of one transformed woman, Corrie ten Boom. Her story is as follows:

> It was in a church in Munich that I saw him—a balding, heavyset man in a gray overcoat, a brown felt hat clutched between his hands. People were filing out of the basement room where I had just spoken, moving along the rows of wooden chairs to the door at the rear. It was 1947 and I had come from Holland to defeated Germany with the message that God forgives.

> It was the truth they needed most to hear in that bitter, bombed-out land, and I gave them my favorite mental picture. Maybe because the sea is never far from a Hollander's mind, I liked to think that that's where forgiven sins were thrown. "When we confess our sins," I said, "God casts them into the deepest ocean, gone forever. . . ."

> The solemn faces stared back at me, not quite daring to believe. There were never questions after a talk in Germany in 1947. People stood up in silence, in silence collected their wraps, in silence left the room.

> And that's when I saw him, working his way forward against the others. One moment I saw the overcoat and the brown hat; the next, a blue uniform and a visored cap with its skull and crossbones. It came back with a rush: the huge room with its harsh overhead lights; the pathetic pile of dresses and shoes in the center of the floor; the shame of walking

naked past this man. I could see my sister's frail form ahead of me, ribs sharp beneath the parchment skin. *Betsie, how thin you were!*

[Betsie and I had been arrested for concealing Jews in our home during the Nazi occupation of Holland; this man had been a guard at Ravensbruck concentration camp where we were sent.]

Now he was in front of me, hand thrust out: "A fine message, Fräulein! How good it is to know that, as you say, all our sins are at the bottom of the sea!"

And I, who had spoken so glibly of forgiveness, fumbled in my pocketbook rather than take that hand. He would not remember me, of course—how could he remember one prisoner among those thousands of women?

But I remembered him and the leather crop swinging from his belt. I was face-to-face with one of my captors and my blood seemed to freeze.

"You mentioned Ravensbruck in your talk," he was saying, "I was a guard there." No, he did not remember me.

"But since that time," he went on, "I have become a Christian. I know that God has forgiven me for the cruel things I did there, but I would like to hear it from your lips as well. Fräulein," again the hand came out—"will you forgive me?"

And I stood there—I whose sins had again and again needed to be forgiven—and could not forgive. Betsie had died in that place—could he erase her slow terrible death simply for the asking?

It could not have been many seconds that he stood there—hand held out—but to me it seemed hours as I wrestled with the most difficult thing I had ever had to do.

For I had to do it—I knew that. The message that God forgives has a prior condition: that we forgive those who have injured us. "If you do not forgive men their trespasses," Jesus says, "neither will your Father in heaven forgive your trespasses."

I knew it not only as a commandment of God, but as a daily experience. Since the end of the war I had had a home in Holland for victims of Nazi brutality. Those who were able to forgive their former enemies were able also to return to the outside world and rebuild their lives, no matter what the physical scars. Those who nursed their bitterness remained invalids. It was as simple and as horrible as that.

And still I stood there with the coldness clutching my heart. But forgiveness is not an emotion—I knew that too. Forgiveness is an act of the will, and the will can function regardless of the temperature of the heart. ". . . Help!" I prayed silently. "I can lift my hand. I can do that much. You supply the feeling."

And so woodenly, mechanically, I thrust my hand into the one stretched out to me. And as I did, an incredible thing took place. The current started in my shoulder, raced down my arm, sprang into our joined hands. And then this healing warmth seemed to flood my whole being, bringing tears to my eyes.

"I forgive you, brother!" I cried. "With all my heart!" "For a long moment we grasped each other's hands, the former guard and the former prisoner. I had never known God's love so intensely, as I did then."[13]

Freedom. On the deepest and most personal level, Corrie Ten Boom experienced it. You can too! There is a path to freedom from bitterness. There is a road to restoration and renewal. The pertinent question hangs in the balance. Are you willing to follow the path? Are you willing to walk the road? "You reveal the path of life to me; in Your presence is abundant joy; in Your right hand are eternal pleasures" (Psalm 16:11). Will you take the first step?

Recognize bitterness in your own life. Sometimes the most difficult place to fix your gaze is your own reflection. Often, we see a distorted image when we look in the mirror. Pause now and ask God to reveal any root of bitterness that may have germinated in your life. Ask Him to allow you to see what He sees. "Search me, God, and know my heart; test me and know my concerns. See if there is any offensive way in me; lead me in the everlasting way" (Psalm 139:23–24). Who is on your grudge list? One name, multiples names, many names? The very hint of an invisible grudge list indicates a root of bitterness. According to God's Word, love "does not keep a record of wrongs" (1 Corinthians 13:5). If your mental scorecard continues to tally a record of wrongs against someone, beware! You have entered bitter territory.

Bitter territory gives way to full-blown resentment when we allow our minds to chew and ruminate over a record of wrongs. Perhaps you have heard of the term "chew the cud." As cows eat and digest their food, it passes into a sort of holding tank or first stomach. "Cud is the partly digested food that cows bring back into their mouths from their first stomach, to chew at leisure."[14] This illustration may seem unpleasantly graphic, but it serves as a powerful word picture for resentment. When you continue to bring back and ruminate on an offense or a wrong suffered, you are chewing the cud. When you bring it back up in conversation

---

13   Excerpted from "I'm Still Learning to Forgive" by Corrie ten Boom. Reprinted by permission from *Guideposts* Magazine. Copyright © 1972 by Guideposts Associates, Inc., Carmel, New York 10512.

14   Phrases.org.uk, "Chew the cud," http://www.phrases.org.uk/meanings/91100.html

(without the motive of reconciliation), you are chewing the cud. And it allows a root of bitterness to germinate and spring up to mature growth.

◊ Take a moment (or a few) and ask our Holy Father to identify anyone you are holding a grudge against. Record the names below:

Resentment gives way to the urge for retaliation. Retaliation is simply the desire to "get back" at someone. Retaliation wants to see the offender pay for his or her offense. Retaliation births the heart attitude, which seethingly says, "I sure hope you get what you deserve." Retaliation may be overt and aggressive, or it may be more passive. How familiar are you with the silent treatment? If you recognize the principle of the silent treatment, then you understand passive retaliation. The desire to retaliate (if left unchecked) will eventually express itself in an outward display of anger, hatred, or violence. Someone is bound to be harmed. The heartbreaking and terrible irony is that expressions of anger, hatred, and violence often manifest as self-destructive behaviors. All too often, a wounded person becomes a resentful person. A resentful person becomes an angry person. An angry person does damage to either those around her or to herself. How many incidents of self-harm, addiction, eating disorders, and suicide could be prevented if bitterness was not allowed to fester? It is serious business, and it demands a radical response.

◊ So, how do you respond if the Lord has revealed even a hint of bitterness in your life?

Repent and renounce bitterness. Follow King David's pattern in Psalm 51. Throw yourself on the mercy of an ever-loving God. Fall into the arms of a forgiving, redeeming God. Agree with Him about your offenses. Ask Him for pardon. Ask Him for cleansing. "Wash away my guilt, and cleanse me from my sin . . . purify me with hyssop, and I will be clean; wash me, and I will be whiter than snow" (Psalm 51:2, 7). Hallelujah! Rejoice in the blood of Jesus Christ, Who has the power to wash away every spot and every stain! "Though your sins are like scarlet, they will be white as snow; though they are as red as crimson, they will be like wool" (Isaiah 1:18). Forgiveness! His cleansing waters wash over you with refreshment and renewal. Transformation is under way. But there's more.

Your path to freedom has gloriously begun, and your next step will catapult you forward in your faith journey. "Freely you have received, freely give" (Matthew 10:8, NIV). God's Word instructs us to liberally give that which we have received of His Spirit. God, in His lavish graciousness, granted you forgiveness without any cost to you. Now, He asks that you do the same by His Spirit. Take your grudge list and work through it one name at a time. Forgive. Forgive. Forgive.

The worthiness of the offender is of no consequence. The worthiness of the Redeemer is all that matters. "Do not judge, and you will not be judged. Do not condemn, and you will not be condemned. Forgive, and you will be forgiven" (Luke 6:37).

Read and record what you learn about forgiveness from the following verses:

◊   Matthew 6:14–15

◊   Mark 11:25–26

◊   Ephesians 4:32

As you work through your grudge list, write out a prayer of forgiveness. Declare that you hold each of these offenders harmless and that you willfully release them from any perceived debt they owe you.

Amen! Forgiveness leads to freedom. "If the Son sets you free, you really will be free" (John 8:36). Now it is time to walk in that wonderful freedom!

Refuse to focus on offenders. As you move toward your glorious future, you can expect two obstacles to arise in your path. First, your enemy (the devil) will try to snatch away your precious freedom. He would love nothing more than watch you fall back into the binding vice grip of bitterness. He will tempt you to go back . . . to recall (again) the oppressive offenses of the past. Remember, dear sister, to "run the race that is set before you" (Hebrews 12:1, NASB). Refuse to go back and focus on the offenders of the past! You released them. Let them remain released.

Read the following verses and record your insights. How do these instructions encourage you to protect your mind?

◊   Philippians 4:8

◊   2 Corinthians 10:5

While your enemy desires to see you fall, your Redeemer desires to see you stand. Take every thought captive to the obedience of Christ. Refuse to dwell on anything that is not worthy of praise. "And the peace of God, which surpasses every thought, will guard your heart and your mind in Christ Jesus" (Philippians 4:7).

Your future will present new opportunities for a budding root of bitterness. As you walk forward in freedom, you continue to walk in the midst of a fallen and filthy world. You will experience disappointment, loss, and grief—again. But this time will be different. You are armed with Scripture and Truth. In the power of Almighty God, you can respond as a new creature, with a new nature. "You took off your former way of life, the old self, that is corrupted by deceitful desires; you are being renewed in the spirit of your mind; you put on the new self, the one created according to God's likeness in righteousness and purity of the truth" (Ephesians 4:22–24, NASB). Scripture is profitable for teaching, correcting, and training in righteousness (2 Timothy 3:16). By it, you not only learn the precepts of God, but you also benefit from the examples of faith-filled people.

◊ Take time to read Genesis 37 and 39–45:15. Record the offenses and disappointments in Joseph's life. How was Joseph able to avoid bitterness? On whom did he focus in the midst of his trials? What difference did it make in Joseph's life? How could you apply his example to your life?

Joseph refused to focus on his offenders. He resolved to remain focused on his God, and it allowed him to fulfill his calling, preserve his family, and bless an entire nation! Beloved sister, the Redeemer has wonderful plans for you, plans to give you a hope and a future (Jeremiah 29:11). Set your eyes on the prize. Press forward with a fixed gaze. Run with endurance the race set before you, fixing your eyes on Jesus, the Author and Finisher of your faith (Hebrews 12:1–2).

Finally, remember the goodness of God. Bring to mind often the faithful deeds of your faithful Father. Recount His displays of kindness to you. Revisit the times He delivered you. Record the ways He has provided for you. Memorize His Word as a memorial to His faithfulness.

◊ Read and meditate on Psalm 103:1–22. How do these verses prompt you to remember God's goodness? Choose several of these verses and commit them to memory.

◊ Read Psalm 34:1–4 and record your insights. How can you apply these verses to your current circumstances?

◊ Read Hebrews 13:15 and record your insights. How would you characterize or describe a person who continually offers praise from her lips? How does that compare to a bitter person?

Praise reveals a gracious heart of gratitude. "An evidence that our will has been broken is that we begin to thank God for that which once seemed so bitter, knowing that His will is good and that in His time and in His way, He is able to make the most bitter waters sweet."[15] Gratitude and bitterness are mutually exclusive. They just don't go together. Keep your lips occupied with praise and thanksgiving. Train your tongue to bless those around you. Your words will serve as soothing balm to others, and you will leave little room for bitterness to reemerge.

Naomi's transformation provides an occasion for celebration. Through loss and grief, a pleasant woman soured and temporarily lost the disposition and destiny intended for her. But God stepped into the picture (in the form of an earthly redeemer), and He restored Naomi in every way possible. He renewed her hope. He refreshed her disposition. He moved her from blaming to blessing. He changed her from bitter to sweet, all through His kindness expressed through Boaz. Never underestimate the power of kindness! "When we consider how potent our kindness may be in quickening the sense of God's kindness and compassion in a neighbor's heart . . . we may well tremble at the responsibility which may fall upon us at any moment."[16]

God desires that you, too, would break free from the pain of your past and embrace your glorious future. His heart delights in revealing the kind intention of His will toward you. You are destined to be a woman who receives the kindness of God, who is transformed by the kindness of God, and who becomes a channel by which the kindness of God is poured out on others. Will you accept His offer? His arms of mercy are open wide. This is your invitation; this is your time. "Now may the God of hope fill you with all joy and peace as you believe in Him so that you may overflow with hope by the power of the Holy Spirit" (Romans 15:13).

---

15   Nancy Leigh DeMoss, *A Place of Quiet Rest* (Moody, 2000), 70.

16   Samuel Cox and Thomas Fuller, *The Book of Ruth* (Klock and Klock Publishers, 1982), 100.

RUTH 3:1–5

Ruth's mother-in-law Naomi said to her, "My daughter, shouldn't I find security for you, so that you will be taken care of? Now isn't Boaz our relative? Haven't you been working with his female servants? This evening he will be winnowing barley on the threshing floor. Wash, put on perfumed oil, and wear your best clothes. Go down to the threshing floor, but don't let the man know you are there until he has finished eating and drinking. When he lies down, notice the place where he's lying, go in and uncover his feet, and lie down. Then he will explain to you what you should do." So Ruth said to her, "I will do everything you say."

CHAPTER EIGHT

Beth Reed

Entering into Spiritual Rest

Introduction

> "Then Naomi her mother in law said unto her, My daughter,
> shall I not seek rest for thee, that it may be well with thee?"
> (Ruth 3:1, KJV).

Frantic. Harried. Hurried. Are there better words to describe the current pace of life for the average woman? Today's typical female has mastered multitasking, is savvy with social media, and regularly rotates multiple hats of responsibility. Seriously, has there ever been a time when so much can be accomplished on the drive home from work? Before exiting the parking lot, one quick look at e-mail reveals that a friend has been admitted to the hospital and the electric bill is due tomorrow. No worries. A few "thumb maneuvers" and the electric bill has been paid. To avoid "distracted driving," it's time to switch to voice command. "Call florist." After a few quick questions and the recitation of memorized credit card information, a beautiful arrangement is on its way to the hospital. The next call addresses the perpetual question: What's for dinner? "Call pizza place." Whew! The dinner dilemma is solved. Now, enjoy a few moments of quiet before pulling into the driveway. Remember the mounds of laundry piled up in the laundry room? (It would be an impressive engineering feat if it weren't so intimidating.)

Start with whites. No. They can all go in the dryer. Start with dark colors because some of them need to air dry. Ahh . . . home is in sight! Who is that in the driveway? What is today anyway? Oh, NO! Can it already be the second Thursday of the month? Booster club meeting . . . and it's my month to host! I better order more pizzas. I NEED A BREAK! I NEED REST.

Can you relate? Your level of activity may vary, and your flavor of responsibility may differ, but your innate craving for rest resonates all the same. Your soul was created to seek rest, not simply physical rest but spiritual rest. As we continue our journey with Naomi and Ruth, we see the beautiful offer of rest—lasting rest. Everlasting rest. The invitation to enter into a state of rest is both exclusive and all-inclusive. The *exclusive* nature of this glorious rest rises from the simple fact that there is one single, solitary source of eternal repose—the person of Jesus Christ. The *inclusive* nature of this marvelous rest derives from the free and open invitation to come and receive—whosoever will. So, what about you? How would you describe your life right now? Are you laboring or are you resting? Jesus' offer of rest is, at once, both universal and intensely personal. While His perfect atonement made rest available for all of mankind, He is profoundly attentive toward you. He is fiercely passionate about your future, your destiny, and your spirit. Will you consider His offer of rest today? "Come to Me, all of you who are weary and burdened, and I will give you rest" (Matthew 11:28).

Trials

Over a prolonged period, the demands of life begin to wear on a woman. Seasons of stress, burdens, and toil begin to take their destructive toll. Have you ever wondered why life can seem so laborious? Toil is not a respecter of persons. Whether you work in the corporate world, own your own business, or manage your household full time, you understand the concept of "the daily grind." Have you ever heard the biblical explanation for the daily grind? In the beginning (THE beginning), God created a man and a woman. He placed them in a garden of paradise, and He gave them a job. "So God created man in His own image; He created him in the image of God; He created them male and female. God blessed them, and God said to them, 'Be fruitful, multiply, fill the earth, subdue it. Rule the fish of the sea, the birds of the sky, and every creature that crawls on the earth.'" (Genesis 1:27–28) Paradise, the Garden of Eden, was not a place of unending leisure. It was designed and ordained as a place of work (the ideal place of work) and a place of rest.

Paradise is not characterized by the absence of work but by the absence of the *burden* of work. Adam and Eve enjoyed days of work and days of rest. Work days were joyously fulfilling, and rest days were joyously fulfilling. Why? Because they enjoyed unbroken, unhindered fellowship with their Creator, the One Who designed them for life, work, and eternity. Even while their bodies were at work, their souls were at rest. It was perfect. Really, truly, spiritually perfect. They were as blessed as any two people could possibly be! They enjoyed every blessing—loving marriage, perfect home, and satisfying work. Until . . . until temptation came to visit, and they entertained his offer. They sinned; they disregarded the clear, simple instruction of their Creator and Friend. Fellowship was broken, and consequences were incurred. There was a curse for the tempter, the serpent. There was a curse for the woman (and all of womankind.) Finally, there was a curse for the man (and all who would participate in any form of work.) "The ground is cursed because of you. You will eat from it by means of painful labor all the days of your life . . . You will eat bread by the sweat of your brow until you return to the ground . . ." (Genesis 3:17, 19). Death was ushered in by their sin—both physical and spiritual. Shame and guilt were ushered in by their sin. Broken relationships were ushered in by their sin—both horizontally and vertically. The fractured relationship between man and his Creator gave rise to a fallen, restless soul, a soul that no longer enjoyed perpetual peace and joy. Ultimately, the toil of work was ushered in by the curse. Work was not the result of the curse but the burdensome nature of work was. And so began the elusive search for rest. So, what is rest anyway? Rest means the cessation of work or movement in order to relax or recover strength. Rest means freedom from anxiety or disturbance. Rest means freedom from work, toil, or strain. "The body is at rest when it ceases to move. The mind is at rest when it ceases to be disturbed or agitated."[17] John McArthur offers further insight on rest:

> **Rest** also means freedom from whatever worries or disturbs you. Some people cannot **rest** mentally and emotionally because they are so easily annoyed. Every little nuisance upsets them and they always feel hassled. **Rest** does not mean freedom from all nuisances and hassles; it means freedom from being so easily bothered by them. **Rest** means to be inwardly quiet, composed, peaceful. To enter God's **rest** means to be at peace with God (Ro 5:1-note), to possess the perfect peace He gives (Is 26:3). It means to be free from guilt and even unnecessary feelings of guilt. It means freedom from worry about sin, because sin is forgiven. God's **rest** is the end of legalistic works and the experience of peace in the total forgiveness of God. [18]

Before we dive more fully into the implications of rest, it seems an appropriate time to examine the opposite of rest. What are some antonyms for rest? Restlessness. Strain. Toil. Drudge. Grind. Do any of those sound familiar? Do any of those sound a little *too* familiar? Have you ever heard of the soap opera entitled *The Young and the Restless?* Though the characters changed, the story line always seemed to remain the same. Looking for love in all the wrong places. Betrayal. Revenge. Illicit affairs and so on and so on. Is it a raunchy and ridiculous plot? Or is it a regrettable reflection of our days and our times? Unfortunately, it is probably both. We live in a world where life is not only stranger than fiction, but it is often raunchier and racier than fiction. Day after day, we see overwhelming evidence of restless hearts, restless souls, and restless spirits. *Restless souls seek out resting places.* If the innate craving for rest is a God-given desire, then how does the search for such a good thing turn so horribly wrong? It seems like such a paradox. But there are two important truths that bring the puzzle pieces together.

---

17   PreceptAustin.org, "Rest in the Bible," http://www.preceptaustin.org/rest_in_hebrews_4.htm

18   Ibid.

First of all, we are fallen creatures who are influenced (to one degree or another) by selfish thoughts and motivations. "The heart is more deceitful than all else and is desperately sick; who can understand it?" (Jeremiah 17:9, NASB) Even the believer, who has become a new creation in Christ and has been given a new nature in Him, can rely on deceptive and fallacious emotions. She can fall back into old patterns of thinking. Wrong patterns of thinking, self-serving patterns of thinking, and distorted patterns of thinking. In this case, the search for rest morphs into a search for gratification or satisfaction. *If I could only have _____, then I would be happy and at peace.* Fill in the blank. *If I could only attain _____, then all would be well. If only . . .*

Restless souls seek out resting places.

Second, our adversary (the serpent) disguises himself as an angel of light. (2 Corinthians 11:14). As if it weren't enough that our own hearts can be deceitful, we also have an active enemy who is committed to deceiving us. He knows our innate desire for rest, and he falsely promises rest even as he sets a trap of destruction. The sweet wife, whose husband has been distracted by work lately, longs for companionship and the security of feeling loved. She works hard to clean the house, make an appetizing dinner, light the candles, and dress her best. Her hopes are dashed as she receives the call . . . late again . . . no time for dinner . . . don't wait up. Her mind is a jumble of voices. *Why am I not enough? What do I have to do to get his attention? I should be more . . .*

Her heart is restless and her emotions raw. Not much to do at home but eat dinner alone, surf the Internet, and check up on social media. Hey! There's a face from the past. Wonder how he is doing these days? There's nothing wrong with a quick message. Quick message evolves into lengthy exchange . . . lengthy exchange evolves into lunch plans . . . lunch plans evolve into dinner and drinks . . . you know the rest of the story. *Restless hearts seek a resting place.* Her enemy sold it to her as a place of love, appreciation, and contentment. He lied.

She is not alone. In fact, she is afloat amidst a sea of women (and men) who have gone looking for rest and found turmoil and tumult instead. She finds herself alongside the woman who has not yet been physically unfaithful, but she spends hours reading about illicit relationships with otherworldly beings. Sometimes those thoughts even turn to fantasy. She finds herself alongside the woman who has become obsessed with her physical appearance. It started with a simple exercise class, which led to hours of workouts a day, which led to eating habits that had to be hidden, which led to rapid weight loss, which led to a little "cosmetic" surgery, which led to an all-out, all-consuming obsession. She finds herself alongside the woman who bears her fair share of scars from life's disappointments. Letdown after painful letdown and she finds herself in physical pain as well as emotional pain. She just needs a little something to take the "edge" off of the pain. A few more pills won't hurt . . . it's under control . . . until it becomes a full-blown addiction.

Restless souls seek out resting places.

◊   Take a moment to record the evidence of restlessness around you.

◊   Take another moment to record any evidence of restlessness within you.

◊   Perhaps you can relate to the elusive search for rest. Perhaps you have seen it play out in the life of a friend or family member. Perhaps you relate because it resonates somewhere deep within you. However, at this point, the previous examples may seem foreign or detached from you. You live a morally clean and well-balanced life. You believe the Scriptures, and you serve the Lord. You really serve the Lord. You volunteer, you teach, you give, and you lead. You rarely miss a Sunday, and you regularly attend inspirational conferences. And yet, something just seems amiss. Women around you are whistling and smiling . . . who has time for that? Women around you are talking about their sweet times of private worship . . . what is up with that? Amidst the serving and the "doing," your soul longs for something more. What is it? REST. Yes, even the Christian soul can be restless.

Restless souls seek out a resting place.

Would you like to hear the most wonderful news? There is a place of rest available. And it is available to you. His name is Jesus. You were created (knit together in your mother's womb) to find rest in Him—and in Him alone. You may have searched high and low. Or you may just now be awakening to your craving for rest. His offer ever stands. "The soul never finds its true resting place till it can lean on the bosom of the Christ."[19]

So, how does all this relate to Ruth? Ruth is not only a real, historical figure, but she is also a symbol. She represents all women. She had a need for rest. Under the guidance of Naomi, she sought her rest in the right place. She was greatly blessed for her obedience and faith. Her story serves as an encouragement for us today. Her story could be your story. Let's examine how she positioned herself to become the beneficiary of rest and blessing.

Truth

"My daughter, shall I not seek rest for thee?" (Ruth 3:1, KJV). Naomi's question must have stirred the memory of a previous conversation for Ruth. After the death of Elimelech, Mahlon, and Chilion, Naomi was determined to return to Bethlehem. In the midst of tearful good-

---

19   Henry Briggs, *Sermons on the Book of Ruth* (London, 1901), 75.

byes, Naomi expressed concern and care for the future of her daughters-in-law. "May the Lord grant that you may find rest, each in the house of her husband" (Ruth 1:9, NASB). Naomi fully understood the likely options for each girl's future. A new husband would provide security and protection—rest. Without a new husband, a young widow's outlook for the future would be quite dim with limited opportunity to provide for herself. As Naomi urged the young women to stay behind, Ruth declared her loyalty to Naomi and determined to adopt her homeland and her God. Together, the two women returned to Bethlehem where Ruth was providentially led to the fields of Boaz. Ruth worked through the barley season and the wheat season. Scripture indicates that she worked long days in the fields to provide for herself and Naomi. As the harvest season ended, Naomi recognized that Ruth would no longer have the means to provide for herself. Her heart focused once more on the well-being of her beloved daughter-in-law. Naomi suggested rest.

What type of rest was she suggesting? Certainly, there was the implication of rest from her physical labors. "No man is strong enough to endure ceaseless labor. Even our Savior needed to relax His efforts and retire to the mountains for repose."[20] Ruth shouldered the burden of providing for the two women throughout the harvest season. Ruth also shouldered the burden of carrying hope for Naomi throughout her bout of bitterness. Ruth needed rest. But there was a much richer meaning to the rest Naomi suggested. Naomi wished *menuchah* rest for Ruth. The Hebrew word *menuchah* means "abode or quiet, a still resting place." It is the place of honor, freedom, and peace, which a Hebrew woman would find in the home of her husband.[21] Naomi understood that neither man nor woman was created to be alone. She longed for Ruth to enjoy the refuge of hearth and home. Naomi knew, by experience, that a good marriage was a shelter from the storms of life. Naomi also cared deeply about Ruth's future security and protection. "My daughter, shall I not seek rest for thee, that it may be well with thee?" (Ruth 3:1, KJV). In other words, Naomi was seeking the absolute best for this precious daughter-in-law and her future. Oh, that we would share such a concern

---

20   Henry Briggs, *Sermons on the Book of Ruth* (London, 1901), 69.

21   Samuel Cox and Thomas Fuller, *The Book of Ruth* (Klock and Klock Publishers, 1982), 155.

for those around us! Naomi made it her mission to help secure rest for beloved Ruth. What if we shared the same concern to see those around us find rest, everlasting rest?

Naomi, who progressed from bitter victim to strategic planner, began to reveal her plan. She offered a proposition. "Now isn't Boaz our relative? Haven't you been working with his female servants? This evening he will be winnowing barley in the threshing floor" (Ruth 3:2). Naomi proposed the invocation of a legal right. Boaz was a kinsman or kinsman-redeemer (a *goel*). Jewish law listed several redemption opportunities under the law of *goel*, including the responsibility of the nearest relative marrying the childless widow of his brother. By law, it was both Ruth's privilege and responsibility to ask Boaz to exercise the right of kinsman-redeemer. Naomi's wise and watchful eye did not miss the special interest Boaz had taken in Ruth. Her intuition rightly interpreted Ruth's admiration of Boaz. Consequently, her bold and daring plan was developed.

Not only did Naomi offer a bold *proposition*, but she followed it with a meticulous prescript for *preparation*. "Wash, put on perfumed oil and wear your best clothes" (Ruth 3:2). Naomi's instructions were both practical and symbolic in nature. Wash. Moabites were not known for good personal hygiene. In fact, they were notorious for quite the opposite. Ruth was a field worker. No doubt Boaz had often seen her in a soiled and dirty state. If she were to present herself as his potential bride, she must present herself in cleanliness. Symbolically, cleanliness is regarded as "a type of purity of the mind and spirit."[22] Ruth was presenting herself to Boaz with the intent of securing hope, help, and home. But she was also laying claim to an inheritance. Therefore, she must keep clean. Her hands, her eyes, her ears, and her lips must be kept clean as a steward of such rich inheritance.

Anoint yourself. Again, the instruction carries practical and symbolic meaning. Ruth was poor, and it is doubtful that she possessed costly ointment. Unlike Mary, who anointed Jesus with nard, Ruth had no precious jar of oil for such an occasion. She likely used a common oil such as olive oil, which was plentiful and cheap. Perhaps she added spices to the oil to produce a fragrant aroma. By anointing herself, she

---

22   Henry Briggs, *Sermons on the Book of Ruth* (London, 1901), 85.

made her face to shine, and she conveyed a pleasing aroma. Physically, her preparation served to enhance her natural beauty. Symbolically, the anointing set her apart for a new role. She practiced the protocol of prophets, priests, and kings who were anointed to signify God's blessing and calling on their lives. Ruth's adherence to this instruction illustrated her assent to God's call on her life. Oh, the blessings of obedience! At the point of her obedience, Ruth could only hope that God intended to bless her marriage and her offspring. Could she have guessed that her grandson would by the great king of Israel? Could she imagine that this bold proposition would draw her in to the line and lineage of Christ, the Messiah? Could this childless widow even begin to comprehend the future fruit of her womb? And yet, she obeyed. She accepted the instruction of Naomi and, by extension, the will of God without question. Would you do the same? Would you accept the call of God on your life without question or clarification? Would you set yourself apart for an, as yet, undisclosed new role in His service?

Put on your best clothes. Naomi did not instruct Ruth to buy new garments. She simply told her to show up in her best. Remember, Ruth was a young widow. She had been wearing garments of grief. It was time to shed the garments of mourning and put on the garments of celebration—garments suitable for a wedding feast. "I will turn their mourning into joy, give them consolation, and bring happiness out of grief" (Jeremiah 31:13). By clothing herself in her best garments, Ruth expressed faith that future blessings were running to meet her. She expressed confidence in the future based on her submission to God's will for her life. By faith, she reached out and grabbed the blessings that were intended for her, even though the magnitude of those blessings was yet unknown.

Following the specific details for *preparation*, Naomi lays out her plan for *presentation*. "Go down to the threshing floor; but do not make yourself known to the man until he has finished eating and drinking. It shall be when he lies down, that you shall notice the place where he lies, and you shall go and uncover his feet and lie down, then he will tell you what you should do" (Ruth 3:3–4, NASB). Bold, daring, and a little bit suspenseful. What a plan! If one suggested such a plan today, it would seem scandalous. Certainly in modern culture, this would be interpreted as a highly sexual overture. (Bear in mind that we live in a hypersexualized culture, which influences our interpretation.) What was Naomi thinking? On what basis did she suggest such a forward plan? Naomi trusted the wisdom of the plan because she trusted the character of those involved. Naomi had ample opportunity to observe the integrity of both Ruth and Boaz. Ruth consistently displayed modesty and loyalty. She chose to stay with Naomi rather than seek a young husband in her homeland. She chose to stay in the fields of Boaz (as he requested) rather than glean in any other fields. She chose to remain close to his female maids to avoid any hint of impropriety among the male field workers. Her reputation of purity preceded her. ". . . all the people in my town know that you are a woman of noble character" (Ruth 3:11). If ever there was a woman to be trusted with such a delicate situation, it was Ruth. The same could be said of Boaz. He demonstrated a protective kindness towards Ruth, a kindness born out of respect and compassion. Boaz also upheld a reputation of integrity. "Now Naomi had a relative on her husband's side named Boaz. He was a prominent man of noble character from Elimelech's family" (Ruth 2:1). Naomi trusted each one to act in a right and righteous manner. Furthermore, she trusted the righteous nature of the claim. Jewish law "allowed Ruth to act in a manner which would otherwise have been improper and indelicate."[23] Naomi's spiritual eyes had been opened to recognize the goodness and the providence of God. She trusted God to bless the forthcoming union, and she trusted Ruth and Boaz not to spoil the opportunity. Buoyed by Naomi's confidence and instruction, Ruth prepared to move forward "with holy boldness as she pressed her claim."[24]

Finally, notice the sweet submission with which Ruth received her instructions. "All that you say, I will do" (Ruth 3:5, NASB). Naomi offered a *proposition* for the purpose of securing rest for her beloved Ruth. She specified a deliberate and symbolic method of *preparation*. And she gave detailed instruction regarding the method of *presentation*. Ruth's spontaneous response offers great insight into her soul. It reveals her *predisposition*. Predisposition is an inclination or preference toward something. Ruth's inclination was to trust the counsel of the woman

---

23   Henry Briggs, *Sermons on the Book of Ruth* (London, 1901), 77.

24   W. G. Heslop, *Rubies From Ruth* (Zondervan, 1944), 77.

she followed to a new land and a new faith. Ruth witnessed enough of God's faithfulness in the life of Naomi that she herself leaned toward faith. The evidence of God's goodness in her past was so strong that she leaned toward Him for her future. "All that you say, I will do." She leaned to the point of absolute surrender. She leaned to the point of no return, no compromise, no questioning, and no justifying. She leaned forward in faith, with the assurance that the plans for her were good. "For I know the plans I have for you—this is the Lord's declaration—plans for your welfare, not for disaster, to give you a future and a hope" (Jeremiah 29:11). How does her example encourage you? How could you follow her example in a practical way today?

Transformation

Have you ever thrown your hands in the air and uttered the words, "I can't take it any more"? Have you ever sat with your head in your hands and thought, *I'm emotionally spent . . . I have nothing left?* Several years ago, I was leading a small group of adults through Bible study. I invested heavily in the lives of my class members. I spent a few hours teaching them each week. I spent immeasurably more time shepherding them! I loved them dearly, and it was a joy to serve them. We went through a period of difficult life circumstances together. Some lost jobs. Some lost babies in the womb. Some nearly lost children to acute disease. Some nearly lost marriages. I spent time in hospitals, living rooms, and prayer closets. In many ways, it was a wonderfully glorious season—a true picture of the Body of Christ operating as intended. But, all of a sudden, it caught up with me. I poured out everything I had, and I landed on empty. I continued to "minister" on empty for a while. (Pure misery, just in case you wondered.) Until finally one night, I poured out my heart to the Lord in prayer. I admitted that I was tired. I admitted that I was empty. I admitted that the job of shepherding was a little overwhelming. I cried out, "I NEED A SHEPHERD!" And the unmistakable, inner voice of the Holy Spirit answered my heart cry. "The Lord is my shepherd; there is nothing I lack. He lets me lie down in green pastures; He leads me beside quiet waters. He renews my life; He leads me along the right paths for His name's sake" (Psalm 23:1–3). It was like a cup of cold water to a parched soul. I needed rest, and the Lord was gently reminding me where to find it. I would love to report that I have remained in that sweet rest continually. But that's not the case. Occasionally, my Good Shepherd has to lead me back to the quiet waters. The marvelous truth is that there is a blessed rest available. Even better, Scripture illumines the pathway to His blessed rest. Are you willing to go there? Are you willing to follow that path marked out in His Word? His offer is as timely as it has ever been. "Come to Me, all of you who are weary and burdened, and I will give you rest" (Matthew 11:28).

How do quiet waters sound to you? If they sound even slightly appealing, they are about to sound even better. Guess what the word for *quiet* is in Psalm 23? Yes! *Menuchah*. Remember the rest that Naomi wished for Ruth? An abode or quiet dwelling place. A place of honor, freedom, and peace. A place of security and protection. Menuchah. The Good Shepherd leads His sheep to menuchah. Oh, what a delightful Shepherd!

◊ Take time to read Psalm 23. Personalize the chapter by replacing the pronouns "me" and "my" with your name. How does this chapter encourage you today?

Simply put, you were born with a restless heart, a restless soul—a consequence of the Fall. You will continue to seek rest until you find the genuine specimen, and, once found, you will delight in its bliss. Ruth, as our universal representative, was a woman in need of rest. Her rest was not found in a place but in a person, Boaz. As Ruth represents mankind, Boaz represents the matchless Christ. "Christ is our great-hearted Boaz willing to act the part of kinsman, in whose love we may find rest for our souls."[25] Naomi's great love for Ruth prompted her to seek a favorable

---

25   Henry Briggs, *Sermons on the Book of Ruth* (London, 1901), 77.

marriage with the willing redeemer. God's great love for you prompts Him to draw you into relationship with the great Redeemer, Jesus Christ.

◊   Look up 2 Corinthians 11:2 and write out the entire verse.

◊   What insight do you gain from this verse?

Almighty God has prepared a blessed marriage for you. He has offered His Son as the faithful Bridegroom. Marriage is a symbol of the spiritual union between Christ and the Church. But is also a symbol of spiritual union between Christ and the individual believer. All the benefits that Ruth recognized in a relationship with Boaz, the Lord offers to His bride . . . and more! The Lord assumes toward His beloved people the duty of protection and support—to guard them from danger and meet all their needs. He assumes the responsibility of headship. He gives directions for conduct and service, and He provides the power for fruitfulness.[26]

◊   Have you accepted His proposal? Have you entered, by faith, into the relationship He offers?

---

26   Philip Mauro, Ruth, *The Satisfied Stranger* (Bible Truth Depot, Swengel, PA, 1963), 181.

"Behold I stand at the door and knock; If anyone hears My voice and opens the door I will come into him and will dine with him, and he with Me" (Revelation 3:20, NASB). Have you ever answered the loving "knock" of salvation? The Bridegroom of glory and perfection stands ready to accept you into His arms of mercy. If you are willing to love Him and believe in Him, He stands ready to enter your very innermost being and make His abode with you (John 14:23). This, sweet sister, is the rest of salvation. Have you entered into this glorious rest?

◊ Take time to record your own story of salvation. How did you recognize the "knock" on the door of your heart? How did you respond?

Grace is the love language of our wonderful Bridegroom. He took note of our insurmountable sin debt, and He offered full payment, relieving us of the overbearing burden. He recognized our abject helplessness, and He offered power, protection, and provision. He had compassion on our restless souls, and He offered an eternal resting place—Himself. "If it is true that the natural affections of woman find rest in married love, it is no less true that the finer and more spiritual cravings of the human heart find a rest in the love of God, as revealed in the Son."[27] There is no true rest outside of the person of Jesus Christ. "Come to ME," He said. Not come to church. Not come to Bible study. Not come to Christian counselors. (Though they are all good and useful in the Kingdom of God.) Come to Jesus! He is the single, solitary source of true rest.

So, what about the believer? Once the balm of grace has been applied, is there still a need for rest? Yes, yes, a resounding yes! Entering into salvation delivers you into a one time (for all time) rest. This rest offers reprieve from the wrath of judgment, freedom from the guilt of

---

27   Henry Briggs, *Sermons on the Book of Ruth* (London, 1901), 75.

unforgiven sin, and eternal security concerning the future of your soul. But there remains a continuing rest . . . a day-by-day rest . . . a moment-by-moment rest . . . a quiet waters rest. "Seeking rest in a world of unrest and sin should be the one supreme business of all who have found grace."[28]

So, how does a woman remain in "quiet waters" amidst the frantic, frenzied world of today? First, she adopts an accurate view of her yoke. "Come to Me, all who are weary and heavy laden, and I will give you rest. Take my yoke upon you and learn from Me, for I am gentle and humble in heart, and YOU WILL FIND REST FOR YOUR SOULS. For my yoke is easy and my burden is light" (Matthew 11:28–30, NASB). Rest is not idleness. Rest is not the absence of a yoke. Christ does not invite us to throw off our yoke and breeze through life "yokeless." When we come to Christ, we don't lose all yokes and burdens, but we are invited to wear a new yoke and assume a new burden.[29] He offers us a trade. Trade your yoke for His. Take off your yoke of striving and struggling in your familiar manner of self-sufficiency; take on His yoke of gentleness and lightness. Take off the yoke of law; put on the yoke of grace. Take off the yoke of self; put on the yoke of death to self. The yoke of meekness. Much of our burden is rooted in a soul that feels mistreated, unappreciated, unjustly offended, or inconvenienced. "Who does not see that many of our most biting cares, if not all of them, spring from our self-love, our self-assertion, our high thoughts of ourselves? Instead of being meek, we are quick and sudden to resent slights and wrongs, and even to imagine them."[30] Why is Christ's yoke so easy and light? Because He is meek, gentle, and humble in heart. Thus, the yoke sits lightly upon Him. He invites us to learn from Him. He invites us to put on His yoke. Every day.

---

28   W. G. Heslop, *Rubies From Ruth* (Zondervan, 1944), 74.

29   Samuel Cox and Thomas Fuller, *The Book of Ruth* (Klock and Klock Publishers, 1982), 159.

30   Ibid., 162.

◊ This is particularly applicable in the home. For women, home is both a place of labor and a place of rest. How would your home be different if you put on Christ's yoke of gentleness and meekness as you served your family?

◊ Read the following verses and compare the different images of a woman in her home: Proverbs 21:9, Proverbs 21:19, Proverbs 27:15, 1 Peter 3:1–4, and Titus 2:3–5.

Whether you work exclusively in the home or whether you also work outside of the home, you desire for your home to be a place of rest for you, for your family, and for all who enter. In order for a home to be a place of true rest, it must be a godly home. Your role in creating a godly home of sweet repose is to put on the yoke of Christ. As you walk in meekness, gentleness, and humility of spirit, your home becomes a safe harbor for those who seek shelter from the storms of life, especially your husband and children.

A second way to remain beside quiet waters is to focus your attention on the upcoming wedding feast. "Blessed are those who are invited to the marriage supper of the Lamb" (Revelation 19:9). Your heavenly Father has betrothed you to His glorious Son, the Bridegroom, the Spotless Lamb. All of heaven and creation await the splendor of the promised wedding feast. Just as Naomi prescribed specific steps of preparation for Ruth, your Holy Father has called you to be diligent in your preparation for the celestial celebration. The instruction to cleanse, anoint, and put on your best clothes is a parallel for the Bride of Christ.

Wash. Just as Ruth became soiled in the fields, it is easy for us to "contract spiritual filth by daily contact with the evil influences of the world."[31]

◊   Read John 13:3–10 and record what you learn about washing.

Jesus offered to wash Peter's feet, and Peter's lack of understanding caused him to balk at the offer. As Peter began to understand the nature of the washing, he wanted it all over, not only his feet but his head and hands also. Jesus tenderly explained that Peter had already been washed completely; now, he need only wash his feet to remain clean. So it is with the believer. At salvation, the believer is washed completely clean. Jesus washes His bride with the washing of the water of the Word that He may present her a spotless bride. But, at present, His bride walks around in a filthy world. Her feet need to be cleaned to remove the grime. Wash. Confess. Seek forgiveness where you have wronged; offer forgiveness where you have been wronged.

Anoint yourself. It is the glory of the believer to be anointed by the Holy Spirit. He has sealed us and set us apart. He is the deposit and guarantee of our future inheritance and glory. He is the surety that all of God's promises will be found true. He is the indwelling evidence that Christ has taken up residence in our hearts. "Now it is God who strengthens us in Christ and has anointed us. He has also sealed us and given us the Spirit as a down payment in our hearts" (2 Corinthians 1:20–22).

Put on your best garments. In 1 Peter 3, Scripture instructs us to place more emphasis on our inner nature than our outer adornments. It is of utmost importance that our soul and spirit are properly arrayed.

---

31   Henry Briggs, *Sermons on the Book of Ruth* (London, 1901), 85.

◊ Read the following verses and record how the believer is to be arrayed: Colossians 3:12–14 and Ephesians 4:24–2.

Only through the blood of Christ are acceptable garments found. The garment of Christ is the only garment that will be acceptable at the wedding feast of the Lamb. Praise God for the blood of the Lamb! "I greatly rejoice in the Lord, I exult in my God; for He has clothed me with the garments of salvation and wrapped me in a robe of righteousness, as a groom wears a turban and as a bride adorns herself with jewels" (Isaiah 61:10). "If we would be among the bridehead saints, we, too, must keep clean outwardly, stay under the anointing of the Holy Spirit inwardly, and adorn ourselves as becometh the saints."[32]

"Uncover his feet, and lie down. Then he will explain to you what you should do" (Ruth 3:4). As Ruth desired to draw near to Boaz, so the believer desires to draw near the protective canopy of our Lord and Master. We must come in the same manner as Ruth—in full submission and full humility, grateful to find available space at His feet. "Seek Him in private, when no eye but that of heaven is upon Thee; come secretly to His feet, and lay thy helpless, desolate state open before His mercy seat . . . He will not despise thee on account of the hole of the pit from whence thou hast digged."[33] True. He will not send you away. Rather, He will lovingly tell you what to do. Lay yourself at His feet and wait patiently for His instruction. "I will instruct you and show you the way to go; with My eye on you, I will give counsel" (Psalm 32:8). Can you hear the soft, sweet sound of the company of quiet waters?

This very day, the Lord offers Himself as your Shepherd. Under His shepherding, you will lack no good thing. He will lead you to rest and quiet waters. Are you willing to follow Him without question or

---

32   W. G. Heslop, *Rubies From Ruth* (Zondervan, 1944), 76.

33   Archive.org, "Ruth the Moabitess," p. 44, http://archive.org/stream/ruthmoabitessac00huntgoog#page/n48/mode/1up

clarification? Are you willing to follow in the same manner as Ruth? She went without compromise, without bargaining, without questioning. She went with a fully surrendered heart and a fully surrendered will. She went with no guarantees of the outcome but full confidence in the one she entrusted herself to. You, too, can have full confidence in the One Who has extended His invitation. "Come to Me, all of you who are weary and burdened, and I will give you rest" (Matthew 11:28). His rest is a blessing. His rest is repose.

"He calls us from the noise, from the contentions and rivalries, from the vulgar ambitions and feverish unrest of life, from shame and remorse, from the fear of change and the fear of evil, into a secure, happy asylum in which we may dwell in honor and freedom, unalarmed by the loud uproars of the world, unfretted by its cares and vexations, untainted by its pollutions, unstained by its guilt."[34] His rest is glorious. His rest is available. It is readily available to you. Cast yourself onto the feet of the Good Shepherd. Enter into His rest.

---

34   Samuel Cox and Thomas Fuller, *The Book of Ruth* (Klock and Klock Publishers, 1982), 158.

RUTH 3:6–18

She went down to the threshing floor and did everything her mother-in-law had instructed her. After Boaz ate, drank, and was in good spirits, he went to lie down at the end of the pile of barley. Then she went in secretly, uncovered his feet, and lay down. At midnight, Boaz was startled, turned over, and there lying at his feet was a woman! So he asked, "Who are you?" "I am Ruth, your slave," she replied. "Spread your cloak over me, for you are a family redeemer." Then he said, "May the Lord bless you, my daughter. You have shown more kindness now than before, because you have not pursued younger men, whether rich or poor. Now don't be afraid, my daughter. I will do for you whatever you say, since all the people in my town know that you are a woman of noble character. Yes, it is true that I am a family redeemer, but there is a redeemer closer than I am. Stay here tonight, and in the morning, if he wants to redeem you, that's good. Let him redeem you. But if he doesn't want to redeem you, as the Lord lives, I will. Now lie down until morning." So she lay down at his feet until morning but got up while it was still dark. Then Boaz said, "Don't let it be known that a woman came to the threshing floor." And he told Ruth, "Bring the shawl you're wearing and hold it out." When she held it out, he shoveled six measures of barley into her shawl, and she went into the town. She went to her mother-in-law, Naomi, who asked her, "How did it go, my daughter?" Then Ruth told her everything the man had done for her. She said, "He gave me these six measures of barley, because he said, 'Don't go back to your mother-in-law empty-handed.'" Naomi said, "My daughter, wait until you find out how things go, for he won't rest unless he resolves this today."

CHAPTER NINE

Beth Reed

Embracing Submission

Introduction

"Humble yourselves, therefore, under the mighty hand of God, so that He may exalt you at the proper time" (1 Peter 5:6).

Love stories. We grew up with them. They captured our imagination and drew us into a world where fantasy seemed real. We identified with favorite characters. We shared their excitement. We experienced their heartbreak. Their stories became our stories, and we left our trail of tears on their pages. They were childhood companions, and they shaped our tender views of romance. How many a young girl has envisioned herself as Cinderella? Who else has completely lost track of time engrossed in books like *Gone with the Wind*, *Wuthering Heights*, *The Count of Monte Cristo*, or *The Notebook*? There's just something charmingly compelling about a wonderful love story. And yet, the majority of best-selling love stories are absolutely fictional. Make-believe people in a make-believe setting with a make-believe love. What if there were a love story just as compelling, just as suspenseful, just as romantic . . . but it was true? Well, there was. And there is.

The timeless tale of Ruth and Boaz is arguably the most beautiful love story of all time. Theirs is a love born of mutual respect for character and integrity. Theirs is a love born of Providence and purpose. Theirs is a love born of purity rather than passion. And underneath this story of rich and tender love lies a beautiful spirit. What makes this story so beautiful? What makes Ruth such a beautiful heroine? The spirit of submission.

Ruth's spirit of submission opened wide the doorways of promise and blessing for her. Her submissive spirit enabled her to walk with abandonment into a dwelling place of love, protection, and security. Her story is as glorious as it is compelling. And her story could be your story. Unlike the fictional stories of your childhood, this story invites you to enter, not on some imaginary level but in the most real and everlasting way possible. God, the Father, is inviting you into a dwelling place of love, security, protection, and purpose. He is seeking a heart of submission in which He can release a literal storehouse of spiritual treasures. The eyes of the Lord roam throughout the earth to show Himself strong for those whose hearts are completely His (2 Chronicles 16:9). When His eyes landed on Ruth, He saw a heart of surrender and submission. His mercy and grace provided more than she ever could have wished or dreamed. What will He find when His eyes land on you?

Trials

Submission. Some consider it a controversial word. Some ascribe a negative connotation to it. Some even misuse it. In any case, its meaning has certainly become tangled and twisted in recent years. Somehow, in Christendom's marginal understanding of God's Word, we have relegated the term to a "female" word with implications exclusively for wives and women. It has become a word associated with oppression. Its delicate beauty has been diminished. In God's eyes, however, submission is altogether needful, profitable, beneficial, and beautiful for all creation. All creation.

Even animals instinctively understand the concept of submission. Did you realize that animals speak the body language of submission? Wolves, dogs, horses, cats . . . they all know how to show submission. Years ago, our family went to pick out a new puppy. We had already determined the breed of dog we wanted, and we found a reputable breeder. When the puppies were old enough to leave their mother, the breeder invited us to come choose our puppy. We could choose any puppy from the litter. As we sat on her floor (with puppies crawling and sprawling all around) she explained the distinctive signs of their personality. She told us about dominant puppies, aggressive puppies, and submissive puppies. Thus, the obvious question, how do you know which one is which? She explained that a submissive dog would readily roll over on its back and expose its belly to you—a sign of submission, a posture of submission, a willingness to be vulnerable. In a dog! If God created dogs to express signs of submission to a master, how much more has He wired men and women to express submission to Him! And, sure enough, as I sat there a pudgy little puppy crawled into my lap, rolled onto her back, and exposed her little pink belly to me. She's still our sweet Sophie—gentle, mild, and loyal. Her early sign of submission accurately predicted her temperament and disposition. Oh, that the same could be said of us!

So, what is submission? Submission means to yield, to subject one's self to another, to subordinate or to arrange under. Submission means yielding your will or authority to another. Submission is an absolute necessity in the Kingdom of God. It is an essential and fundamental principle of discipleship. It requires humility and trust. Humility and trust. Perhaps that's why we don't see it in practice more often. What is the opposite of humility? Yes, you guessed it. Pride. Pride is the enemy of submission. Pride is the gigantic obstacle between you and submission. Pride is a sneaky, stealthy blessing-blocker. And pride is the prevailing and predominant attitude of men and women today.

Pride comes in many shapes and flavors. The most obvious and overt expression of pride is self-aggrandizement. Perhaps you know someone of this flavor. They love to share their accomplishments—sometimes with a side helping of embellishment. They love to share numbers. *Gross revenue, gross profit, miles per minute, minutes per mile, price per square foot, exactly how many square feet, test scores, measurements, and on and on.* Everything is a competition to them, and they intend to win. They are, after all, winners. *Oh, and did I mention that I won . . . that I was named . . . that I was elected . . . that I was honored?* Pride.

Whew! You may have a mental image of someone who displays a similar type of overt (almost cartoonish) pride. You may even be feeling some relief that you are not THAT person. But there are other, more subtle, flavors of pride. Have you tasted the false humility flavor? The person with false humility tends to belittle herself or speak in self-deprecating terms. *I'm such a loser . . . such a failure . . . can't do anything right . . . nobody cares what I think or say.* Pride. Although it is more subtle, it is still a preoccupation with self. Pride can think too highly of one's self or too poorly of one's self. The problem is the focus on self. One expresses superiority while the other expresses inferiority, but opposite extremes of self-esteem share the same root: self. Each will find it difficult to submit—one out of arrogance and the other out of fear.

There remains an even more subtle flavor of pride. This flavor may not find expression in spoken words, but it communicates loudly in the mind. *It's not that I'm picky . . . I just want it the way I want it. My way is better. I want it my way.* Pride.

No wonder interpersonal relationships are a mess! Let's get some insight from our furry friends. Let's reevaluate some animal behaviors. What happens when a cat is threatened? Yes. It arches its back. It "bows up." Pride can cause similar emotional reactions within humans. What happens when you feel offended? Challenged? Rebuked? Corrected? Inconvenienced? Too often, the internal, emotional response mirrors the cat with its back "bowed up." Have you ever watched two cats circle each other, each with its back arched ridiculously high? It may be a silly example, but it illustrates a sad truth. Due to pride, and a misunderstanding of submission, people often circle through life with a "bowed up" back. It's a feeble form of self-protection, a weak attempt at self-preservation. It damages relationships, and it stunts spiritual growth. You see, ironically, submission is the pathway to freedom, not oppression. But pride resists it, ferociously. And the ill-effects begin to permeate every area of life.

Consider a child who does not submit to authority. Stubborn, selfish pride resists the good commandment of the Lord: "Children, obey your parents in the Lord, for this is right" (Ephesians 6:1, NASB). Pride gives birth to rebellion. Rebellion gains a foothold, and disrespect breeds contempt. Correction is rejected at home. Correction is rejected at school. Correction is rejected on teams and in the community. Before long, an angry, insolent, and isolated youth circles through the teenage years. Perhaps there are outward manifestations of rebellion—rule breaking, law breaking, risky behaviors, and violence. Perhaps the effects are internalized—depression, withdrawal, and self-loathing. Without grace, broken kids grow into broken adults. Without grace, disrespectful children grow into disrespectful employees, spouses, and parents. They leave a wake of destruction behind them. "Pride goes before destruction and a haughty spirit before stumbling" (Proverbs 16:18, NASB). Unfortunately, damage and destruction are not limited to the prideful. Collateral damage occurs. Family, friends, and coworkers get caught in the cross fire—needless casualties of the ravages of pride and rebellion.

Consider the grown man who does not submit to authority. Under his breath, he questions every decision. He mentally criticizes those in leadership. His selfish, stubborn pride tells him that he knows better than his boss. *There's a more efficient way . . . a more productive way . . . this guy is an idiot . . . I'll just do it my way.* Why does he always seem to get passed over for promotions? Why do other people seem to get credit for his ideas? *Am I the only one who can see things around here? What's wrong with these people?* "Pride goes before destruction and a haughty spirit before a fall" (Proverbs 16:18, NASB).

In His infinite wisdom, God established headship and authority. He established headship within the family, within the church, and within society. According to the kind intention of His will, He commanded submission to authority and headship. Submission is not for the detriment of the believer. Quite the contrary! Submission is for the benefit of the believer, and for society as a whole. But believers have resisted this command on every level. Now we are corporately reaping the fruit of the rebellion we have sown. Divorce rates within the Church mirror the rates of society at large. Children and teenagers are dealing with all manner of addictions, immorality, and self-destructive behaviors. Congregations are splitting. Denominations are splitting. Pastors are leaving ministry in droves. Rivalries have emerged within our churches, within ministries. Manipulation and control have crept in and crowded out love. Jealousy and envy have drowned out the spirit of cooperation. Some are too busy devouring one another to be bothered with ministering to one another. How is this so in the house of God? Pride goes before destruction, and a haughty spirit before stumbling. (Proverbs 16:18). Yes. Tragically, even in the household of faith, pride rears its ugly head and wreaks its havoc. Is there any hope? Is there a better way? Praise God! He has shown us a more excellent way. He has commanded us aright. His divine power has given us everything we need for life and godliness (2 Peter 1:3). His Holy Scripture has given us examples to follow. Examples of the right way, the victorious way, and the overcoming way. The way of submission.

Truth

"Humble yourselves, therefore, under the mighty hand of God, so that He may exalt you at the proper time" (1 Peter 5:6). Though the words were not penned until generations after the life of Ruth, she understood in her time the eternal Truth of God's promise. Ruth, the Moabite widow of humble means, reached out and laid hold of the blessing of God. She extended a heart of submission, and God responded with a hand of providence, favor, and honor. Remember her story. She married a man whose family sought refuge from famine in her native land. In her homeland, her father-in-law died, her brother-in-law died, and her own husband died. Her mother-in-law, Naomi, decided to return to the land of Judah when she heard that the Lord had visited His people. Naomi urged Ruth and her sister-in-law to stay in Moab and find young men to marry. Ruth, in her opening display of submission, declared her loyalty to Naomi and Naomi's God. She yielded her desire for protection and comfort and chose to follow Naomi and her God. She yielded her desire for the familiar and chose to embrace something new—a new home, a new faith, and a new God. She accompanied Naomi to Bethlehem, and she sought means to provide for them. By God's providence, she landed in the fields of Boaz. Again, she displayed a spirit of submission by heeding instructions to remain in Boaz's fields and remain close to his handmaids. She worked hard. She showed loyalty. She found favor in the sight of the master, Boaz. And then, the harvest season was over. There would be no more gleaning. There would be no more watchful, protective eye to oversee her in the fields. So Naomi hatched a plan. It was a righteous plan, but it was daring. It was a legal plan, but it was bold. It was a solid plan, but it could be rejected. Naomi instructed Ruth to wash herself, anoint herself, and put on her best clothes. Ruth was instructed to go to the threshing floor, to uncover the feet of the Boaz, to lie at his feet, and wait for his instruction. What?

What could possibly go wrong with a plan like that? Ruth must have been aware of the possibilities. Boaz could have taken advantage of her and sent her away in shame. He could have misinterpreted her offer. He could have outright rejected her. She had to know the possible scenarios as she listened to Naomi's plan. Yet, she did not question. She did not second-guess. She did not negotiate. She never asked, "What if . . ." She simply replied, "All that you say I will do" (Ruth 3:5, NASB). And she did.

Scripture records that she went to the threshing floor and did all that her mother-in-law commanded her (Ruth 3:6). She submitted to Naomi without questioning, arguing, or complaining. She submitted to Boaz without reservation or hesitation. She submitted to God in full expectation that He could be trusted with her life, her livelihood, and her future. Her submissive spirit preceded and prepared her for this critical moment. From the time she arrived in Bethlehem, her sweet spirit had been sowing seeds of righteousness, and she was now poised to reap a harvest of spiritual fruit.

There on the threshing floor, she presented herself. There on the threshing floor, she submitted herself. There on the threshing floor, she entrusted herself to an earthly master and a heavenly Master. And she never stepped out of submission, not even for a moment. She was a woman on a mission, and she never stepped out of her purpose. Throughout this dramatic scene, four characteristics of her submission emerge.

First, she displayed *humility*. When Boaz awoke and realized that a woman was lying at his feet, he said, "Who are you?" (Ruth 3:9, NASB). Ruth gently answered, "I am Ruth your maid. So spread your covering over your maid for you are a close relative" (Ruth 3:9, NASB). Not Ruth the Moabitess. Not Ruth the hard worker. Not Ruth the faithful daughter-in-law. Ruth your maid. She did not assert her own identity. She did not exploit the family connection. She did not focus on herself but on Boaz. Ruth *your* maid. She humbled herself in his sight. Remember, she was coming to claim her "right" under the law of *goel* (or kinsman-redeemer.)

She could have come with an air of entitlement. She could have come with the attitude that he owed her something. She came in *humility*. So spread your covering over your maid. It was not a legalistic demand; it was a humble request. She was asking for his protection. She was asking for his covering physically, emotionally, and spiritually. She was asking. And she asked humbly. *Humility* is a chief characteristic of submission.

Loyalty was also evident in her submission. "May you be blessed of the Lord, my daughter. You have shown your last kindness to be better than the first by not going after young men, whether poor or rich" (Ruth 3:10, NASB). What was her first kindness? What was her first act of loyalty? When Naomi urged her to stay in Moab and find a young man to marry, Ruth chose *loyalty* over opportunity. Ruth chose to follow Naomi and her God rather than chase the youthful lusts of life. Boaz recognized this *loyalty* as a great virtue, an outworking of a submissive heart. But there on the threshing floor, he recognized a more noble expression of *loyalty*. This young woman found her way to his field, and she honored his request to remain in his field. She had not gone in search of other fields, or other men. Her *loyalty* kept her from wandering into another's field.

Integrity was also evident in her submission. The moment of truth had arrived. Ruth had prepared herself and presented herself to her would-be redeemer. She humbly made her request of him. His answer hung in the balance. "I will do for you whatever you ask, for all my people in the city know that you are a woman of excellence" (Ruth 3:11, NASB). Yes! He was willing to redeem her. He was willing to protect her and provide for her. He was willing to bring her into his home and honor her as his wife. Why? Did he agree out of duty? No! He was pleased with her. He, in turn, wanted to please her. I will do for you whatever you ask. What caused this noble man to become so smitten that he would do whatever she asked? It was the beauty of her character. She was a woman of excellence. Her integrity adorned her as a garment. She was known for it throughout the city. And she had only lived there a few months during the harvest season. Character is quickly discernable and readily identifiable. Hers was excellent, and it captured the heart of a generous and tender man. What a great lesson for young women today! Character attracts character. Integrity attracts integrity. Boaz was smitten because her heart beat to the same tune as his. He was a man of integrity. He valued it, and he honored it in others. His integrity was further illustrated by his following remarks. "Now it is true I am a close relative; however, there is a relative closer than I" (Ruth 3:12, NASB).

There on the threshing floor, Boaz could have accepted her offer, expressed his love and desire, and given in to physical temptation. But he didn't. He was a man of integrity. Yes. He wanted to become Ruth's husband. Yes. He wanted to express his love for her. But his strength of character and his honor for the Lord compelled him to act in righteousness. Boaz was mature enough and wise enough to know that if something is worth doing, it is worth doing the right way. "Remain this night, and when morning comes, if he will redeem you, good; let him redeem you. But if he does not wish to redeem you, then I will redeem you, as the LORD lives. Lie down until morning" (Ruth 3:13). Oh, there's a beautiful nugget of truth here! Remember that God intends for all creation to submit to His headship and authority. Boaz submitted under the mighty hand of God. As most of the chapter (and the weight of history) focused on Ruth's submission, Boaz quietly illustrated the strong, complementary male expression of submission. His heart yielded to the authority of another. His heart yielded to the heart of God's law and the rights of another brother. His desire was for Ruth, but his heart was set on righteousness. So he yielded. He yielded to God, trusting that God would provide the best for Ruth. If God would allow another to redeem her, then so be it. He would honor God. He would bless the union. But if the closer brother relinquished his right, Boaz would embrace the privilege of being her redeemer. How great a love is that! How honorable a love is that! Arguably, the greatest love story ever told.

The final characteristic of submission expressed on the threshing floor was *serenity*. Peace. "So she lay at his feet until morning and rose before one could recognize another" (Ruth 3:14, NASB). After the washing, the anointing, and the preparation of clothing, she still didn't have her final answer. After the presentation and the proposal, she still didn't know who her redeemer would be. But she lay at his feet in peace. She had done her part. She had seen his heart. Without final resolution, she lay at his feet in peace. A submissive heart can wait in peace. A submissive heart can *trust* the outcome without *knowing* the outcome.

"Don't worry about anything, but in everything, through prayer and petition with thanksgiving, let your requests be made known to God. And the peace of God, which surpasses every thought, will guard your hearts and minds in Christ Jesus" (Philippians 4:6–7).

Transformation

Have you ever finished a book and just felt sad at the end? It may have had a happy ending, but you were sad that is was over. You had become so engrossed in the story that you still wanted more. You had become so involved with the characters that you were going to miss them as you put the book back onto the shelf. I felt that way about *Redeeming Love* by Francine Rivers. As I turned to the last page, I read each word slowly, deliberately. I knew I was near the end of a beautiful story. I knew I would carry these characters in my heart for a while. I knew I would never forget the demonstration of immense love that unfolded on its pages. I knew I would reread the story, probably multiple times. I simply didn't want it to end.

The story of Ruth and Boaz is just such a story. Timeless and true, their sweet love story causes my heart to leap and soar. Why? Because it is so full of promise—for me and for you. Because I never have to put the book back on the shelf and long for something distant or unattainable. Because everything that was available to Ruth is available to me, and to you too.

Ruth and Boaz were real people in a real world with a real love—for God and for each other. Their story is real. But there's so much more! Not only are they authentic characters, they are also universal symbols. Ruth is every woman. Ruth is everybody. She represents every human who has walked the face of earth since the Fall. She was needy and poor. She needed love, protection, and security. She needed to be redeemed from her situation, bought back from her life of poverty and helplessness. The difference between Ruth and most people in our culture is that she realized her predicament. She acknowledged her neediness and her helplessness. And her heart was ready to accept rescue, and a rescuer, a redeemer.

Boaz was the strong yet gentle hero—the master of the fields, the master of the harvest. He was strong in character and tender in compassion. He was strong in righteousness and gentle in submission. He was able to redeem, and he was willing to redeem. He represents Jesus Christ. Here's where the story becomes timeless. Here's why it is arguably the greatest love story ever told. The great Redeemer, Jesus, still lives today. He is always able to rescue, and He is always willing to redeem. He is available to every "Ruth, "to everyone who is willing to come and lie at His feet and submit to His Lordship. That includes me. That includes you. That includes every person you know with every kind of need that you know of. The threshing floor is open to all. The Lord of the Harvest extends His great offer of rescue to any and all. He offers a safe dwelling place, unconditional love, and eternal security. He offers to cherish His bride and love her sacrificially. Will you come, like Ruth, to the threshing floor? Will you lie at His feet and allow Him to cover you with His everlasting love? You don't need all the answers. You don't even need to know the next step. Just like Boaz, He will tell you what to do.

Perhaps you might wonder who needs this type of rescue. Surely, you have friends whose lives are a wreck. But do they really need *rescue*? Or do they just need a little help? Maybe some good counsel and wise choices could go a long way with them. What about your own life? It's had its ups and downs but overall, it's not too shabby. Who exactly needs this type of rescue (redemption)?

Read the following verses and record what you learn from them:

◊   Ecclesiastes 7:20

◊   Proverbs 20:9

◊   Isaiah 53:6

◊   Romans 3:23

◊   James 3:2

◊   1 John 1:8

◊   According to Scripture, who needs rescue? Who needs a redeemer? We all do! Everyone. Every single one! There is none righteous, not even one. We have all sinned and fallen short of the glory of God. Degrees of "fallenness" don't matter. Your flavor of sin is no better or worse than your neighbor's in terms of righteousness. Without a redeemer, we are all desperate, needy, and poor. We are spiritually bankrupt, and we need to be bought back from our indebtedness to sin. We need a redeemer! We need a Boaz who is willing and able to redeem. Praise God, we have one. His name is Jesus. He is the only One *able* to redeem men spiritually, and by His submission, He is perfectly *willing* to redeem any and all who call upon His great name. "And there is salvation in no one else; for there is no other name under heaven that has been given among men by which we must be saved" (Acts 4:12, NASB). Have you called upon His great name? Have you placed yourself at the feet of this magnificent Redeemer?

◊　Take a few moments to record your personal journey. How did you come to the point of calling upon the saving name of the Great Redeemer?

Whether you are just becoming acquainted with this precious Redeemer or whether you have known Him for a long time, I have great news. There's still more! Whatever you know of Him—however well you know Him—there's so much more. His mercies are new every morning. If you can list one thousand ways He has expressed His love for you, there are countless thousands more. If you can recount story after story of how He has displayed His power in and through you, you have only begun to scratch the surface. He delights to reveal Himself to you in new and fresh ways. "Therefore the LORD longs to be gracious to you, and therefore He waits on high to have compassion on you. For the LORD is a God of justice; How blessed are all those who long for Him" (Isaiah 30:18, NASB). Do you desire Him? Do you long for Him? Do you long for the fullness of His presence and power? Then choose the pathway of submission. The lower you bow, the higher He will take you. The more you release, the more He will give. "For whoever wants to save their life will lose it, but whoever loses their life for Me will find it. What good will it be for someone to gain the whole world, yet forfeit their soul?" (Matthew 16:25–26, NIV).

Submission. Why choose the attitude and posture of submission? Read the following verses and record what you learn about the way of submission.

◊   Job 22:21

◊   Proverbs 3:6

◊   1 Peter 2:13–15

◊   1 Peter 5:5–6

Scripture not only tells us *to* submit to headship and authority, but more importantly it tells us *why* to submit. We are encouraged to submit because God gives grace to the humble, and He opposes the proud. Would you rather have His grace or His opposition? Would you rather have Him working for you or against you? This is what we call a "no-brainer!" You absolutely want to be aligned with God! You absolutely want Him working on your behalf! Consequently, your divine marching orders are crystal clear. Humble yourself, therefore, under the mighty hand of God so that He may exalt you at the right time (1 Peter 5:6).

Mighty hand. What is the significance of the mighty hand of God? Scripture instructs us to humble ourselves under the mighty hand of God. What do we need to understand about the mighty hand of God? Read the following verses and record what you learn about the power of His mighty hand.

◊   Exodus 32:11

◊   Matthew 9:18–25

◊   Mark 1:40–42

◊   Mark 8:22–25

◊   Luke 4:40

According to Scripture, God's mighty hand is able to deliver His people out of oppression and captivity. The mighty hand of Jesus is able to heal, to restore, and to give life. What a mighty hand! There is safety underneath His mighty hand. There is healing and restoration underneath His mighty hand. There is life underneath His mighty hand. Humble yourself, therefore, underneath the mighty hand of God. Hide yourself under the shelter and shadow of His wings. It is a glorious place to be! Covered. Ruth asked Boaz to cover her with his garment, to assume the role of her protector and provider. Your precious Redeemer is willing to cover you with His tender mercy and love. He offers to assume the role of your Protector and Provider. "Then I passed by you and saw you, and you were indeed at the age for love. So I spread the edge of My garment over you and covered your nakedness. I pledged Myself to you, entered into a covenant with you, and you became Mine. This is the declaration of the Lord GOD" (Ezekiel 16:8). Oh, how He loves you! Will you come and lie at His feet? Will you submit to Him and His lordship?

Submit. What does it look like? What does it mean? Is it a matter of obedience? Yes . . . and no. Yes, submission is a matter of obedience in that Scripture *commands* us to submit to the Lord and the earthly authorities He has allowed in our lives. But submission goes beyond obedience. Consider a toddler who misbehaves. His mother corrects his behavior, and she sends him to the corner to sit and consider his actions. He huffs and puffs, and he plops down defiantly on the stool in the corner. His mother gently encourages him by acknowledging his *obedience*. "Thank you for obeying me and sitting in the corner." Through clenched teeth he replies, "I'm sitting down on the outside, but I'm standing up on the inside." His heart has not caught up with his body. The outward display of obedience is not matched by an inward yielding of the will. How often do we offer God the same type of obedience?

Have you ever obeyed with an "I don't want to" attitude? It is true; blessings follow obedience. It is true; obedience wards off consequences. But where is the fullness? Where is the joy? Where is the abundance? These are reserved for submission. Remember, to submit means to yield one's self to another or to place one's self under the authority of another. To submit means to yield your *will* to another. To submit means to yield your *wishes* to another. To submit means to obey out of a heart of love rather than an act of duty. How do you determine the difference? Examine your response to obedience. Is your obedience accompanied by a spirit of grumbling and complaining, even if it's only on the inside? Do you begrudge obedience? How often could God say of you, "She's sitting down on the outside, but she's standing up on the inside"? Humble yourself, therefore, under the mighty hand of God so that He will exalt you at the right time. Learn from Ruth. Learn from Boaz. God had marvelous plans and glorious purpose for each of them. "For I know the plans I have for you"—this is the Lord's declaration—"plans for your welfare, not for disaster, to give you a future and a hope" (Jeremiah 29:11). Ruth and Boaz were destined to be the great-grandparents of King David. They were destined to be part of the lineage of Jesus Christ—the Great Redeemer. They had big roles to fill in the eternal Kingdom of God. They entered into their purpose and calling by their submission. What is your purpose and calling? Girlfriend, it is probably too glorious for you to even imagine or comprehend! "What eye did not see and ear did not hear, and what never entered the human mind— God prepared this for those who love Him" (1 Corinthians 2:9). God's purpose and plan for your life cannot be fathomed, but by His Holy Spirit. Greater works are in store for you. In fact, they were planned before the foundation of the world (Ephesians 2:10). But in order to walk in them, you must walk in submission to God the Father; to Jesus Christ, His Son; to His Holy Spirit; and to the authorities He has allowed in the earthly realm. Do you want to claim His promises and embrace your purpose? Then walk humbly through the circumstances He has entrusted to you right now. Yield to His timing and His training ground. Your current road may seem unpleasant. Your heart may be tempted to rebel inwardly as God asks you to submit to thankless jobs and testy relationships. You may even resent your daily responsibilities. Take heart; your God stands ready to help you walk with grace and submission today and every day. "For the eyes of the LORD move to and fro throughout the earth that He may strongly support those whose heart is completely His" (2 Chronicles 16:9, NASB). What will He find when His eyes rest upon you?

Consider the example of Jesus. He never questioned His Father's guidance or methods. He never suggested a "better way" to the Father. He never complained about the mistreatment, disrespect, or betrayal. He never grumbled about the difficulty of His path or the extent of His suffering. Even as He walked toward a treacherous death and asked if the bitter cup could be taken from Him, His heart was yielded in submission. "Father, if You are willing, take this cup away from Me— nevertheless, not My will, but Yours, be done" (Luke 22:42). Jesus submitted and humbled Himself under the mighty hand of God. "He humbled Himself by becoming obedient to the point of death—even to death on a cross. For this reason God highly exalted Him and gave Him the name that is above every name, so that at the name of Jesus every knee will bow" (Philippians 2:8–10). Scripture urges us to have the same attitude as Jesus—humble and submissive, yielded to His will. He exalted Jesus. He exalted Ruth. He will exalt you at the proper time.

Have you found your place in the greatest love story ever told? There is no reason to remain a bystander. There is no reason to long for a dreamy rescuer to come along and offer you the promise of love and security. HE HAS COME! And He has come for you. You were on His mind before heaven and earth were created. There is no end to His love for you. He has loved you with an everlasting love, and He has drawn you with loving-kindness (Jeremiah 31:3). In light of such compelling love, He has beckoned you to come and lie at His feet. He is calling you to surrender your will and your ways and to seek cover under His mighty hand. You will find that you are not alone there. You will join many who have called upon His name and sought refuge in Him. "The name of Yahweh is a strong tower; the righteous run to it and are protected" (Proverbs 18:10). But He offers so much more than protection. He offers His presence and His power and, indeed, Himself to those who will abandon their hearts in submission to Him. Ruth embraced it. Boaz embraced it. Jesus embraced it. Will you?

"Therefore, since we also have such a large cloud of witnesses surrounding us, let us lay aside every weight and the sin that so easily ensnares us. Let us run with endurance the race that lies before us" (Hebrews 12:1). The only thing that lies between you and the absolute exhilaration of abandonment and surrender is your pride. The areas where you think you know better, the areas where you want to retain control, and the areas where you continue to grumble and complain, they are weights and snares. They will hinder your run. They will hinder your walk. They may even cause you to stop dead in your tracks. What are your hindrances? What are your weights and snares? Jesus is calling you to lay them aside. He is calling you forward—to the race that lies before you. To glory. To freedom. To greater works. The pathway is submission. Decide today to move beyond obedience and to embrace submission. Decide today to honor God with the attitude of your heart as well as the actions of your body. Declare today: Thy will, not my will! Give yourself fully and unreservedly to your Redeemer. Don't be surprised if that mighty hand moves quickly on your behalf!

BETH REED, AUTHOR OF CHAPTERS 7–9

Beth enjoys a variety of roles in life as wife, mother, teacher, and writer. Beth graduated from Mississippi State University in 1991 with a degree in economics. Beth began studying and teaching God's Word as a newlywed. After twenty-two years of teaching and leading Bible study, her quiet study time with the Lord remains her greatest joy. Beth is married to Bob Reed, a homebuilder in the Greater Memphis area. They have three children: Ashley, Joey, and Matthew.

RUTH 4:1–10

Boaz went to the gate of the town and sat down there. Soon the family redeemer Boaz had spoken about came by. Boaz called him by name and said, "Come over here and sit down." So he went over and sat down. Then Boaz took 10 men of the town's elders and said, "Sit here." And they sat down. He said to the redeemer, "Naomi, who has returned from the land of Moab, is selling a piece of land that belonged to our brother Elimelech. I thought I should inform you: Buy it back in the presence of those seated here and in the presence of the elders of my people. If you want to redeem it, do so. But if you do not want to redeem it, tell me so that I will know, because there isn't anyone other than you to redeem it, and I am next after you." "I want to redeem it," he answered. Then Boaz said, "On the day you buy the land from Naomi, you will also acquire Ruth the Moabitess, the wife of the deceased man, to perpetuate the man's name on his property." The redeemer replied, "I can't redeem it myself, or I will ruin my own inheritance. Take my right of redemption, because I can't redeem it." At an earlier period in Israel, a man removed his sandal and gave it to the other party in order to make any matter legally binding concerning the right of redemption or the exchange of property. This was the method of legally binding a transaction in Israel. So the redeemer removed his sandal and said to Boaz, "Buy back the property yourself." Boaz said to the elders and all the people, "You are witnesses today that I am buying from Naomi everything that belonged to Elimelech, Chilion, and Mahlon. I will also acquire Ruth the Moabitess, Mahlon's widow, as my wife, to perpetuate the deceased man's name on his property, so that his name will not disappear among his relatives or from the gate of his home. You are witnesses today."

CHAPTER TEN

Marie Strain

A Love That Redeems

Introduction

Redemption's essence has always been LOVE, and God's LOVE has always been manifested in action. Chapter 4 in the book of Ruth reveals what action love required and God's faithfulness to providentially prepare all circumstances to accomplish His plan for redemption. When God redeems, there is a complete transformation from any crippling situation to deliverance and victory. So many times, one is inclined to think of redemption only in the terms of salvation from their sins, which of course is accurate and a glorious truth, but it is only the beginning of God's redemptive provisions for His children. No one in the land of Moab would have ventured to even think that Ruth's life would end up being included in the most important, the most noble, and the most life-changing human lineage of all mankind. God not only redeemed Ruth from her sins of idolatry but transported her into a king's sovereign lineage that would soon lead to King David and ultimately to our Lord and Savior, Jesus Christ. In this chapter, the focus is on the major truths gleaned from Ruth 4:1–10, but some related principles will have their foundation in Ruth 3.

This road traveled by Ruth is not only an actual Old Testament historical event, but it contains New Testament spiritual realities. There is no limit to the depths of despair, depravity, or rebellion that a person can go where our faithful and merciful God cannot move in divine, redemptive ways to bring him or her safely into His Kingdom. Nor are there any circumstances that God's children can find themselves where He cannot enter into their human experience and bring great redemption and victory, all for the glory of His great name.

On many occasions, genuine followers of Jesus Christ will find themselves in circumstances where there seems to be two realities similar to Ruth's. First, the only choice before them in their present circumstance seems to be rooted in the power of someone else's hands. Second, the only hope they have for the possibility of future deliverance is found in God's faithful love and mighty power. The first is visible with eyes of flesh. The second is visible with eyes of faith. Naomi's guidance to Ruth was based on her knowledge of God's declared instruction for widows of the sons of Israel. Our guidance must also be based on God's declared instruction in His Word because when obeyed, it releases God's awesome and divine workings for deliverance and redemption.

There is an indisputable Truth throughout God's Word. God's purposes are always redemptive in nature. Our good and faithful God is never lacking either in resolve or power to "cause all things to work together for good for those who love God, to those who are called according to His purpose" (Romans 8:28, NASB). The Scriptures assure that all any Christian needs for life and godliness is found through the true knowledge of God and His Son, Christ Jesus (2 Peter 1:3, paraphrased). Most often, the seeming impotence in a person's life to live victoriously in all circumstances boils down to the common denominator of not knowing enough about the God of the Bible to trust Him.

Trials

Up to Ruth chapter 4, there seems to be nothing but trials in the lives of Ruth and Naomi. They were women who lived in the time and culture where women were considered to be not much more than chattel. A widow's life could be brutal and, many times, perilous. But Naomi served a God Who had given His nation Israel laws that, when followed, would protect widows from a fate worse than death. Even though Naomi renamed herself "bitter," it seems clear through Ruth's decision to make Jehovah God her God that Naomi had conveyed enough truth about her God's love, deliverance, and watchcare of His people to impact Ruth in a redemptive way.

Chapter 4 begins with the foundational context of the previous night's occurrences. Ruth had followed Naomi's instruction and had slept at Boaz's feet. It requires only a little imagination to realize the courage it took to obey Naomi's plan. The humiliation she must have felt as she uncovered Boaz's feet and then to lie down at them had to be immense. Keep in mind she had to come into the threshing floor at a time that he would be sound asleep. She needed to keep unrecognized among those who were very familiar with her. This probably necessitated that she travel alone during dark hours.

Whether one is married, widowed, or single, there are times when it is necessary to set out on a journey of obedience that seems as dark and with as little hope as Ruth's. At times, obedience may require walking on a potentially dangerous and seemingly humiliating path. Even though Ruth herself did not encounter any danger on her trip to and from Boaz's threshing floor, it is worthwhile to note the possible dangers of which she had to have been aware. We saw in Ruth 2:15 and 22 that it was dangerous for a woman to even be gleaning in the fields alone. A woman alone was always potentially in danger of robbers, kidnappers, or worse. These roads did not have streetlights on every corner that would have lit her way to keep her from stumbling. A question all must ask on more than one occasion is, has my knowledge of God resulted in a complete trust in obeying His guidance? When the road seems very dangerous and not very sensible to travel according to our own evaluation, trusting in God's goodness and sovereignty is essential.

Living a life of obedience always requires faith. In Ruth's case, her faith was based on Naomi's guidance received from the law of God for the children of Israel. Ruth had made Naomi's God her God and had proclaimed, "where you go, I will go" and "your God *will be* my God" (Ruth 1:16). So, she headed out in the faith of her new God, believing that He would protect her and accomplish His good purposes. One must contemplate the question of just how many of the present-day children of God live life with the same depth of faith and assurance as Ruth.

Another truth we must consider is the ever-present obstacles that test one's faith and that attempt to throw up roadblocks or detours to following God's will God's way. The path that God seems to be leading is often unknown and can be unsettling. There is indeed a powerful and intimidating enemy that is often encountered. Satan is relentless in his schemes to derail or diminish obedience. As Ruth made the trip in spite of the known dangers, believers can accept similar seemingly dangerous assignments to accomplish God's redemptive plans and purposes. Satan is a defeated foe and no plan of God can be thwarted (Job 42:2).

Therefore, our journey requires, as Ruth's did, the knowledge of Who God is, what God's divine purpose is, and that He will overcome all obstacles and dangers that might present themselves. This kind of faith puts every saint of the Most High God in a position of receiving unlimited, immeasurable grace that protects, redeems, and restores. It is essential that one comes to the place of faith that believes God is Who He says He is and that He will do what He has promised He will do. Knowing and believing what God declares in His Word is an essential element to maturing and abiding faith that transforms.

Now back to the difficulties everyone encounters in his or her walk of faith. In Ruth's case, they would have been physical. In one's present walk with the Lord, the difficulties are most often spiritual. Satan seems to be content whether he has convinced one that he doesn't exist or that he is so very impotent that he is not to even be considered a threat or hindrance. Or Satan tries to render one powerless through the deception that he is so very powerful that he can do much harm, and they are unable to stand firm against his schemes. Satan indeed is the father of lies. Error (what is not true according to God's Word) puts a believer in bondage. It is only the Truth that sets us free (John 8:32). The knowledge of who Satan is according to God's Word and who the saints of the Most High God are provide all who believe Him insight, courage, and yes, the faith to proceed on a path in victory that most probably will be fraught with potential dangers. But our God is able to deliver us from every obstacle, every danger, and to redeem every circumstance, all for His glory.

We have read of Ruth's then present trial of waiting for Boaz to accomplish a seemingly unattainable task. There was a closer "kinsman-redeemer," and Ruth was given no assurance by Boaz of what this closest relative would do. Imagine a time when you have been—it could even be now—in God's waiting room for complete deliverance, or redemption, if you will. There is nothing you can do even though every fiber of your being screams for you to do something. This wait feels like it is about to kill you. Another important aspect of God's redemptive love that we must understand is that many times He places us in a time of *waiting faith* for divine and specific reasons. When we get on the other side of this trial and experience a mighty redemptive move of God, we look back with 20/20 vision. Then we can understand what being in "God's waiting room" accomplished. Not only was the *waiting* necessary for God to get every circumstance in place and in order to accomplish His divine purpose, but His presence and provision had proven to be all sufficient, as well as faith building. His loving-kindness was overshadowing you at all times. A common response from God's children, who have waited in faith for Him to work His divine plan is, "I would not change a thing about this trial, even if I could."

Now consider another trial Ruth faced. Her knowledge of what it meant to be the wife of a Hebrew man living in the land of Israel was virtually unknown to her. The text implies that Ruth had learned much from Naomi about the God of Abraham, Isaac, and Jacob. You have learned that the historical timing of the book of Ruth is set in the spiritually dark time of the "Judges." There was much evil being practiced by the children of Israel. There was oppression and wars because of God's judgment. She had returned with Naomi to Israel to serve the God of heaven and was finding herself in need to marry a kinsman-redeemer about whom she knew little to nothing. But her devotion to Naomi and her declared faith in Jehovah God compelled her to follow the guidance given to her by her mother-in-law. Marriage or singleness in women today requires the same faith and obedience shown by Ruth. In the culture of our times, most live life centered on their own selfish desires. Even though our relationship with the living God through Christ may be young and immature, we are granted enough faith all along the journey to follow in obedience and holiness. It has been granted. The question most face is will they trust and obey. One should never cease to be amazed at the creativity and loving-kindness of our good and faithful God. All along the journey in this life of faith, which includes many trials, God's redemptive love always overwhelms us. He continually displays His divine favor and His mighty acts of grace and mercy toward us. The question that begs an answer is, do you recognize them?

Ruth chapter 4 reveals that God had prepared the way for Boaz who had shown much love and compassion for Ruth. It is worth noting that Boaz loved His God and the law of God more than he loved Ruth. Boaz would not disregard the biblical mandates for the "kinsman-redeemer," no matter his emotions. It is never profitable, spiritual or otherwise, to determine in one's heart that God doesn't care how one lives his or her life. God does indeed care about every choice one makes in the minute-by-minute daily decisions. He prefers obedience to sacrifice (1 Samuel 15:22). Ruth waited for God to work through Boaz. Boaz approached the situation God's way, and God wrought a mighty redemptive work for Ruth and Naomi. Only time would reveal the future and eternal rewards of such waiting and obedience.

Truth

We are plainly told in God's Word that trials are not to be considered as unexpected interruptions. They are vehicles through which He refines His children as pure gold. God never changes. He always rewards obedience. Because of His great love for all His children, God must also discipline disobedience. We can be assured because of the sovereignty, omnipotence, and all-loving character of God that all trials a Christ-follower encounters have been selected by God for duel purposes: to make them into the image of His Son AND to manifest His glory in and through them. Whether God has called you to walk a potentially dangerous path or to wait for His perfect timing, He is always faithful to complete what He has begun and to provide all that is necessary to walk through victoriously. A goldsmith carefully watches over the crucible when refining his gold. Gold never fears fire. All fire can do to gold is to make it purer and into a property easily reshaped. So it is with the Creator God of the universe. He is always in control of the height of the temperature and the length of firing. There is never a trial without God's sovereign control over the choice of the trial, the length of its circumstances, and the depth of the pain it causes. The result is pure gold, a choice vessel through whom God can manifest His glory.

You need to see if these previous statements are true by your personal observation of Scripture and by letting the Word of God strengthen and build your faith. Read the three passages of Scripture below. Please summarize the truths God has either revealed to you for the first time or confirmed to your heart from your previous study of Scripture.

1 Peter 4:12–13, NASB

12 Beloved, do not be surprised at the fiery ordeal among you, which comes upon you for your testing, as though some strange thing were happening to you;

13 but to the degree that you share the sufferings of Christ, keep on rejoicing, so that also at the revelation of His glory you may rejoice with exultation.

◊ **Insights**:

◊ **Application**:

James 1:2–4, NASB

2 Consider it all joy, my brethren, when you encounter various trials,

3 knowing that the testing of your faith produces endurance.

4 And let endurance have *its* perfect result, so that you may be perfect and complete, lacking in nothing.

◊ **Insights**:

◊ **Application**:

1 Corinthians 10:13, NASB

13 No temptation has overtaken you but such as is common to man; and God is faithful, who will not allow you to be tempted beyond what you are able, but with the temptation will provide the way of escape also, so that you will be able to endure it.

◊ **Insights**:

◊ **Application:**

It is vital we understand that when trials or temptations are mentioned in Scripture in reference to a child of God, it is never referring to any attempt to make a person sin (James 1:13) and or fail the test. Every encounter, which God chooses to place us in, is for the purpose of proving our faith to be genuine (James 1:12). There was a process in the times in which the New Testament was written to prove a piece of pottery did not have any flaws or cracks. The test was to actually place a piece of pottery up to the light. The light would reveal any crack or flaw that had been covered with wax. A common Greek word of that day, which we would translate as "genuine" in today's English language, was a word that literally meant "no wax." God tests us to prove to ourselves and to the world around us that our faith is genuine and without cracks, i.e. no wax.

It will be helpful for you to look at a couple of biblical characters who show God's testing in order to bring light to the faith God had deposited in them. It seems appropriate to start with Abraham. Even though Abraham failed a few tests along his journey of faith with Jehovah God, he passed the most important test when God told Abraham to offer his son Isaac as a human sacrifice. Please observe the following Scripture passages. Summarize what the Lord revealed to you, and note any application He has given to you.

Genesis 22:1–5, 10–13, NASB

1 Now it came about after these things, that God tested Abraham, and said to him, "Abraham!" And he said, "Here I am."

2 He said, "Take now your son, your only son, whom you love, Isaac, and go to the land of Moriah, and offer him there

as a burnt offering on one of the mountains of which I will tell you."

3 So Abraham rose early in the morning and saddled his donkey, and took two of his young men with him and Isaac his son; and he split wood for the burnt offering, and arose and went to the place of which God had told him.

4 On the third day Abraham raised his eyes and saw the place from a distance.

5 Abraham said to his young men, "Stay here with the donkey, and I and the lad will go over there; and we will worship and return to you."

10 Abraham stretched out his hand and took the knife to slay his son.

11 But the angel of the Lord called to him from heaven and said, "Abraham, Abraham!" And he said, "Here I am."

12 He said, "Do not stretch out your hand against the lad, and do nothing to him; for now I know that you fear God, since you have not withheld your son, your only son, from Me."

13 Then Abraham raised his eyes and looked, and behold, behind him a ram caught in the thicket by his horns; and Abraham went and took the ram and offered him up for a burnt offering in the place of his son.

◊ **<u>Insights</u>**:

◊ **Application**:

One would have to wonder, how could it be that Abraham was so willing, ready, and immediately obedient to sacrifice Isaac? Had not God Himself declared it was only through Isaac that His promises would come? The glorious thing is that God tells us. Look at two more passage before we leave Abraham. Abraham proved to be a person who genuinely believed in God and what God had promised. Observe and make applications from Hebrews 11:17–19.

Hebrews 11:17–19, NASB

17 By faith Abraham, when he was tested, offered up Isaac, and he who had received the promises was offering up his only begotten *son*;

18 *it was he* to whom it was said, "In Isaac your descendants shall be called."

19 He considered that God is able to raise *people* even from the dead, from which he also received him back as a type.

◊ **Insights**:

◊ **Application**:

It is essential that you note God's declared redemptive purpose in this was the testing of Abraham's faith. "He *(Abraham)* also received him *(Isaac)* back as a type." A "type" of what or of whom? Isaac was a pre-figuring of God providing a redeeming substitute for the payment due for each person's sin debt. Abraham was willing because his faith was solid as a rock. He was convinced that God's promises to him were unfailing, and God would raise Isaac from the dead in order to fulfill what He had promised. Oh, that our faith would be that steadfast and sure!

The object of Abraham's saving faith was the same as ours. Look at Galatians 3:8–9 and note below what God preached to Abraham along with any applications from the Lord.

Galatians 3:8–9, NASB

8 The Scripture, foreseeing that God would justify the Gentiles by faith, preached the gospel beforehand to Abraham, *saying,* "All the nations will be blessed in you."

9 So then those who are of faith are blessed with Abraham, the believer.

◊ **Insights**:

◊ **Application**:

Now on to Joseph, who, other than Christ, is a favorite biblical character among many.

Psalm 105:17–19, NASB

17 He sent a man before them, Joseph, *who* was sold as a slave.

18 They afflicted his feet with fetters, he himself was laid in irons;

19 Until the time that his word came to pass, the word of the Lord tested him.

◊ **Insights**:

◊ **Application**:

Let's add some flesh onto the bones of Joseph's testing. God had given Joseph two dreams that indicated his family would one day bow down to him. Because of Psalm 105, we can safely assume that Joseph believed these dreams to be the Word of the Lord. Through overwhelming jealousy on the part of his brothers, he was sold into slavery. Because of Joseph's faithfulness to his God, he was given the favor of God and was made the manager of all that Potiphar owned. Even though all of us would have calculated these circumstances as unjust and bad, the reality is that God had to get Joseph to Egypt.

Through the overwhelming lust of Mrs. Potiphar followed by her anger of being rejected, she falsely accused Joseph of attempted rape. Joseph was thrown in jail. Again, our human evaluation of his circumstances would see it as unjust and bad. But God had to keep Joseph in Egypt and readily available. Through God's favor and Joseph's undiminished faith, Joseph was made an overseer in the jail and was in the place to interpret the dreams of both the Pharaoh's wine taster and baker. Through the inexcusable ingratitude and fear of the wine taster, Joseph was left in prison. The wine taster's promise to remember him was not fulfilled. But the truth was that God needed a witness to bring Joseph to the Pharaoh's attention at God's appointed time. There would be a famine and God was about to fulfill His prophetic words to Abraham in Genesis 15:13. What is astounding and almost incomprehensible is that during the approximate fourteen years between the dreams and the reality, Joseph encountered incredible hardship. Yet throughout, Joseph lived a faith-filled life that brought forth the favor of God wherever he was, becoming a vessel through whom God saved the nation of Israel.

If we didn't know the whole story, we would evaluate Joseph's life as a complete failure and a totally wasted life that was riddled with pain and unjust suffering. Did you know that Joseph spent the last forty-one years of his life in some sort of slavery? God's favor does not always bring sunshine and roses. But His favor does always bring us into the place where God's perfect and redemptive plans and purposes can be accomplished. When we look at the whole picture, there is not a biblical character who surpasses the standard of how Joseph was tested and proven "without wax." The major point that is so needed for the Church of Jesus Christ today is that the God Who brought Ruth out of the land of idols into His Promised Land and royal lineage is the same God Who wants to refine us as pure gold. God is always about proving that He has the devotion and sovereign power to orchestrate and accomplish His purposes in our lives. He also declares them good according to Ephesians 2:10. "For we are His workmanship, created in Christ Jesus for good works, which God prepared beforehand, that we should walk in them."

As Ruth walked by faith and not by sight (2 Corinthians 5:7), so also should every person who has surrendered his or her life to the person and work of the Lord Jesus Christ. Ruth lay at Boaz's feet not understanding how such an unlikely physical act could possibly be the answer to her dire circumstances. But because of her obedience, Boaz responded and proceeded to make plans to redeem Ruth and Naomi— God's way. Boaz's implied love for Ruth did not drive him to take her as his wife his own way. His love for her wanted God's best for her, so he went to the gate where the Jewish elders sat and acted in a way that allowed God to work divinely for both he and Ruth.

Do you ever think that what God has asked you to do is as illogical in our culture as uncovering the feet of a man and sleeping at his feet must have seemed to Ruth? For instance, have you ever wondered what good it could possibly do to forgive someone who has sinned against you and has never expressed any remorse whatsoever much less asked your forgiveness? Or have you argued with God that it is unfair, too much to ask, that you love your enemies, pray for those who have persecuted you (Matthew 5:44), and bless, not curse, those who mistreat you (Luke 6:28)? Since God rarely reveals the exact results of what will happen before we obey, obedience many times seems to us not to be rational or profitable. The joy and rewards come when we see God move divinely on our behalf, removing every obstacle, and accomplishing divine results that we never even thought of, much less dreamed possible. God does indeed bless obedience. He always has, and He always will.

There is one last passage of Scripture that is vital to our understanding of God's redemptive love. Please read Ephesians 1:7–14 and note your insights and applications.

Ephesians 1:7–14, NASB

7 In Him we have redemption through His blood, the forgiveness of our trespasses, according to the riches of His grace,

8 which He lavished upon us. In all wisdom and insight

9 He made known to us the mystery of His will, according to His kind intention which He purposed in Him

10 with a view to an administration suitable to the fullness of the times, *that is*, the summing up of all things in Christ, things in the heavens and things upon the earth. In Him

11 also we have obtained an inheritance, having been predestined according to His purpose who works all things after the counsel of His will,

12 to the end that we who were the first to hope in Christ should be to the praise of His glory.

13 In Him, you also, after listening to the message of truth, the gospel of your salvation—having also believed, you were sealed in Him with the Holy Spirit of promise,

14 who is given as a pledge of our inheritance, with a view to the redemption of *God's own* possession, to the praise of His glory.

◊ **Insights**:

◊ **Application**:

From this Ephesians passage, we know that even though Ruth's redeemed inheritance seemed earthly and temporal, God's purposes were undeniably heavenly and eternal. The same is true for every believer in the Lord Jesus Christ. The work done in and through each one of us is leading toward an eternal purpose—"with a view to the redemption of God's own possession, to the praise of His glory."

Transformation

The biblical account of the life of Ruth stands as such an inspiration to us all. She was formerly a pagan idolater whom God transformed into one of only a few women mentioned in Jesus' lineage. A major issue seems to have been that of getting Ruth from Moab to Jerusalem and becoming Boaz's wife. BUT GOD had a plan of redemptive love. That same redemptive work of love is God's design for each of us today. There is one major difference that is always worth consciously noting. Pentecost changed the way in which Jehovah God relates to His children. When Jesus returned to heaven after His bodily resurrection, He sent the Holy Spirit to permanently indwell all who come to faith in Him.

We are not given the details of Ruth's life after her marriage to Boaz and the birth of Obed, but we do know that God had so infiltrated her life, and the life of Naomi and Boaz, that a book in God's Word was given to relate the account of parts of their lives. What an encouragement it should be to each one who is in a relationship with God through the shed blood of Jesus Christ that God is writing a story, or letter, in and through his or her life for the world to see. In fact, Paul says in 2 Corinthians 3:2–3 that "You are our letter, written in our hearts, known and read by all men; being manifested that you are a letter of Christ, cared for by us, written not with ink but with the Spirit of the living God, not on tablets of stone but on tablets of human hearts." We know that a Christ-follower's life can be so transformed and Christ's life so clearly manifested in their everyday life that they are recognized and categorized by others as a "Christian" (Acts 11:26).

We have been focusing on the faith and courage it took for Ruth to follow God's direction for her through the life and instructions of her mother-in-law, Naomi. Few would disagree that knowing and obeying the will of God is essential to our living fruitful and useful lives for the Kingdom of God. But also, today, there are few who actually obey God's instructions that reveal what the will of God is. It can be confidently assumed that many of you have made the statement that you would really like to know God's will for your life. You can imagine with almost certainty that Ruth was thinking the same thing as she waited for Boaz the following day. The wonderful truth is that God has given an explicit answer to that desire. Many of you will be familiar with Romans 12:1–2 where God implores His children, "Therefore I urge you, brethren, by the mercies of God, to present your bodies a living and holy sacrifice, acceptable to God, *which is* your spiritual service of worship. And do not be conformed to this world, but be transformed by the renewing of your mind, so that you may prove what the will of God is, that which is good and acceptable and perfect" (NASB). We are told that not only can we know God's will but that we can *prove* what God's will is for our individual lives. However, there is a critical, never to be overlooked, condition—one must present their bodies as a living and holy sacrifice to God. As Romans 12:2 also states, walking in the center of God's will is WORSHIP! One cannot explain how worship occurs in service, but the undeniable truth is that God's Word will be accomplished; therefore, sweet and indescribable worship does occur.

A glorious truth of redeeming transformation is that God neither requires nor allows us to accomplish that transformation in our own strength. Ruth was helpless to redeem her situation. The same is true for us today. BUT GOD has provided all we need for life and godliness through the true knowledge of Himself and His Son (2 Peter 1:3). It is vital to note that God's provision has a declared source—the true knowledge of Himself and Jesus. This source is God's inerrant and infallible Word, the Bible.

I was saved at the age of fifteen. I remember my visit with Dr. Robert G. Lee in his office on the old Bellevue campus in downtown Memphis, Tennessee, surrendering my life to Christ Jesus as clearly as if it were yesterday. The fruit of His presence was in my life, and I was slowly, ever so slowly, growing in the wisdom and knowledge of our God. But it was not until one day around the age of thirty, as I humbled myself before my faithful and merciful heavenly Father, confessed the sin of pride, and gave myself unconditionally to Him for a life of service, did rapid sanctification begin to take place. I am convinced that true God-sized, God-paced transformation takes place AFTER a commitment of oneself to God for a life of service. When one commits to serve God, He begins to move mightily in your life to bring a passion for holiness and an insatiable appetite for His Word. God brought to me a vehicle through which I would not only learn Truth for myself from God's Word, but He also brought me a ministry through which I could disciple others to be continually transformed by the inherent power of His Word.

All of us know someone (it may be you) whom God has redeemed from a life of deep sin and degradation. Have you ever wondered why some seem to struggle through life with unforgiveness, guilt, or shame with no apparent victory or joy in many areas of their lives? Then you encounter others who immediately seem to begin to live victorious lives, full of joy, forgiveness, and later effective ministry. One can be assured the difference is found in their love for and earnest desire to study God's Word with a commitment to understanding and obeying. Every word of the Bible is to be believed wholeheartedly and without reservation to be the very word of God. First Thessalonians 2:13 states that His Word performs its work in those who believe; i.e., as to obey. Another similar Scripture is found in the negative in Hebrews 4:2b: "the word they heard did not profit them, because it was not united by faith in those who heard" (NASB).

There is glorious "good news," which is accompanied by glorious promises from God. Redemption and sanctification are offered to each person. All those who will surrender to the gracious drawing to God by His Spirit will be given redemption from all sins and the indwelling of the Holy Spirit. The Holy Spirit will cause you to obey God's commandments (Ezekiel 36:27, paraphrased). A life born into the Kingdom of God is only accomplished by Him, and a life of transformation into the image of His Son is also only accomplished by Him—all because of His great love. We are told that all things are from Him, through Him, and to Him (Romans 11:36), and to Him belongs the glory forever.

Our focus for this section of our study of Ruth has been her great need of redemptive love and the implications and insights we can glean and apply to our lives. We have seen that as women we find ourselves in very similar conditions that Ruth did in Ruth 4:1–10. Her future redemption seemed to rest in the lives of humans she did not know nor was she certain as to what they might do. However, we also saw that

Ruth followed Naomi's instructions that paralleled God's law. In faith she believed that God would accomplish what His law intended. God had provided a way for the widows of the sons of Israel to be redeemed by a "kinsman-redeemer." Through Ruth's obedience and God's faithfulness to His promises, not only were Ruth and Naomi redeemed from these very desperate circumstances, but incredible blessings followed as they obeyed God's will God's way. This chapter's portion of Ruth 4 ends in verse 10, stating that the purpose of Boaz becoming their kinsman-redeemer was "so that the name of the deceased may not be cut off from his brothers or from the court of his birth place." We'll look at this purpose in greater detail in a later chapter.

We have seen through our study of specific Scriptures that we have a sure Word from God. We are assured that no matter the circumstance, no matter our seeming impotence, no matter the raging storms of life, we have a Kinsman-Redeemer Who is ready and able to deliver us with compassion and power. You may find yourself in a marriage in which saying it is difficult would be an understatement. You may have before you decisions to be made where none seems desirable. You may have health issues where there seems to be no evident remedy. BUT we have a God Who is able to deliver. Get to know Him through is infallible and inherently powerful Word.

Let's close our study with the intentional and conscious commitment to walk in the truths we have learned. The true and unadulterated revelation of God's character and His ways are found only in His Word. Living a life of obedience and trust is most challenging when we are in periods like Ruth's and Naomi's—times when God has us in the furnace of testing. These are times when He is purifying us as gold to make us into vessels of honor (2 Timothy 2:20), vessels that are useful and fruitful in His Kingdom work (2 Peter 1:8), all for the glory of His great name.

John 17:3 tells us, "This is eternal life, that they may know You, the only true God, and Jesus Christ whom You have sent" (NASB). Get to know your God. Experience the most glorious redemption and transformation possible because of God's great love for you. Let His immeasurable, unquenchable, loving-kindness overshadow you by His glory, goodness, and grace! You will never be sorry you did!

◊ Did you learn anything that might help you deal better with the very difficult circumstances you now find yourself, or may find yourself in the future?

◊ Are you finding it hard to live in victory and joy most of the time? If so, did you learn any biblical principles that might encourage you toward a pathway to experiencing victory, joy, and peace?

◊ What did you learn from your study of Ruth about God's redemptive love that is to be expressed in the lives of all Christ followers?

◊ How would you explain to another person what God's intention was for Ruth as described in Ruth chapters 3 and 4?

◊   Do you think there are some important lessons that could be learned from observing Boaz's handling of his love for Ruth and the law's requirements of a kinsman-redeemer? If so, what?

◊   Are there any biblical principles you have learned as you studied how God worked out His redemptive plan and purposes for Ruth, Naomi, and Boaz?

◊   Are there any circumstances you are encountering today that could be helped by following the biblical principles found in the book of Ruth?

RUTH 4:11–22

The elders and all the people who were at the gate said, "We are witnesses. May the Lord make the woman who is entering your house like Rachel and Leah, who together built the house of Israel. May you be powerful in Ephrathah and famous in Bethlehem. May your house become like the house of Perez, the son Tamar bore to Judah, because of the offspring the Lord will give you by this young woman." Boaz took Ruth and she became his wife. When he was intimate with her, the Lord enabled her to conceive, and she gave birth to a son. Then the women said to Naomi, "Praise the Lord, who has not left you without a family redeemer today. May his name become well known in Israel. He will renew your life and sustain you in your old age. Indeed, your daughter-in-law, who loves you and is better to you than seven sons, has given birth to him." Naomi took the child, placed him on her lap, and took care of him. The neighbor women said, "A son has been born to Naomi," and they named him Obed. He was the father of Jesse, the father of David. Now this is the genealogy of Perez: Perez fathered Hezron. Hezron fathered Ram, who fathered Amminadab. Amminadab fathered Nahshon, who fathered Salmon. Salmon fathered Boaz, who fathered Obed. And Obed fathered Jesse, who fathered David.

CHAPTER ELEVEN

Marie Strain

Marriage—A God-Designed Covenant Relationship

Introduction

What is marriage anyway? Is it something God created just as a wonderful idea but left to humans to regulate? Are its detailed instructions to be adjusted according to each person's desires as time passes and the culture changes? This week we will focus on some of the biblical principles that are prompted by Ruth 4:11–22. This is where all the barriers had been sovereignly removed, and Boaz and Ruth are married. What a great love story! What a great work of redemptive love God has wrought. But the real spiritual profitability for us today is to closely examine what happens because of God's creative design of marriage.

Many of you are already aware of the biblical answers to the previous questions. Marriage was the first institution God created. God saw that it was "not good for man to be alone" (Genesis 2:18). You know the story. But what most do not intentionally focus on is the fact that God's answer to Adam's "not good" situation was not simply to bring a female to Adam. God created and brought to him a WIFE. God joined them together in "holy matrimony," as it is commonly referred.

God's Word calls this institution of marriage a covenant (Malachi 2:14). In this chapter, our primary focus will be on what God has to say about the covenant of marriage. Also, we will briefly touch on the two places where blessings are proclaimed as recorded in Ruth 4:11–22.

There are two separate blessings given in Ruth 4. The first is the blessing proclaimed by the elders to Boaz in verses 11–12 and the second by the women to Naomi in verses 14–15. Hopefully, through this brief examination of the text, you will become more aware of the foundational truth of proclaiming blessings.

It is an awesome thing to note that the blessing these elders proclaimed on Boaz was actually three distinct prophesies. First, the house of Boaz would be like that of Jacob and multiplying the sons of Israel. Second, Boaz's name would be great in Judah. Third, Boaz's lineage would produce the Messiah. This third and final aspect of this blessing is not as explicit but refers to what God had designated to be the messianic line by the mention of the birth of Judah in Genesis 49:10.

The blessing proclaimed to Naomi after the birth of Obed is also prophetic. Obed's birth represented God's redemptive love and restoration of life to the sons of Israel through a promised Messiah. It would be just two generations until the birth of David. Then another twenty-eight to the birth of this prophesied Messiah, Jesus Christ, the Nazarene, the very Son of God (Matthew 1:17).

Proclaiming blessings, founded on the truths of God's Word, are powerful in their influence and out-workings in the lives of the recipients. "Blessings" themselves originated, as did marriage, on the sixth day of creation in the Garden of Eden. Genesis 1:28 states, "And God blessed them; and God said to them, 'Be fruitful and multiply, and fill the earth, and subdue it; and rule over the fish of the sea and over the birds of the sky, and over every living thing that moves on the earth'" (NASB). God's blessing was endued with the power to accomplish its contents, and such also are those proclaimed from the truths and precepts of God's Word when believed and obeyed.

The major emphasis we will study in this chapter is found in the commitment and blessings that God intended through the covenant of marriage. A genuine tragedy in the North American church today is that very few individuals in these congregations are biblically literate regarding the full counsel of God's Word on the subject. God has clearly defined and given instructions regarding this all-important, first institution established by a holy and all-wise God. The family, since Adam and Eve, has been the vehicle through which God would "picture" His love relationship to His children and extend His glory through holy and righteous children. Therefore, it is extremely profitable for us to examine God's truth regarding marriage and the family.

Trials

There is no record of explicit trials that Boaz and Ruth faced after their marriage. But we can assume that even in a love story as sweet and inspiring as Ruth and Boaz's, they had to live life day by day. They would have raised their family in an evil, rebellious, and idolatrous environment such as is described in the details of the book of Judges. What they did have were the blessings and favor of God to guide and protect them through life because they had a heart for obedience evidenced clearly in this book. This is also true for believers today, but the added component for all who are believers in the Lord Jesus Christ is having the indwelling Holy Spirit and the promises of a new and better covenant (Hebrews 8:6). These promises of God are huge and cannot be overestimated or overemphasized. Ruth, Boaz, Naomi, and all the children of Israel lived under the Covenant of Law, which did not contain the inherent power to obey.

Now back to our major emphasis for this chapter—the covenant of marriage. Moses' God-given narrative added for explanation in Genesis 2:24 (KJV) and repeated verbatim by Jesus in Matthew 19:5 and by Paul in Ephesians 5:31 regarding marriage is explicit and profound: "For this cause a man shall leave his father and his mother, and shall cleave to his wife; and they shall become one flesh." In these passages, both the Hebrew and Greek words translated "cleave" means to cling to, to be joined with, to be glued together. It carries with it the idea of sticking two pieces of paper together with glue. Of course, there were other commandments given in the Law of Moses, which would have also been the guiding principles for Boaz and Ruth. What will be the most profitable for us in this chapter, however, is for us to concentrate on what has been explicitly and clearly defined for us today in the New Covenant of grace.

Since God originated the institution, He has full prerogative and authority to set the rules and boundaries. As is clearly declared over and over in God's Word, God blesses obedience, and He must judge and discipline disobedience. What seems to be the greatest trial today is that both men and women are most often governed by what they see and what they feel rather than by what God's Word clearly teaches. It is tragic that there is so little known and understood by Christians today about what **God** says about marriage. Many Christian couples' mind-set about what each are to do in their respective roles and how to respond in difficulties is most frequently *not* governed by what God instructs. God never makes a commandment that He does not also provide the power and means to obey. God's indwelling power by His Spirit when appropriated is sufficient for all obedience. However, we continue to have churches filled with couples making decisions on what seems to be culturally acceptable and what their flesh desires, rather than what God requires. Making decisions based on emotions is one of the most dangerous things a person can do.

There seems to be equal but contrary circumstances in the life of women in the time of Ruth versus the time and culture in which women live today. As mentioned in a previous chapter, in the times of Ruth, women were considered by culture to be not much more than chattel, or property. They most often lived at the whim and fancy of their husbands. Clearly, this was not God's design. The wife has been designed by God from the beginning to be a "helper suitable, completer" (Genesis 2:18). The husband is to cleave to her as a part of his own flesh. Today, we have a cultural mind-set that is the opposite, yet it is just as destructive. Now, the majority opinion regarding wives is that she is not a person under the authority of her husband, as clearly commanded in Ephesians 5:23, but is free to do whatever she pleases whenever she pleases to do it. There is a principle and reality from Scripture that gives consternation to almost every person living in this sin-contaminated human flesh. The truth is every person is under some authority. We are told that even within the Godhead there is an authoritative structure. "God is the head of Christ" (1 Corinthians 11:3). In marriage, God has also established an authoritative structure, which declares that "man is the head of the woman," also found in 1 Corinthians 11:3. It is imperative to note that positions in authority were never intended to mean or even intimate one's value or usefulness to God.

However, in our bodies of flesh, which have not as yet been redeemed from the sin nature of Adam (Romans 8:23), one often rebels against submitting to any authority. This is an area hard for women, but especially for women of today's culture and humanistic mind-set. It seems needful for us all to be reminded that to rebel against the God-given authority of one's own husband is ultimately rebellion against our God and Savior. Rebellion can basically be defined as "you have no right to be in authority over me," when that authority has been clearly given by God in His Word. God's intended purpose is to bring stability, peace, and order. Institutions (including governments) without an established authoritative structure provide no peace, stability, or protection, but instead many times create chaos and vulnerability. So also is the case with the institution of marriage.

As women whose wifely role has been clearly defined by God in Scripture, it should thrill your heart to know that "in Christ" there is neither male nor female, for we are all one in Christ (Galatians 3:28). Women have been given the same presence and power of the Holy Spirit in their lives as the men to whom God has given the headship, or leadership, of the family and the local church. Women are equally given gifts of the Holy Spirit and ministries of service in the Body of Christ.

As the Lord begins to reveal the wondrous Truths of His Word, one's thinking begins to be transformed and to be set free from a mind-set sculpted by this present worldview of marriage. God's Kingdom advances in profound and eternal ways when women determine that God's design for marriage is the only way to achieve God's plans and purposes in and through them. That was certainly true in the life of Ruth. One can only imagine what would have been the outcome if Ruth had said something like, "I'm my own boss and I don't need to do anything so demeaning as to sleep at the feet of a man lying on a harvest floor."

Truth

The family is a foundational element of the Church of Jesus Christ. Therefore, there are major truths in the New Testament about marriage that are essential for all Christians to know. Few, even in the Church, know, much less follow, these clearly defined principles. Thus, the enemy of our souls has been able to ravage and destroy so many of our families. We have previously looked at God's authoritative structure. Now it is time for you to go to the Scriptures to learn and confirm by your own examination what God has clearly designed and intended.

You might have asked the question, "Why is following God's design so important?" Or you might even ask, "Why does it seem as though Satan has put a bull's-eye on the family in particular?" Glad you asked. God gives us one major reason for both. God designed marriage to be, to this lost and dying world, His living picture of Christ's love for and relationship to the Church, which He purchased with His blood (Ephesians 5:32).

The remainder of our time in this section will be primarily spent in studying to understand and apply a few major passages in Scripture that contain life-changing principles on marriage. You have heard it said that it takes two to change a bad marriage into a better one. It certainly sounds reasonable, but it is not biblical. One spouse truly devoted to learning and obeying God's handbook on marriage—the Bible—can significantly influence their marriage for the better. This is not my opinion; it is proven fact. God's Word and the principles He reveals in His infallible, inerrant Word work. There is inherent power in God's Word that is released to do divine and redemptive work when it is believed and obeyed (1 Thessalonians 2:13).

It seems profitable for us to begin in a very unlikely place. You will be blessed and encouraged to know that God promises a sanctifying benefit to a believer's spouse and children (1 Corinthians 7, NASB). We will look at this passage a little later in more detail, but the English words "sanctified" and "holy" used in verse 14 are from the same Greek root. This root used in this context can be interpreted accurately as "set apart to God for His blessings and protection." This passage does not imply a promise of "salvation," although verse 16 certainly implies the wife could be used as an instrument of God to lead her husband to Christ. However, many have chosen to believe the promise of God's sanctifying work and, through their own obedience to God's Word, have provided an avenue through which God worked miraculously and redemptively in their own marriages and families.

We will briefly examine 1 Corinthians 7 at this time, but doing a thorough study of this entire chapter at a later date will prove invaluable. When one outlines the structure of the truths in 1 Corinthians 7, we discover the following:

1. **Verses 1–7** give general information regarding sexual morality and behavior among all believers.

2. **Verses 8–9** speak to Christians who are unmarried or widows. Paul tells them it is good for them to remain "unmarried," but if any do not have their sexual appetites under control it is better for them to marry.

3. **Verses 10–16** speak to Christians who are married, ". . . the wife should not leave (the context makes it clear this means divorce) her husband." Verse 11 is interesting in that it virtually says if you choose not to obey My command not to divorce, know that you have only two options: a) never to remarry, or remain unmarried, or b) be reconciled to her husband. To ignore or to choose to disobey this command leaves many women and their children vulnerable to the evil and destructive works of Satan. There are too many casualties today to innumerate, which contain horror stories too many of us have heard too frequently, of those who chose to believe the lie of Satan and not obey God. However, verse 15 states that if an unbelieving husband should choose to leave (again in this context means to divorce), then the wife is to let him leave. That wife is then freed (not under bondage) from obeying all marital covenant vows she made with regard to her husband being in authority over her. He has broken them by initiating and completing a divorce against her; therefore, he is no longer her authoritative head.

4. **Verses 17–31** speak to those adults who have just gotten saved. Bottom line is that it is a repeated command to remain in the marital condition in which one is saved.

5. **Verses 32–35** state that to be "unmarried" is good; it ". . . secures undistracted devotion to the Lord."

6. **Verses 36–38** detail a father's authority over his virgin daughter regarding marriage. There are few fathers today who believe God has given him the authority and responsibility over if, when, and to whom his daughter is to marry. It's just not our culture! But it is God's mandate.

7. **Verses 39–40** clearly state that a widow is free to be married or re-marry; i.e. it is a "lawful" choice for a widow or widower to re-marry.

"Free to be married?" you must have asked yourself. "Freed from what?" You can know from Scripture (Romans 7:2–3) that the above-mentioned passage is implying the freedom from becoming an adulterer or adulteress. We are going to observe a few passages that specifically address divorce because it is a major issue that is devastating the family today. The frequency of divorce among members of the Body of Christ continues to be horrific. Based on the fact that Truth makes us free, but error keeps us in bondage (John 8:32), it is imperative that all believers personally examine the Scriptures themselves. This allows the God of all glory and grace to fill their hearts and minds with God's redeeming love and transforming Truth. Marriage was designed by God to be "until death do us part," which you will see in the following study of Matthew 19 and other passages. Most of you know God's declared opinion of divorce. He hates it (Malachi 2:16)!

It will be not only extremely profitable but vitally important for you at some future time to examine every New Testament passage that speaks to this subject. It is true that any doctrinal belief determined personally from a thorough examination of God's Word keeps one anchored in Truth—not tossed to and fro by every wind of doctrine. However, because of limited time and space, we will cover only a few New Testament passages that speak clearly and powerfully.

Jesus was asked about divorce in a culture where a man could divorce his wife for any reason at all. Sound familiar? Let's look at one such occasion and observe what Jesus said. Closely examine Matthew 19:3–10. Please keep in mind as you read that Jesus' major point in His answer here was that they "not become an adulterer" (NASB). Please add your insights and points of application in the spaces that follow.

Matthew 19:3–10

3 *Some* Pharisees came to Jesus, testing Him and asking, "Is it lawful *for a man* to divorce his wife for any reason at all?"

4 And He answered and said, "Have you not read that He who created *them* from the beginning made them male and female,

5 and said, 'For this reason a man shall leave his father and mother and be joined to his wife, and the two shall become one flesh'?

6 "So they are no longer two, but one flesh. What therefore God has joined together let no man separate."

7 They said to Him, "Why then did Moses command to give her a certificate of divorce and send *her* away?"

8 He said to them, "Because of your hardness of heart Moses permitted you to divorce your wives; but from the beginning it has not been this way.

9 "And I say to you, whoever divorces his wife, except for immorality, and marries another woman commits adultery."

10 The disciples said to Him, "If the relationship of the man with his wife is like this, it is better not to marry."

◊ **Insights:**

◊ **Application**:

To be sure that you didn't miss a couple of important points, please note the following observations and conclusions from this passage.

1. Jesus knew the Pharisees came to Him to test him. He did not explicitly answer their question but took them back to when God first created marriage. Jesus' unmistakable implied answer to their question was **NO**—"what God has joined together let no man separate." Since they were not satisfied with Jesus' answer, they brought in Moses. Jesus' bottom line response was that Moses, not God, had permitted divorce because of the hardness of their hearts. Jesus said categorically that what Moses permitted was contrary to what God had intended from the beginning.

2. The second major truth Jesus addresses here is what re-marriage can cause. A dangerous consequence from divorce, among many others, can be that a re-marriage after a divorce that was *not* caused by immorality can result in one becoming an "adulteress." In Hebrews 13:4, God states, "Marriage *is to be held* in honor among all, and the *marriage* bed *is to be* undefiled; for fornicators and adulterers **God will judge**," (emphasis added).

This warning about the issue of committing adultery is also addressed in Matthew 5:32, Mark 10:11–12 (Mark 10:2–12 is a companion passage to Matthew 19), Luke 16:18, and Romans 7:2–3. At some point, you should examine these passages for some very pertinent and profound insights. It is needful and profitable for us to be reminded here that, at times, Scripture itself convicts us that what we have believed or what we have done in the past contradicts the clear teaching of God's Word. When that happens, and it does to all born-again believers, we can be assured that there is always forgiveness and redemption available. First John 1:9 clearly promises that "If we confess our sins, He is faithful and righteous to forgive us our sins and to cleanse us from all unrighteousness." There is no sin that 1 John 1:9 does not cover.

Another admonition that all believers need to be reminded of is that we must be students of God's Word so that when life gets tough, when life gets seemingly unbearable, when we begin to see no hope, we can know, believe, and obey the clear teachings of Scripture. We all are assured by God that His grace is sufficient for all life's troubles and hard choices. God is always on His throne. He never departs from His sovereign position. Our circumstances are never a surprise to Him. Our good and faithful God has promised and is forever committed to providing a way for His children to living life victoriously (1 Corinthians 10:13). Our responsibility is to "trust and obey," and on occasion confess our sins and receive God's unconditional and unqualified forgiveness and restoration.

It's time for you to examine two more passages before we leave this section: Ephesians 5:22–24 and 33b. In the culture in which we live, these could be the most hated and resisted passages of all and possibly two of the most misunderstood. We must always keep in mind that God gets to make the rules; we don't. But we must also remember that one of God's greatest joys is to bless obedience. God truly and unconditionally loves us, and His heart's desire is always to bless. One never ends up on the short end of the stick, so to speak, by continually adhering to God's instructions. In fact, He will move heaven and earth to bless those who walk in faith following His commandments. Before you examine the following Ephesians passages, it is necessary that you understand the Greek word translated "subject" in verse 24 (NASB) and implied in verse 22. This word can be accurately interpreted "voluntarily submit yourself under the authority (headship) of your own husband." Nowhere does Scripture teach that the husband is to *make* his wife submit.

After you have closely examined Ephesians 5:22–24 and 33b, please note below any insights and applications you observe from these passages.

Ephesians 5:22–24, 33b, NASB

22 Wives, *be subject* to your own husbands, as to the Lord.

23 For the husband is the head of the wife, as Christ also is the head of the church, He Himself *being* the Savior of the body.

24 But as the church is subject to Christ, so also the wives *ought to be* to their husbands in everything.

33b . . . and the wife must *see to it* that she respects her husband.

◊ **Insights**:

◊ **Application**:

It was impossible for you to have missed that not only are wives to place themselves voluntarily under the headship, or authority, of their own husbands, but the comparison is made to what the Church, the Bride of Christ, is to do. It is worth warning any woman who is contemplating marriage that she should make sure she knows enough about this man's habitual behavior that she is willing to submit herself under his authority and to respect his position as head of the family "as long as they both shall live." If that is not true, then she should not marry that man unless he becomes someone she is willing to respect and submit to. There is no way to overestimate the value of such an examination. There seems to be a "game killer" on the husband's side. God seems to have placed in every husband's DNA the absolute need for leadership and respect. The individual man might not be a respectable person, but his position of authority, according to God's mandate, is to be held in honor and respect.

Let's end this section on Truth with a close look at 1 Peter 3:1–4. This passage is not a suggestion but God's commandment. It is worth noting that verse 1 starts with the phrase "In the same way." You will do well to examine 1 Peter 2:18–24 in which "the way" is clearly given. First Peter 2:21 ends with, "Christ, leaving you an example for you to follow in His steps." Again, please add your insights and applications below.

1 Peter 3:1–4, NASB

1 In the same way, you wives, be submissive to your own husbands so that even if any *of them* are disobedient to the word, they may be won without a word by the behavior of their wives,

2 as they observe your chaste and respectful behavior.

3 Your adornment must not be *merely* external—braiding the hair, and wearing gold jewelry, or putting on dresses;

4 but *let it be* the hidden person of the heart, with the imperishable quality of a gentle and quiet spirit, which is precious in the sight of God.

◊ **Insights**:

231

◊ **Application**:

There are several observations worth reiterating here. Another aspect of most every husband's DNA is that seldom to never will a husband be taught by his wife. So wives, you will not be able to save your husband through continually preaching the Gospel to him, leaving Scripture taped to his bathroom mirror, etc. In fact, if this practice is continued, the husband could very well rebel against, not be drawn toward, the Gospel. This passage makes it clear that it is the godly behavior of the wife that wins a husband over "as they observe." Please circumspectly answer the following question. "Is my habitual behavior at home chaste (holy, free from sin, pure) and respectful?"[35] It is always great counsel for any wife who has a husband who is disobedient to the Word to make her primary focus her own spiritual growth and obedience. Spiritual maturity results in a behavior that is attractive and winsome to her husband. Be confidently assured that the rewards for doing so are immeasurable and eternal!

The word *gentle* in verse 4 is often translated "meek." These English words are a translation of a Greek word that means bridled strength—strength that is harnessed as a horse is trained to use its strength in useful, controlled, and productive ways. The word translated "quiet" in the same verse means "tranquil." This word implies that the emotions and mouth are under control, thus bringing peace. It is imperative that wives know silence is not what is meant here. Therefore, being silent is not a wife's instruction or "role." A wife's assigned role is to be "a helper suitable, completer," as previously mentioned. She brings to the marriage information and insights that are invaluable and necessary to every marriage. Often, it is the wife who is more sensitive to underlying circumstances and consequences in the family. Frequently, it is the wife

---

35   Spiros Zodhiates, ThD, *The Complete Word Study Dictionary, New Testament* (Chattanooga, TN: AMG Publishers, 1992), 73.

who has the emotional engagement to bring in aspects for decision making that a husband has neither detected nor considered. So, Wives, bring your God-given wisdom, understanding, and sensitivity to every important decision. A wise wife helps her husband make wise decisions by providing him the accurate and sufficient information he needs to make good ones. Many times, God gives wives insights into the possible future ramifications of proposed decisions. A wife obeying this passage and always remembering her husband is the final authority will make any marriage better! Try it, if you have not already. The rewards are not only experienced in this life, but in eternity as well.

Transformation

There is an interesting passage in Titus that brings a whole new insight to wives who learn to "love their husbands, to love their children, to be sensible, pure, workers at home, kind, being subject to their own husbands." There is an effect that few are conscientiously aware—"that God's Word may not be dishonored" (Titus 2:4–5). The phrase "workers at home" used in this Titus passage is such an unfortunate translation. In the parallel passage of 1 Timothy 5:14, NASB, this is also an unfortunate translation. Here the Greek word *oikodespoteó* is translated "keep house" but literally means "master of the house, ruler of the house."[36] In other words, the home is the domain in which the wife manages. One can accurately say the president of a manufacturing company rules the company in oversight and making major decisions and creating guidelines. But the plant manager rules over the daily operations of his assigned plant under the general guidelines of the president. So it is to be with a marriage. The husband makes the final decisions for working guidelines with the wise input of his wife. The wife should be given and empowered to make everyday working decisions concerning the management of the home.

There should not be a happier husband than one who has a wife who has been given the freedom and authority to run her own household well. He will indeed be a "man honored at the gate" (Proverbs 31:31). When the wife is granted this honor by her husband, as the manager

---

36   Ibid., 1030.

of the home, there is most often peace, tranquility, order, and many blessings.

It is pertinent for you to know that the Greek word that is used three times and translated "manage his household," as a qualification for overseers (we most often call pastors) and deacons in 1 Timothy 3:4, 5, 12, is *proistêmi* and means "to rule over or to be set over"[37]—a different word entirely from that which is used in Titus 2 and 1 Timothy 5. There is no contradiction of God's ordained roles between the Titus 2 and 1 Timothy 3 and the 1 Timothy 5 passages.

There was a young woman who regularly attended my Sunday school class. During this time, we were studying the Precept Upon Precept course "Marriage without Regrets." She made it clear that these truths were not workable, and she was not going to follow them. She even went to other Christian authorities who agreed with her. She left our Sunday school class and the city with the full intentions of getting a divorce and going her own way. She was choosing to follow the cultural mind-set and her emotions and refusing to be obedient to God's Word. One of the most thrilling and gratifying occasions of my discipleship ministry came the day I received a phone call from her. She acknowledged that she had recently made the decision to follow God's instructions for wives and, as a result, her marriage had been fully restored. She had determined to be obedient to the Lord and applied what she had learned through our study of marriage, and God did a merciful and gracious redemptive work. Hallelujah, what a Savior! The truths shared in these chapters have mostly been gleaned from personal in-depth study of God's Word through many such courses produced by Precept Ministries, International.

Another lady who was estranged from her husband for years was repeatedly advised by Christian friends to divorce her husband. He had no interest in filing himself. She had a sister who wrote her a letter, which contained the principles outlined in this chapter. After reading this letter, she was convicted by the Spirit of God that she was to obey His Word and not her emotions or the advice of so many others. It is her testimony, and that of her husband's, that her years of obedience to the Lord Jesus in His Word and her loving ministry to him during ongoing

---

37   Ibid., 1220.

illnesses eventually led Him to Christ and their marriage being restored. The truths of these two actual accounts are not isolated ones. Living life in obedience to God's revealed truths WORKS.

As you can imagine, those who are in a ministry of discipleship are very often approached for advice concerning marriage on various subjects and conditions. There seems to be a simple principle that when followed helps bring peace to a marriage and fewer confrontations. Suggestions or advice brought to a husband by his wife once is "she is his helper." The same information brought to him twice is "she is reminding." The same brought to him three times is "she is making an appeal." But the same advice brought to him a fourth time or more "she is being a nag." (Note: This principle was gleaned from Jesus' rebuke of Paul after asking the third time to be healed of the thorn in his flesh in 2 Corinthians 12:7–8.)

There is another principle of communication I have learned over the years. The following has been proven to be true with many husbands. Many men communicate through stories. If you haven't noticed before, listen to men in conversations with other men and count the different stories told. When there is a very important issue to be addressed, including your husband's behavior that is hurtful to you, you will most likely find it profitable to communicate your need through a story that will engage him emotionally. These stories, when related with compassion and without accusation, many times bring to realization insights into behavior that had before been unconscious and, many times, unintended.

Marriage is primarily what God uses to raise up godly children—where we are to bring them up in the discipline and instruction of the Lord (Ephesians 6:4). Children who witness their mothers living a life of respect and submission to their fathers and their fathers loving and honoring their mothers are the ones most likely to experience a seamless transition from being under authority at home to being under the authority of a good and faithful God as an adult.

In closing, let's review the most important truths we have gleaned from our studies in this chapter. Nothing has changed since the sixth day of creation when God established this holy institution of marriage. Its intention is to be between one man and one woman until parted by death. God clearly has appointed the man to be the head of the authoritative structure. The wife has been appointed the role of manager of the home under her husband and is a necessary and invaluable resource of wisdom and understanding. A woman's role is in no way inferior to the husband's. It is just different. God established the difference to compliment and empower the family! All for the glory of His great name!

No woman needs to fear or be threatened by God's commands to wives because every commandment of God is designed for greater intimacy with Him and for greater spiritual work in the family. Thereby, the Kingdom of His dear Son is nurtured and expanded. You can believe wholeheartedly and without reservation that following God's "Handbook on Marriage," the Bible, will bring you great earthly *and* eternal rewards. It is clear that marriage is the union that Satan is most interested in destroying. The reason is clear. As we noted before, marriage is God's living picture to the world of Christ's relationship to the Church. Guard it carefully and with all diligence, all for the glory of His great name.

The underlining principle for us all is that when God's Word is obeyed it transforms one into the image of the Lord Jesus Christ. Let us each commit today to throw away all our cultural biases, beliefs, and influences that are contrary to God's Word. Let us determine today to delve deep into the treasure chest of Scripture and to live by faith based on His inerrant, infallible Word. Then, watch Him work divinely and supernaturally in you and your family. Experience the abundant life that only He came to provide. "The thief comes only to steal and kill and destroy; I came that they may have life, and have *it* abundantly" (John 10:10, NASB).

◊   Is there anything you have learned from God's Word in this chapter that was brand-new to you? If so, what?

◊ Did God reveal to you any change that you might need to implement in your marriage? Or if not married, in your mind-set or belief system about marriage?

◊ If God has convicted you of not following His instructions regarding your explicit role as a wife, use this time to confess it to our merciful and gracious heavenly Father, ask His forgiveness, and then ask Him for the empowerment to change.

◊ How would you describe the most commonly held beliefs about marriage today that you have discovered are contrary to the clear teaching of God's Word?

◊ What would you describe as the greatest need in the marriages in the United States in the twenty-first century?

◊ What strikes you as the most challenging aspect of God's instruction for wives in today's society and culture?

◊ Do you believe that God could bring revival to His Church through marriages being brought into compliance with His clearly declared instructions? If so, in your opinion how can this change begin to be accomplished?

RUTH 4:11–22

The elders and all the people who were at the gate said, "We are witnesses. May the Lord make the woman who is entering your house like Rachel and Leah, who together built the house of Israel. May you be powerful in Ephrathah and famous in Bethlehem. May your house become like the house of Perez, the son Tamar bore to Judah, because of the offspring the Lord will give you by this young woman." Boaz took Ruth and she became his wife. When he was intimate with her, the Lord enabled her to conceive, and she gave birth to a son. Then the women said to Naomi, "Praise the Lord, who has not left you without a family redeemer today. May his name become well known in Israel. He will renew your life and sustain you in your old age. Indeed, your daughter-in-law, who loves you and is better to you than seven sons, has given birth to him." Naomi took the child, placed him on her lap, and took care of him. The neighbor women said, "A son has been born to Naomi," and they named him Obed. He was the father of Jesse, the father of David. Now this is the genealogy of Perez: Perez fathered Hezron. Hezron fathered Ram, who fathered Amminadab. Amminadab fathered Nahshon, who fathered Salmon. Salmon fathered Boaz, who fathered Obed. And Obed fathered Jesse, who fathered David.

CHAPTER TWELVE

Marie Strain

Jesus, the Real and Final Kinsman-Redeemer

Introduction

How does the Old Testament law, which provided for a kinsman-redeemer, actually relate to those of us who are genuine followers of Christ Jesus? Are there any promises or aspects in the New Covenant of Grace that you may not be aware of? What is a covenant anyway? The answers to these questions, if you do not already know them, are life changing. In this chapter, you will come to a better understanding of the first covenant's "shadow" of a kinsman-redeemer illustrated by Boaz. This will be accomplished by contrasting the "shadow" with the "Real." Jesus became the reality when He inaugurated the New Covenant of Grace, by His blood (Hebrews 12:24). Therefore, the primary focus in this chapter will be to guide you toward a deeper understanding of the major aspects of this second covenant, the Covenant of Grace.

Many, who surrender their lives to the person and work of the Lord Jesus Christ, enter into the New Covenant of Grace with little to no understanding of genuine covenant principles and benefits. Many are less able to appreciate and live in the light of this New Covenant because they are virtually unaware of the implications of entering into covenant, both its obligations and expectations. The very heart and intention of biblical covenant is "relationship."

There is great evidence that those who come to a clear understanding of biblical covenant have a greater commitment to live as good and faithful covenant partners. They seem to claim the many clearly stated promises without reservations and live by the New Covenant's commandments. You can be confident that when you finish with this brief but life-changing study on biblical covenant you will never view your personal relationship with our Most High God and Christ Jesus in the same way. You most likely have heard of or even have said something about "having a personal relationship with Christ Jesus." That relationship is based on a covenant with incredible promises but also with great expectations from those who decide to enter in through faith.

Boaz and Ruth were included among those who had entered into the Covenant of Law along with its promises and judgments. Because of time and space, this chapter is not intended to give an exhaustive study on covenant but to whet your appetite for later study in God's Word on the subject.

It is clearly seen from Ruth 4:11–22 what the law required the kinsman-redeemer to provide. Boaz needed to redeem the land Elimelech had inherited as a son of Judah. Elimelech had most likely sold it before leaving Bethlehem for the land of Moab. The text does not tell us, but it is clear that Naomi did not return with the expectation or ability to claim her husband's inheritance without a kinsman-redeemer. Under the law, the land could not be permanently sold outside each tribe. There was a cost to gain back the land, and Boaz was willing and able to pay that cost. But more importantly, he was a kinsman of Elimelech from the tribe of Judah. He was therefore *qualified* to be a kinsman-redeemer. This was an unmistakable foreshadowing of the work of Jesus Christ. It was required that He come into the "human" tribe, so to speak, to be qualified to do the work of the world's Kinsman-Redeemer. So God prepared a human body for Jesus to enter (Hebrews 10:5). He did so by creating a human egg that was fertilized by the Holy Spirit, not contaminated with the sin of Adam. God implanted this pure, sinless embryo into the womb of the virgin Mary into which the very Son of God entered (Luke 1:24–35).

Trials

Our Kinsman-Redeemer, Jesus Christ, came to reclaim *our* inheritance—all of earth's creation, as well as redeem man from his helpless, hopeless, and sinful condition. I'm sure you recall learning of the original sin when Adam and Eve disobeyed God and ate of the forbidden fruit. They had been created in the image of God with a human body, a soul, and a spirit. The spirit was created by God as the place where He would communicate with them individually. Just as God had declared, Adam and Eve died spiritually the moment they disobeyed Him. Death also entered into the world that day when God had to kill an animal to cover their nakedness. Humans from that point would be born spiritually dead and would eventually die physically (Hebrew 9:27). Adam died physically some 900+ years later (Genesis 5:5).

Furthermore, their inheritance was lost. God had given Adam and Eve the dominion and authority to rule over all the earth's creation. When they obeyed Satan and not God, they literally turned over their dominion to Satan. Jesus called Satan the "ruler of this world" (John 12:31, 14:30, and 16:11). In Ephesians 2:2, the devil is described as the "prince of the power of the air" (NASB). So there was an inheritance—all earth's creation—to reclaim. The price was Jesus' blood. Jesus' blood paid for the redemption of the sins of the whole world for all time (Matthew 26:28; Hebrews 10:10–12). What we rarely think about is that Jesus also paid for the redemption of all creation (Romans 8:19–23). At Jesus' return, He will literally take back what was forfeited by the first humans, Adam and Eve. Revelation 20:4 says we will rule and reign with Christ for a thousand years. Revelation 22:5 states that we will rule and reign with Christ also after the new heaven and the new earth are created—forever and ever. So there was not only a sin debt to be paid, but also an inheritance to be taken back. No man was willing, able, and qualified. It took the God Man, Jesus Christ, the Nazarene, by the will of His Father, to reclaim all of what had been forfeited by sin.

When as an act of faith a person accepts Jesus Christ as their Lord and Savior, i.e., when a person surrenders his or her life to His person and work, they receive a "new spirit" (Ezekiel 36:26). We'll later address this passage, and Jeremiah 31, where the promise of a New Covenant was prophesied. As mentioned before, this New Covenant of Grace was inaugurated by Jesus Christ through His blood (Hebrews 12:24).

It was not revealed what price Boaz paid to redeem the land of Elimelech. However, we do know the cost for the redemption from our sin debt and the restoration of the lost inheritance to us. It cost Jesus everything. Not only was the cost great for our Savior, but we cannot fathom what the cost was for our heavenly Father. He was compelled to tell Jesus on the night of His betrayal, as He was in agony sweating great drops of blood, "Son, there is no other way." The cost was beyond imagination physically, but the cost spiritually was incalculable. Because Jesus, Who knew no sin, was made to be sin on our behalf (2 Corinthians 5:21), He had to experience separation from His Father for the first time from all eternity past to that hour. But praise be to His great name, God raised Him bodily from the grave—victorious over sin *and* death. Jesus' sinless and spotless blood was accepted by God as just payment for all the sins that had been and would ever be committed in all the world for all time. Hallelujah, what a Savior! The sin debt we owe our Lord and Savior can never be repaid, but we can spend our lifetime praising, worshiping, following, and serving Him for so great a salvation—all for the glory of His great name.

Boaz not only paid the price for the redemption of Elimelech's land but also for a bride. In the law, if at all possible, a kinsman-redeemer took the wife of the dead husband and produced a son to carry on the lineage of the deceased. Boaz accomplished this with the birth of Obed. Lightbulbs must be turning on in your mind. Jesus also took a bride. You got it! The Church is Christ's bride bought by His redemptive love and sacrifice. The Church was created on the Day of Pentecost through the work of the promised coming of the Holy Spirit. According to 1 Corinthians 12:13 and other passages, each person, at the moment of their surrender in faith to the Lord Jesus Christ, is placed by Christ using the agent of the Holy Spirit into the Body of Christ. Even though we are as yet still the "betrothed," or engaged, there is a wedding coming! When Christ comes in the clouds for His bride, we'll meet Him in the air and be taken to a wedding feast beyond all wedding feasts. Oh, that we each will be found a faithful bride until He returns for us.

As mentioned previously, there was no power to obey provided in the Old Covenant of the law. The Old Testament is filled with the inability of the sons of Israel to live in obedience to God's commandments. As much as Boaz, Ruth, and Naomi would have desired to live holy and righteous lives, they had hearts of stone, which had not been replaced with new hearts of flesh (Ezekiel 11:19, 36:26). Therefore, they could not have fellowship with God on a personal level. Their fellowship was a corporate one provided through being a Jew and keeping God's law. However, when we enter the New Covenant of Grace, we begin an immediate personal relationship and fellowship with both our heavenly Father and our Lord Jesus Christ. Not only have we been given a new spirit at our new birth, but the Holy Spirit has been given to permanently indwell all believers in their new spirits (John 14:17).

This is not the place for a complete study about Jesus pouring forth of the Holy Spirit on the Day of Pentecost (Acts 2:1–21), but it will be helpful to mention just a few of the works of the Holy Spirit that are inherent parts of this New Covenant of Grace. He guides us into all Truth (John 16:13). Our access to the Father is through Him (Ephesians 2:18). He has been given to us as a pledge of our inheritance with a view to the redemption of God's own possession (Ephesians 1:14). He bears witness with our spirits that we are children of God (Romans 8:16). He intercedes for us (Romans 8:26). He sanctifies us, transforming us continually into the image of Christ Jesus (1 Peter 1:2). God seals us within this New Covenant by His Spirit (Ephesians 1:13). Therefore, once a person enters into this New Covenant, God Himself provides His Spirit to assure that no one, no thing, or no circumstance can change, remove, or invalidate this awesome and all-powerful New Covenant of Grace's promises and provisions.

It seems relevant to make it clear at this point that a person has always been saved by faith starting with Adam and Eve (Genesis 3:15). Before Jesus Christ's incarnation and death, salvation came through the personal belief of God's promise of a coming Messiah. The promised Messiah has come in the person of Jesus. After Jesus' death, resurrection, and ascension into heaven, salvation comes to all who put their faith in Him. This belief includes believing that Jesus is God's Son, that He came into the world in human flesh to pay all sin debt by His death on the cross, and that He was raised bodily from the dead. An individual personal relationship with a holy God can only come through the New Covenant of Grace inaugurated through Jesus' blood.

You need to examine several pertinent Scriptures for yourself to better understand the fullness of the New Covenant mediated by Jesus Christ (Hebrews 9:15). A biblical covenant is a solemn, binding, irrevocable agreement between two persons or groups of people that has been entered into voluntarily, deliberately, and consciously. Some covenants that God initiates do not stipulate any conditions, such as God's covenant with Abraham and Noah regarding the earth after the Flood. We call these unconditional covenants, which cannot be broken because God Himself has made them. There are other covenants where the covenant is "conditional." These require some action(s) on the part of the parties entering into that covenant for it to be valid. Such was the case with the Covenant of Law and is with the New Covenant of Grace. There is always a reason for establishing a covenant whether stated or implied. There are also stipulated consequences for breaking it and blessings for keeping it. Entering into biblical covenant establishes a stated relationship. With the Old Covenant of Law, God's relationship with the nation of Israel was through the priests as mediators. With the New Covenant of Grace, there is a personal relationship between a holy God and each individual who chooses to enter via its stated terms and conditions. In this New Covenant, we individually have access to the presence of the Creator and Sovereign God of the universe on His throne in heaven through the "veil of Jesus' flesh" (Matthew 27:51; Hebrews 10:20, NASB). In God's presence, we receive mercy and find grace to help in time of need (Hebrews 4:16).

Truth

You were given much to ponder in the preceding sections. Is that an understatement?

In this section, you will delve into some selected Scriptures and learn for yourself from God's Word some of the principles previously presented. Here we will primarily focus on what God tells us about biblical covenant. Even though you have already been given a definition of covenant, it is profitable to reiterate that entering into a "conditional covenant" is a voluntary, deliberate, and conscience choice.

We learn from the Old Testament several important aspects of making a conditional covenant: 1) there was a reason(s) for making it; 2) there was blood shed to consummate the covenant; 3) there were established terms and conditions; 4) there was an exchange of vows; 5) there was an established "sign of the covenant"; and 6) there was usually a commemorative meal.

It will be helpful for you to learn how these were accomplished when God and the sons of Israel entered into the Covenant of Law (literally twice). Exodus 24 records the first time and Deuteronomy the second. It is important to note that the remaking of this Covenant of Law as described in Deuteronomy was approximately forty years after the first. All the adults who first made the covenant at Mt. Sinai had died in the wilderness. This brand-new generation of adults needed to enter into this covenant themselves. This was the generation that would go into the Promised Land and would be required to follow its laws and commandments. They would receive its blessings for obedience but also its curses and judgments for disobedience.

The reason is not stated here, but the Covenant of Law was made to enable our holy God to dwell among His people until Christ Jesus would come. We will not look at Galatians 3:19–25 during this study, but this passage gives additional, invaluable insights about the law. The location of His presence among the sons of Israel was in the tabernacle that Moses built according to God's blueprint. God's presence resided over the "mercy seat"—the lid of the Ark of the Covenant—which was placed in the Holy of Holies. When Solomon's Temple was completed and dedicated, God's presence moved into this new Temple. His Shekinah Glory would remain there until He left as recorded in Ezekiel 10:18–19, just before the Babylonians would invade Jerusalem and completely destroy the city and the Temple.

Moses read the terms and conditions of the Covenant of Law to the sons of Israel at Mt. Sinai, and he recorded them in a book. Exodus, Leviticus, Numbers, and Deuteronomy are the books that contain these covenant laws along with the blessings for obedience and the curses for disobedience. Exodus 24 records the exchange of vows between Jehovah

God and the sons of Israel. This passage also gives us the account of the blood of a sacrifice that was sprinkled on the book of the law and the people who consummated the covenant. They also ate a commemorative meal. The sign of this covenant was circumcision.

What is so awesome about the New Covenant of Grace inaugurated, or mediated, by Jesus Christ is that it is a better covenant enacted on better promises (Hebrews 8:6). But interestingly enough, it was first promised to the Jews through Ezekiel and Jeremiah, the prophets. You need to observe these "better promises" for yourself in Ezekiel 36 and Jeremiah 31. But first, let's address the reason for a new covenant. God wanted a personal and intimate relationship with His children. The old one only provided a distant and corporate relationship as described previously. God had been planning this New Covenant all along, but it could not be established until the fullness of time, when the Son of God would take on flesh and pay the sin debt for all the world. Because of this New Covenant, God could now "tabernacle," or dwell, *in* His children because of their purification from sins and the imparted righteousness of God (1 Corinthians 1:30; 2 Corinthians 5:21). God intended all along to sovereignly orchestrate time and events so, at the right time, man could be prepared and given a new spirit through which He could manifest and extend His glory. Only then would God be able to personally communicate and fellowship with man—man who had been redeemed by the blood of the Lamb.

The Jews who had believed that Jesus Christ was the Son of God, the promised Messiah, were the first to enter the New Covenant of Grace. This occurred on the Day of Pentecost when Jesus sent the Holy Spirit to spiritually place them into the Body of Christ, the Church. It seems as though God did not see fit, initially, to reveal all the promises and instructions in this New Covenant. There would be a continuing revelation of these through the apostles and prophets, which were completed and written in the form of the New Testament. The terms to enter into this covenant and to receive the promise of salvation—eternal life—were simple and are articulated in Romans 10:8–10. Please closely observe these three verses and note your insights and applications below.

Romans 10:8–10, NASB

8 But what does it say? "The word is near you, in your mouth and in your heart"—that is, the word of faith which we are preaching,

9 that if you confess with your mouth Jesus *as* Lord, and believe in your heart that God raised Him from the dead, you will be saved;

10 for with the heart a person believes, resulting in righteousness, and with the mouth he confesses, resulting in salvation.

◊ **Insights**:

◊ **Application**:

It is important to point out a commonly misguided belief. I am sure you have heard someone say, "I was such-and-such age when I made Jesus my Savior, but it was not until such-and-such a time that I made Him my Lord." If Jesus is not your Lord, then neither has He become your Savior. Genuine salvation requires each person to "confess with your mouth Jesus *as* Lord, and believe in your heart that God raised Him from the dead." Then, and *only* then, does one receive the free grace gift of salvation. So the clearly stated terms for any person to enter into

Jesus' New Covenant were established. Each individual would have to declare Jesus as Lord and that God had raised Him bodily from the dead. John 5:18 and 8:24 make it clear that to confess Jesus as Lord includes also believing that He *is* God. When these terms are met, entrance into the New Covenant is assured and immediate.

I'm sure you remember that these promises were made to the sons of Israel. But it is interesting to note that both Ezekiel and Jeremiah prophesied during the days just prior to, during, and after the three sieges by the Babylonians on Jerusalem from 605–586 BC. Ezekiel was taken captive to Babylon in the second siege in 597 BC and appointed God's prophet to the exiles in Babylon. Jeremiah remained in Jerusalem during the entire time and prophesied to the Jews in Judah and Jerusalem. You can understand the importance of these prophesies that were given to them during the darkest days of their existence as a nation. We will connect these Old Testament passages with the New Covenant mediated by Jesus after you examine the Ezekiel and Jeremiah Scriptures.

Let's observe Ezekiel 36. Keep in mind, these are promises given to those who had already been taken from their Promised Land of Israel and the Temple in Jerusalem in which God dwelt. They had been taken away from the only place where they could worship God with His required sacrifices and offerings. Please note your insights and applications below. From this passage, also make a list of the promises that were to be given.

Ezekiel 36:26–27, NASB

26 Moreover, I will give you a new heart and put a new spirit within you; and I will remove the heart of stone from your flesh and give you a heart of flesh.

27 I will put My Spirit within you and cause you to walk in My statutes, and you will be careful to observe My ordinances.

◊ **Insights**:

◊ **Application**:

For confirmation of your insights, the promises from this passage regarding what God would do for and give to those who would enter into this New Covenant are listed below.

◊ **New Covenant Promises from God in Ezekiel 36:26–27**:

1. given a new heart
2. a new spirit put within
3. the heart of stone removed
4. given a heart of flesh
5. have God's Spirit put within
6. God's Spirit will cause them to walk in and observe His statutes and ordinances

Now observe Jeremiah 31:31–34. Keep in mind these are the promises God made to those who remained in Judah and Jerusalem. They were still able to bring their prescribed sacrifices and offerings to Solomon's Temple in Jerusalem. But the sieges by the Babylonians were fierce and overwhelming. Please note your insights and applications below. From this passage, also list the promises that are mentioned.

Jeremiah 31:31–34, NASB

31 "Behold, days are coming," declares the Lord, "when I will make a new covenant with the house of Israel and with the house of Judah,

32 not like the covenant which I made with their fathers in the day I took them by the hand to bring them out of the land of Egypt, My covenant which they broke, although I was a husband to them," declares the Lord.

33 "But this is the covenant which I will make with the house of Israel after those days," declares the Lord, "I will put My law within them and on their heart I will write it; and I will be their God, and they shall be My people.

34 "They will not teach again, each man his neighbor and each man his brother, saying, 'Know the Lord,' for they will all know Me, from the least of them to the greatest of them," declares the Lord, "for I will forgive their iniquity, and their sin I will remember no more."

◊ **Insights**:

◊ **Application**:

Here again, for confirmation of your insights, the promises from this passage regarding what God would do and give them in the New Covenant are listed below.

◊ **New Covenant Promises from God in Jeremiah 31:31–34:**
1. it will not be like the Covenant of Law, which they broke
2. the law will be put within them, written on their hearts
3. God will be their God
4. they will be God's people
5. all will know God
6. God will forgive their iniquity
7. God will remember their sins no more

Now it is time to connect these promises of a new covenant given in the Old Testament to the New Covenant of Grace. To do so you need to examine Hebrews 8:6–13. It will be helpful for you to know that Hebrews is purported to be among the first of the New Testament books to be written. One can only imagine the great difficulty new Jewish believers were experiencing when they had lived their lives striving to obediently practice the Covenant of Law. This letter was written to these Jews by an unidentified author while the Temple was still standing and in operation. They needed to hear and to understand why the New Covenant Jesus mediated was a better one enacted on better promises. They needed to have it explained that Jesus was a better High Priest than those ministering in the Temple. They needed to know that Jesus was always living to make intercession for them (Hebrews 7:25). They needed to know, or to be reminded, that Jesus had provided a way for them personally to go into God's presence through His flesh. Please observe the following verses carefully and note your insights and applications below. Also note any passages included that you have studied from Jeremiah 31.

Hebrews 8:6–13, NASB

6 But now He has obtained a more excellent ministry, by as much as He is also the mediator of a better covenant, which has been enacted on better promises.

7 For if that first *covenant* had been faultless, there would have been no occasion sought for a second.

8 For finding fault with them, He says, "Behold, days are coming, says the Lord, when I will effect a new covenant with the house of Israel and with the house of Judah;

9 Not like the covenant which I made with their fathers on the day when I took them by the hand to lead them out of the land of Egypt; for they did not continue in My covenant, and I did not care for them, says the Lord.

10 "For this is the covenant that I will make with the house of Israel after those days, says the Lord: I will put My laws

into their minds, and I will write them on their hearts. And I will be their God, and they shall be My people.

11 "And they shall not teach everyone his fellow citizen, and everyone his brother, saying, 'Know the Lord,' for all will know Me, from the least to the greatest of them.

12 "For I will be merciful to their iniquities, and I will remember their sins no more."

13 When He said, "A new *covenant*," He has made the first obsolete. But whatever is becoming obsolete and growing old is ready to disappear.

◊ **Insights**:

◊ **Application**:

Hopefully, you noted that Hebrews 8:8–11 quotes Jeremiah 31:31–34. Hebrews 8:8 is a quote from Jeremiah 31:31. Hebrews 8:9 is a quote from Jeremiah 31:32. Hebrews 8:10 is a quote from Jeremiah 31:33. Hebrews 8:11–12 is a quote from Jeremiah 31:34. Hebrews makes it undeniably and unequivocally clear that the New Covenant inaugurated and mediated by Jesus is the One prophesied by Ezekiel and Jeremiah.

There were obstacles to inaugurating this New Covenant though. Gentiles were welcome to God in the Old Covenant, but they could no longer remain a Gentile. They had to become Jewish and obey all its laws to be able to worship and serve Jehovah God. The answer to this seemingly overwhelming and insurmountable problem is clearly explained in Ephesians 2:13–22. It will be very enlightening for you to closely examine this passage. Please also note your insights and applications below.

Ephesians 2:13–22, NASB

13 But now in Christ Jesus you who formerly were far off have been brought near by the blood of Christ.

14 For He Himself is our peace, who made both groups into one and broke down the barrier of the dividing wall,

15 by abolishing in His flesh the enmity, *which is* the Law of commandments *contained* in ordinances, so that in Himself He might make the two into one new man, *thus* establishing peace,

16 and might reconcile them both in one body to God through the cross, by it having put to death the enmity.

17 And He came and preached peace to you who were far away, and peace to those who were near;

18 for through Him we both have our access in one Spirit to the Father.

19 So then you are no longer strangers and aliens, but you are fellow citizens with the saints, and are of God's household,

20 having been built on the foundation of the apostles and prophets, Christ Jesus Himself being the corner *stone*,

21 in whom the whole building, being fitted together, is growing into a holy temple in the Lord,

22 in whom you also are being built together into a dwelling of God in the Spirit.

◊ **Insights**:

◊ **Application**:

In order for the second covenant to be established, the first one had to be abolished in Jesus' flesh, verse 15—put to death, verse 16. The enmity and barrier, which was the law of commandments, had to be broken down. Jesus Himself being our peace has now made the two groups into one new man so that He might reconcile both in one body to God through the cross. Both Jew and Gentile are being built together into a dwelling of God in the Spirit. What so great a salvation God has wrought!

Transformation

Lest we become arrogant and think less of the Jews today, it is good to be reminded that the Body of Christ was initially composed entirely of Jews who had believed that Jesus was their promised Messiah and had entered into the New Covenant of Grace. It would be approximately eight years after Pentecost before the first Gentiles were brought the Gospel. Peter went to Cornelius' house, a Roman centurion, in Caesarea and proclaimed the Gospel. Cornelius' whole household was saved. Gentiles had then entered in the New Covenant of Grace as a Gentile and did not have to become a Jew to worship and serve the living and holy God.

We are told that the Jews are the branches of the natural olive tree and the Gentiles are the branches of a wild olive tree, which have been grafted in (Romans 11:24). Gentiles are to remember that God is the root that sustains this hybrid olive tree. In Christ, there is neither Jew nor Greek (Gentile), for all are one in Christ Jesus (Galatians 3:28). There is no distinction between Jew and Greek, for the same Lord is Lord of all (Romans 10:12). At the foot of the cross, there is neither male nor female, neither Jew nor Gentile. This was all brought about by Jesus establishing a New Covenant through His blood. Hallelujah, what a Savior!

There was a watershed truth that was hidden from the Jews that would be revealed to the apostles and prophets after the death of Jesus and the establishment of the Church. Paul called this a "mystery of Christ." We learn from Paul that the mystery of Christ was that God had always intended for the Gentiles to be fellow heirs and fellow members of the Body of Christ and fellow partakers of the promise in Christ Jesus through the Gospel (Ephesians 3:4–6). In fact, the law, which had been prophesied in the Old Testament to be written on hearts, was not to be the Law of Moses but the "letter of Christ" (2 Corinthians 3:3, NASB), the "law of the Spirit of life in Christ" (Romans 8:2, NASB). Jesus had said, "If you love Me, you will obey My commandments" (John 14:15, NASB). How was it that Jesus could make such a definitive declaration? It was because He knew that His commandments would be written on the hearts of those who entered into His covenant. The Holy Spirit was given, in part, to cause believers to obey Jesus' commandments. The New Covenant would provide both the means and the power to obey.

Let's now go through the points of "covenant making" you learned earlier. You learned how they were met in the making of the Old Covenant of Law. They are also fulfilled in the inauguration of the New Covenant of Grace. Even though these points were either stated or alluded to earlier, it should be helpful and encouraging to specifically apply them to the New Covenant at this time.

1. The reasons for the need of a New Covenant are several, but one of the major ones is to enable the only true and holy God to have a personal, individual, and intimate relationship

with His children. God's children are intended to be made into vessels through whom He can extend His glory.

2. There was blood shed to consummate the covenant—the spotless, blameless blood of God's own Son. Jesus' blood was the only blood pure and sinless enough to pay humanity's total sin debt once for all time and thereby satisfy God's wrath against sin (Matthew 26:28). Without the shedding of blood, there is no forgiveness of sins (Hebrews 9:22).

3. The terms and conditions for entering into this New Covenant are to repent of your sins, acknowledge Jesus as Lord and the only payment for your sin debt, and surrender your life in faith to Him. There are many promises God makes on His part, but two major ones are that your sins are forgiven and forgotten and that you receive eternal life, never to be separated from God.

4. The vows are exchanged when you make a public profession of your faith in the Lord Jesus Christ. Even though water baptism is commanded after salvation, it is not part of the "vow."

5. The established "sign of the covenant" is that all who enter become a "new creature" in Christ Jesus—this new person is no longer a slave to sin (Romans 2:29; Colossians 2:11).

6. The commemorative meal is the Lord's Supper. At this meal, believers are to examine themselves before God for any unconfessed sins. God established an event to be repeated—an occasion for which the corporate cleansing of sin would be the focus. In partaking of the Lord's Supper, we proclaim Jesus' death until He returns.

Talk about Truth that transforms! We are transformed from glory to glory into the very image of the Lord Jesus Christ. Not only did our great and gracious God provide a way for His children to have a personal relationship with Him but one that would provide a way for us to be LIKE HIM (Romans 8:29). One day, when it is time, Jesus will return for His bride. At that moment, in the twinkling of an eye, all those who have trusted Christ, who have either died or are alive when He returns, will receive a gloried body just like Jesus'(1 Thessalonians 4:15–17). Then we will live forever and ever ruling and reigning with Him. We cannot image, comprehend, or contain its majesty. We can simply know that it is true.

Come, Lord Jesus. Come!

Even though we have only touched the hem of the garment, so to speak, prayerfully you have been encouraged, inspired, and transformed more into the image of the Lord Jesus Christ by the truths you studied in this chapter about our Real and final Kinsman-Redeemer. The truths about the new and better covenant Jesus inaugurated and mediated should have been personally life changing.

Most likely, you are familiar with Jesus' words that describe Himself as the "bread of life" and the "living water." John 6:35 states, "Jesus said to them, 'I am the bread of life; he who comes to Me will not hunger, and he who believes in Me will never thirst'" (NASB). Jesus also stated in John 7:37–38, "Now on the last day, the great *day* of the feast, Jesus stood and cried out, saying, 'If any man is thirsty, let him come to Me and drink.' He who believes in Me, as the Scripture said, 'From his innermost being shall flow rivers of living water'" (NASB). There is a great tragedy in our North American churches today. Many genuine born-again believers, even though their physical bodies may be well fed and watered, have spirits that are emaciated and dehydrated. The object of this chapter has been for you to believe in the Lord Jesus Christ, i.e., surrender your life to the person and work of Jesus. Come to Him! Eat and drink of Him through His Word by the power of the Holy Spirit.

Jesus is not only our Kinsman-Redeemer, but He is our brother and our friend (Matthew 12:50; John 15:14–15; Galatians 3:26). The more we become intimately acquitted with Jesus, the more we become like Him. Entry into God's family was created through the establishment of the New Covenant of Grace through Jesus' blood. Have you entered yet?

Boaz foreshadowed (pictured) some of what Christ Jesus would accomplish in future centuries. Boaz was qualified, willing, and able to pay the price for the redemption of both Elimelech's land and lineage. Jesus was qualified, willing, and able to pay the price for the redemption of all creation (Romans 8:19–21). Also, Jesus was qualified to pay for the redemption of the sins of the whole world, bringing forgiveness to each person who puts his or her faith and trust in Him. He frees us from both the penalty and the slavery to sin, which results in being made the righteousness of God in Him (2 Corinthians 5:21). You are beseeched to come to Jesus and allow Him to live His life in and through you. Enter into the New Covenant of Grace by a new and living way, by the blood of God's innocent, blameless, and perfect sacrificial Lamb. If you have already entered into Jesus' New Covenant, if you have been made a new creature in Christ (2 Corinthians 5:17), He bids you to come to His banquet table and be nourished, and to come to His fountain of living water and be satisfied.

◊ Were there any life-changing truths that you learned from this chapter about your covenant relationship with the God of heaven and the Lord Christ Jesus? If so, what?

◊ Did you discover any new insights into Jesus Christ being the "reality" of the Old Covenant Kinsman-Redeemer? If so, how have you applied them to your life?

◊ Did you possibly discover that you have yet to enter into the New Covenant of Grace, which provides a personal and intimate relationship with God? If so, why not enter now?

◊ Is there a particular truth that has grown from a deeper understanding of covenant that has blessed you?

◊ How would you best describe *covenant* to someone who is unfamiliar with the concept?

◊ Has anything in this chapter given you greater clarity about what the Church is? If so, has this affected how you plan to be a better covenant partner in the Body of Christ? Will your new or reinforced understanding of covenant and Jesus being the "real" Kinsman-Redeemer affect how you live? If so, how?

◊ Write down anything you have learned in this study on covenant that may have changed your perspective of eternal life.

MARIE STRAIN, AUTHOR OF CHAPTERS 10–12

Marie and Lee Strain will celebrate fifty-seven years of marriage in August 2016 and live in Collierville, Tennessee, a suburb of Memphis. She has dedicated her life and ministry to teaching the Truths of God's Word and training others how to study the Bible for themselves, so that they can know their God more intimately and serve Him more faithfully. They have two grown daughters who presently live with their families in Tennessee and Alabama. Lee and Marie attend Germantown Baptist Church where Marie teaches a Sunday school class of ladies in various "life stages." She has been leading a weekly Precept Upon Precept Bible study class for the past thirty-six years. Marie wishes to acknowledge that Kay Arthur and Betsy Bird, through Precept Ministries International, have invested much time, energy, knowledge, and love, which have contributed immeasurably to her own personal spiritual growth and in the equipping and effectiveness of her God-given ministries.

Marie Strain

Col. 1:28-29

CPSIA information can be obtained
at www.ICGtesting.com
Printed in the USA
LVOW04s0727110216

474459LV00002B/2/P